THE BOYS FROM
WHITE HART LANE

In Memory of Tony Fuller

MARTIN

To Mum, who wondered if me going to see this team was a good idea, and to Cath, Daniel and Tom

ADAM

For all the family and for much-missed dad, who first took me to see the boys from White Hart Lane

THE BOYS FROM
WHITE HART LANE

MARTIN CLOAKE
& ADAM POWLEY

VSP

Vision Sports Publishing Ltd
2 Coombe Gdns
London SW20 0QU

www.visionsp.co.uk

First published by Vision Sports Publishing in 2008
This paperback edition published by Vision Sports Publishing in 2011

ISBN 13: 978-1907637-08-7

Editor: Jim Drewett
Design: Doug Cheeseman
Copy editor: Ian Turner

Special thanks to Panini for kindly allowing us use of the
fantastic football cards on the front cover.

www.paninigroup.com

Typeset by Palimpsest Book Production Limited, Falkirk, Stirlingshire

Printed and bound in the UK by CPI Mackays, Chatham, ME5 8TD

A CIP catalogue record for this book is stored at the British Library

MIX
Paper from
responsible sources
FSC® C020471

CONTENTS

ACKNOWLEDGEMENTS

Producing this book has been an inspiring experience for us, not only because it gave us the chance to meet the players we watched as kids and get the inside story of the team we still think of as 'ours'. What's also been inspiring is the goodwill and enthusiasm we've encountered along the way.

First mention must go to Steve Perryman. Without him, this book would never have happened. He has spent long hours speaking to us about his experiences, contacting the players and vouching for our integrity as Spurs-supporting writers when we were pestering his old team-mates to give us an insight into the close-knit world of the dressing room. Along the way, Steve has provided many thoughtful suggestions and much background information. He is also one of the most genuinely friendly and straightforward people we've ever had the pleasure of working with – as he would say, a proper fella.

Jim Drewett and Toby Trotman at Vision Sports Publishing also deserve a special mention. They have showed enormous faith in us and their understanding of and passion for sport has enabled us to produce something which, we hope, provides a portrait of the times in line with the vision they had when establishing VSP. Their support and style of work on editorial and marketing matters is much appreciated, as is their willingness to respond to our frequent and varied questions with good humour and honesty. We are pleased to count them as good friends as well as colleagues.

Many other people have played their part in helping produce

this book. The knowledge and accessibility of Spurs historian Andy Porter and statistician and historian Bob Goodwin have been invaluable, and we thank them for providing definitive answers to our questions. Paul Allen at the Professional Footballers' Association also put in some much-appreciated effort on our behalf, as did Pablo Ardiles.

Thanks to Doug Cheeseman for his creativity and expertise in designing a cover that really does convey the spirit of the times and to Clive Batty for bringing his keen eye to bear on what must have been painful reading for a true Blue!

We've had many conversations with fellow Spurs fans, friends, and sports writers, all of whom have informed our approach to writing this book. For this, we would like to thank, in no particular order, Jim Duggan, Julie Welch, Bruce Lee, Bernie Kingsley, Steve Davies, Annelise Jespersen, Nick Auer, Julian Richards, Rick Mayston, Justyn Barnes, Phil and Ian Katz, Rabbi Crackers, Crocket, Pete Panayi and Andy Breckenbridge.

As always, our families have had to put up with us hiding away tapping at keyboards until late into the night, heading off at short notice to do interviews and spending vast amounts of time emailing and phoning each other to discuss the production of this book. Their support and understanding does not go unnoticed.

The last word of thanks must go to the players themselves, who gave up hours of their time to speak to us in depth about their experiences, and who in some cases welcomed us into their homes as well as their confidences. It was a pleasure to meet them, and to be reminded of what football and footballers used to be. Thank you to Ossie Ardiles, Ricky Villa, Tony Galvin, Graham Roberts, Paul Miller, Garry Brooke, Tony Parks, George Mazzon and Peter Shreeve - the boys from White Hart Lane.

INTRODUCTION

There is a time in a football fan's life when one team comes to symbolise all that is best about his or her club. For a large number of Tottenham supporters now comfortably settled into middle age, that side was the one managed to cup-winning glory by Keith Burkinshaw. It was this team that gave us our legends, won trophies with a generous dose of style and swagger and, perhaps, laid a few ghosts to rest.

Burkinshaw's Spurs were appreciated by a wider audience too. While football fans, more than the fans of any other sport, tend to follow teams rather than the sport itself, a side occasionally comes along that commands respect or admiration across the partisan lines of the football tribes. Brian Clough's Nottingham Forest were one such team, their rise from second tier also-rans to double European Champions in four consecutive seasons still fondly remembered because it kept alive the very essence of sport – that everyone has a chance of winning.

Tottenham Hotspur commanded similar emotions between 1978 and 1987. *The Guardian*'s Patrick Barclay captured the mood, writing in 1982 when the team was riding high: "If every team played like Spurs, football's only problem would be in pacifying the herds of supporters unable to get into packed grounds. They bring beauty to the game, and people like that."

We all have our favourite recollections of that era. The games themselves naturally stand out: 1984's epic UEFA Cup final and the vocal support for Danny Thomas following his missed penalty that still brings a lump to the throat at the memory; the first half demolition of Feyenoord in the same campaign; the fans' takeover of Highbury for the 1981 semi-final replay and the titanic, title-deciding clash with Everton in 1984/85. Even for those not present to witness Ricky Villa's extraordinary FA Cup final goal in 1981, it became our 'JFK moment': we all remember where we were when it happened.

But it's the personal memories, the individual rites-of-passage details, that really forge the link between fans and a team. The authors of this book are no exception.

Adam Powley remembers: Unable to get a ticket for the 1981 FA Cup final replay, I was forced to watch the match on TV in a schoolmate's front room in Southgate, north London. We were wearing naff silky quartered caps that seemed quite snazzy at the time. Villa's goal prompted bedlam. We danced out into the road, a gaggle of 14-year-olds unsure how to react to our hitherto under-achieving team threatening to win something of significance. We could hear cheers ringing out around the whole area, before every-one hurriedly rushed back inside to sit through the longest, most painful 12 minutes, until the final whistle brought unconfined relief.

Later that evening my older sister arrived with her then boyfriend to suggest we drive down to Tottenham High Road, "on the off chance there might be a few fans celebrating". We had no compre-hension of just how many there would be. Nearing the Angel, Edmonton, where the North Circular meets Fore Street, the traffic had come to a halt. Diving around the back streets, we eventually managed to work our way onto the High Road via Lordship Lane, a couple of hundred yards from the ground. The scene that greeted us will never leave my memory.

There were thousands, maybe tens of thousands of people, flooding the street, cheering, hugging, kissing, crying. They swelled the throng from every direction, car horns blared, residents hung out from their windows, a thousand stereos blasted out *Ossie's Dream*. It was carnival time. Men, women and children were dancing, pubs heaving with humanity spilled their customers onto the pavements. A huge roar greeted a flat-bed van transporting some of the fans who had actually been at Wembley to see the triumph, as it inched its way down the road. The beer flowed, the laughter flowed, the tears flowed too. It may seem a glib comparison, but it resembled the newsreel footage of VE Day celebrations. The police shut the High Road that night. Tottenham fans had brought a corner of the capital to a standstill.

It was only a game of football that had caused such happy chaos, but for the first time I realised what the game meant to people. It gave us a cause for celebration and a fiercely strong sense of togetherness that transcended, if only for a brief while, the differences that existed between us. This was at a time when the prevailing political ethos was every man for himself and there was apparently no such thing as society. But most of all it gave us joy – pure, blissful, unadulterated joy. No one knows how many babies may have been conceived that delirious evening. But it's safe to say that a fair few were later christened Glenn, Steve, Ricky, Graham, Paul and Tony – who knows, there may well have been one or two Osvaldos as well!

Martin Cloake remembers: I was one of the fans who had been at Wembley on that unforgettable night, a ticket secured after queuing through the small hours following the Saturday game. The chaos of the massive terrace behind the goal meant I wasn't able to fully appreciate Ricky Villa's winner until the TV replays in the days that followed, but it was fitting that it was the South American's goal that won the cup as I watched.

Several years before, the arrival of a pair of Argentinian superstars had captured my imagination as nothing had ever done before. I vividly remember the morning they signed. I was burying myself deep in the bedcovers to avoid getting up for school when my mum shouted something genuinely extraordinary up the stairs. "It says on the radio that Spurs have signed two Argentinians." It certainly got me downstairs fast. A thing like that simply didn't happen in 1978. Except that day it had. Two players I had watched on TV play football on the other side of the world in that summer's World Cup had signed for my team, Tottenham Hotspur. They were from Argentina. And they were coming to play in England, in Haringey, my little bit of north London. "Spurs Scoop the World" roared the headlines on the back pages, and that day at school all Tottenham fans walked a little taller, relishing the envy of classmates who had stuck it to us a year before when our team went down.

I was at an impressionable age, and how could that team fail to make an impression? A potent mix of skill and steel, led by one of the greatest sporting captains ever and managed by a quietly spoken romantic genius, they entertained on the pitch and off it too, crashing the pop charts with a classic cup final ditty. They were at Wembley every season, they conquered Europe, and they did it all with style.

Those events instilled a lifelong devotion that still makes us talk about "our" team, "our" club. At the time we'd say it was because, as we used to sing, Tottenham Hotspur FC were "by far the greatest team the world has ever seen". And we really believed they were. But as the years have passed and times have moved on, our affection for that team has grown as our feelings about the club have changed. It's as well to be wary of nostalgia, even that's not what it used to be, but the regard our generation has for that team is not just because the players that came after have never scaled the same heights.

The 1980s side's standing as the last great Tottenham team, incidentally, is something some of the players we interviewed for this book find uncomfortable or even irritating, the sporting drive within them somehow affronted by the fact that their successors have not bettered their achievements. But what makes this group so special is about more than just what they achieved. They were, arguably, the last generation of players with whom the fans could really identify. They came from similar backgrounds as the vast majority of the supporters, and while they enjoyed a comfortable and glamorous lifestyle, they took home only a fraction of what today's often remote and aloof superstars can expect to earn.

This is the story of those men and how they made those special times happen. In their own words, they explain how a successful squad brimming with flair was built and nurtured, reveal what went on behind the scenes and share the secrets of the dressing room. They talk of their collective triumphs and setbacks, their personal highs and lows, and the friendships that endure to this day. There will inevitably be some favourites missing from these pages. Some players were unsure about contributing, others have their own projects. We have also tried to select a broad cross section of characters to give as full a picture of the time as possible. So there is no Glenn Hoddle, because so much is known already about the greatest player of his generation, and because Glenn is, naturally, a little wary of further media scrutiny. As it turns out, what his teammates have to say about him proves revealing. Steve Archibald and Garth Crooks both decided to keep their own counsel, but feature large in these pages – as they should. Chris Hughton's responsibilities with Newcastle United prevented him from taking part. And Keith Burkinshaw, in typical style, was uneasy about doing what could be seen as blowing his own trumpet.

The ten who appear in this book are a representative sample of a great team, and their selection implies no judgement on the abilities or contributions of either them or their teammates.

In another 25 years, we won't be sitting in Ledley King's front room discussing his time at the club. We won't be drinking tea served by Luka Modric's wife as he tells us of his life in football, and we won't be going for a pint and a chat with Jermaine Jenas. The connection we as fans once had with the game and those who played it at the top level has gone, probably forever.

The interest many fans expressed when they heard we were writing this book stems from a realisation that, for all the riches in modern football, something has been lost. The stories that the players tell in this book reveal a world that has slipped away, a world where the finest English player of his generation could walk unaccosted into his local pub, where players simply loved playing football rather than the football lifestyle.

These were men who worked hard and played hard, gaining the respect of their team-mates and fans alike. Some have moved on to successful careers in or out of football, others have slipped quietly into relative anonymity. They have aged, of course, and their achievements will eventually become part of Spurs history rather than living memory. But as long as football fans talk about Tottenham Hotspur, their legacy is ensured: they are, and always will be, the boys from White Hart Lane.

Since this book was first published we've been delighted with the response it had drawn from Spurs fans who remembered the great days of the early '80s and the players featured here. Since then, a new group of heroes have emerged in a Spurs team which is again winning admirers for the quality of its football.

In a rather neat link, at the time of writing Tony Parks, who in these pages provides a fascinating insight into the world of the 1980s footballer, is back at the club, working with Harry Redknapp's coaching staff to ensure the current crop of goalkeepers perform at their best. His return is said to have been key in helping Heurelho Gomes through a difficult start, and it has been a source of great pleasure to see him back as the current team attempt to fulfil Tony Galvin's wish, stated in his chapter, that fans have a more modern set of heroes to laud.

We hope new readers of this paperback edition will enjoy reading the book as much as we enjoyed writing it – and that the exploits of the current crop of Spurs provide a distraction!'

Martin Cloake and Adam Powley, April 2011

1
STEVE PERRYMAN

"IF YOU'RE HONEST, IF YOU DO IT RIGHT, I'M YOUR MAN"

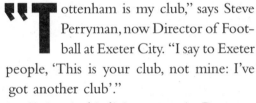

"**T**ottenham is my club," says Steve Perryman, now Director of Football at Exeter City. "I say to Exeter people, 'This is your club, not mine: I've got another club'."

Sitting in his living room in Devon, a view through the living-room window over the Exe estuary providing a picturesque backdrop, Steve appears relaxed in the rural, peaceful and quiet environment that's a million miles from the grit and bustle of London N17. But as he casts his mind back to great times for Spurs, Perryman clearly still holds the memories dear. The choirboy looks have matured, the figure may be slightly fuller and the thick mop of hair now grey, but the characteristic twinkle in the eye remains, as does the unequivocal belief in shouldering responsibility and doing the right thing. Steve Perryman is, even today, the captain his former charges follow, admire and listen to.

"Some players still call me Skip now," he says. He talks to many of them on a regular basis, organises the reunions and get-togethers, and if something is OK by Steve, it's reasonable to assume it's OK by the rest of them. It is a rare skill to be able to earn and retain that respect but from the beginning, when he was first made captain at just 20, Perryman showed himself to be a born leader.

"Being captain came naturally to me. I think I'm a really good communicator, particularly about football, about strengths and weaknesses and how to improve them. It was my specialist subject. I don't think when Bill Nicholson made me vice-captain there was a particular speech from him that said, 'This is how you've got to be', but if I hadn't been captain I would still have spoken in the same way. Bill Nick noticed that and realised I'm a leader type. One of the players at Exeter said to me the other day, 'I don't want to be a captain because I don't want to be a yes man.' But that's not right: you can be a leader without having to compromise what you think and feel."

It was this willingness to lead from the front, coupled with his work rate and nuggety toughness that made Perryman such an instant terrace favourite. 'He's one of us' was the feeling of the fans, who warmed to the industrious midfielder with the suede-head haircut he sported at the time. By the time Tottenham were relegated at the end of the 1976/77 season after several years of struggle, the hairstyle had lengthened but it was an older, wiser and more determined head on Perryman's shoulders, one which saw relegation as the harsh remedy Spurs required.

"Going down was like a breath of fresh air for us," says Steve. "All the seasons before when it didn't quite happen and we got away with it, it didn't change anything. The club had not been living in the real world. We could not compete for the best players, we were well down the wish list of where people wanted to go. We just lost our glamour. We weren't the Tottenham that I'd joined."

Relegation had been emphatically confirmed with a 5-0 defeat at Manchester City. "I think the recovery started then. We went into the last game [a 2-0 win over Leicester] playing with a freedom and with the crowd displaying a great attitude. How could you play for that club and listen to the support the fans gave you and not take that seriously as some sort of indication of their desire to get back to where we should be?"

The rebuilding of a fallen giant began with the board making the bold move not to sack Keith Burkinshaw. "The decision to keep Keith in charge was just unbelievable. How could that happen today? Credit to them, because it turned out to be a fantastic decision." The willingness to make difficult choices continued with the shock transfer of goalkeeper Pat Jennings to deadly rivals Arsenal amid disagreement over a new contract. Burkinshaw was determined to assert his authority on the club but maintained continuity by retaining Perryman as his leader on the pitch. The pair shared, and still do share, a close and trusting relationship that was fundamental to Tottenham's revival.

"I was captain under Terry Neill when Keith first arrived at the club, so when Keith was made manager he could have changed that. Thankfully he didn't want to; it just carried on. I've always found Keith really, really easy to talk to. He's not that approachable actually, but I just clicked with him. We spent hours talking on the phone, especially Sundays after games, and more so if we'd lost or were having a difficult time.

"Keith was young and new to management. But I noticed how much he improved, and we improved together, by talking to each other a lot. It was obvious Keith cared. He cared about the team, about it improving, about Tottenham Hotspur; he cared about living up to the tradition. And he was absolutely committed. He said to me once, 'I am going to make this a team.' It might have been at the point when we were looking all right but not quite there, before Steve Archibald and Garth Crooks arrived [in 1980]. He said, 'Trust me, Steve, I am going to make this a team.' And he did."

Tottenham's renaissance began with an end-of-season tour to Norway. "We played to a particular style that Keith felt was going to get us back up. It was a Tottenham way of playing; we passed the ball through midfield with the emphasis on skill and expression, but we needed to tighten up in defence a bit. After Norway, we went on to a pre-season tournament in Sweden where we carried on playing that way and in every situation we got more 'football serious' using that style. Not that we weren't serious before, but we didn't enjoy it; it was hard work being at Tottenham and struggling. Double hard work. Now, all of a sudden it was fresh, it was like the chains were off us. We were going to play this style of football and get out of the division. But we had to win promotion. We were being outmanoeuvred in the transfer market."

Tottenham's squad was little altered for the season in Division Two, but results and performances improved, with Steve one of those who prospered the most. "It was possibly the best season I ever had, I enjoyed it as much as anything. I played one of my best ever games at Bolton in that league," he says. "I played at the back and just controlled the game from start to finish – though we got beat so I couldn't have been that happy with it. People were sending me cuttings from the local paper two weeks on with readers writing in – northern people writing to a northern paper saying, 'How can this fella not be playing for England?' I was that good on that day.

"I just had such a fresh approach. I think the previous years of playing as a midfield workhorse amid all that hurry and scurry gave me the experience to cope with being pressurised on the ball. Playing at the back I didn't have that same degree of pressure and had more time on the ball. I could now run 20 metres, cut it to Glenn Hoddle, we'd surge forward – wonderful. It really was me drawing a line under a career low.

"My start at Tottenham was lovely, with cup wins at Wembley and all that. The middle part was a bit of a depression. Being a person who felt responsibility I took it hard, all the disappointment of relegation, the demise and criticism, it was tough. So it was like going into a new world as a player in the Second Division. I shouldn't say it was my best season but it was for all sorts of reasons, it gave me fresh impetus to carry on and have a long career with the club, because if it hadn't gone well in that division maybe it would have been time to go. You never know how it quite works out."

Steve and Tottenham's futures were uncertain up until the end of the campaign, but a goalless draw at Southampton gave each side the point they needed to go up. "The last step is always the hardest one to take," says Steve. "You want something so bad, but we lost at home [3-1 to Brighton] and we had to play our way out of it. I just think about those big games towards the end and our crowd – our crowd had been brilliant when we were relegated, but how were they going to act when we needed that final push for promotion? We needn't have worried – they were fantastic. You feel it now sometimes, some very mundane games away and there are 6,000 Tottenham people shouting their hearts out. That's not just happened today – that's been built up over a number of years. In a way that's what fed us: we gained power off the crowd."

'Tottenham people' – it's a Perryman refrain when he talks about Spurs fans, an acknowledgment that it is the supporters in large part who are the club. In contrast to the modern era when top players can seem remote from supporters, existing in their own closed-off, well-heeled world, Perryman and his teammates had the common touch. Steve's bond, honed over the years by his role as captain and man-of-the-people outlook, was stronger than most.

"When I was on the pitch I heard every 'ooh' and 'aah' that 50,000 people could make. At any stage of my career, I knew how the crowd were thinking – I knew. And I think they knew that I knew as well. Therefore I accepted the responsibility of all that. White Hart Lane can be a tough old place to go back to when you've lost the away game to Arsenal and the home game before that and you're playing at home to, say, Birmingham; it wasn't an easy stage to be on at times. But if they saw that you were 'right', that you were committed, honest and doing your best, they backed you: that's how I saw it. Of course if you weren't 'right' they let you know as well, which is everyone's prerogative. It was warranted."

Unsurprisingly, Steve does not hold much truck with the notion of footballers being particularly special or courageous in having to perform in a physical and pressurised environment. By way of example he cites the case of his young daughters. Aged 10 and 12, both are budding gymnasts. There is a photo in Perryman's house of the younger girl poised on the beam. Asked if, as a father, he isn't terrified by the kind of gravity-defying back flips and risky exercises she has to do, he answers, "It's unbelievable. Don't ever tell me that footballers are brave."

An interview with Steve is peppered with such observations about character, and consistent themes emerge: responsibility, leadership, honesty. These are the traits he admires in others and qualities he prides in his own personality. And they were required in abundance for the return to Division One, where Burkinshaw's fundamental faith in attack was to be severely tested.

The initial boost came with the spectacular signing of the World Cup-winning Argentinian duo, Osvaldo Ardiles and Ricardo Villa. Inevitably this led to the partial breakup of the promotion-winning side, and more change for Tottenham's longest serving player to digest. "Prattie [John Pratt] and Terry Naylor were going. I loved those people. I don't remember any suddenness to it; it just sort of evolved. You play with people and then they move on, that's just how it goes.

"In some ways I suppose it needed to happen. The club had to start competing in the transfer market. Of course, you needed some kind of home-grown player, but they were coming up, be it Maxie [Paul Miller], or Chris [Hughton]. When you think of the balance of all that with two non-league players from Goole Town and Weymouth [Tony Galvin and Graham Roberts respectively] – can you imagine players like that getting in Tottenham's team now? With two World Cup winners, two strikers later bought for big money, home-grown full backs? The mix of all that was fantastic.

"Teams evolve. It's one of the things I look back on. I was on the list of players who, every year, someone had to judge. I now know how it works as a manager with budgets and stuff, to say 'You gotta go'. That's what happens. I guess I just survived the cull for 20 years."

Steve's presence was invaluable for the first season back in the top flight. After a good start away to Nottingham Forest in which a Ricky Villa goal earned a draw, Spurs came resoundingly back to earth in front of their own fans with a 4-1 reverse to Aston Villa. Humiliation later ensued with a 7-0 thumping at Anfield, a record defeat in which Spurs had no answer to the relentless red machine that was the Liverpool side of the time.

"I don't think we ever went to away games saying, 'Let's just get a draw,'" Steve recalls. "The day we got beat 7-0, we changed everything we normally did – we flew when we normally went by bus, in fact the only thing we didn't do differently was walk there. On this day, Keith filled the team with footballers. And guess what – we never had the ball. We got overrun. Ossie said to me afterwards, 'Stevie, no problem'. I said, 'What do you mean? Ossie, we've just lost 7-0, I think that's a problem.' Ossie replied, 'Stevie, trust me. This Liverpool team is on drugs!'"

As time wore on, however, it wasn't just Ardiles's humour that impressed Perryman. His intelligence, quietly expressed initially as he and Villa adapted to a British football culture and learned the language, began to tell and helped mould Burkinshaw's side.

"We'd been on tours, we'd seen the World Cup, but it was just staggering that we'd signed these two players. Everyone was thinking, 'What were they going to be like, how were they going to train, how would they be in the winter in the snow and the mud?' Ossie was just very, very clever, as a footballer but also as a person, very intelligent. He smashed everyone to bits in a table-tennis competition in his first training camp in Holland, wiped Prattie away who was our best player. He got through life with English or without by being very funny: his face was funny, his actions were funny, he was just a proper live wire.

"He could cope with the mickey-taking from when he first came in. Someone in the dressing room might have had a cheap shot about a foreigner who didn't understand the language. I think Ossie maybe didn't understand the words, but he saw the face and thought 'OK' and laughed. And his expression would be, 'You wait and see'. Very clever."

As the South Americans adapted, so too did Spurs. The 1979/80 season climaxed with a narrow 1-0 defeat to Liverpool in the quarter-final of the FA Cup, but the run provided vindication of the club's direction. "It started to turn, we were scoring goals, competing against the best teams. When Ossie and Ricky came, we started to get the glamour back and therefore neutrals would come to watch us play. We got our sense of value back, I suppose. I watched a DVD of the 1-0 win away at Man U in the third round cup game from that season the other day, which Don McAllister sent to me. The Ricky goal at Wembley – he did that at Old Trafford about 10 times in this game, but no one remembers because it didn't end up as a goal. He did that type of thing, taking the pressure off us. To win there at Old Trafford in that style – fantastic. It was nailed on we were going to get beat for that replay, but we won it.

"That was when Ossie really began to show his worth. Ossie is so mentally strong. You could see the wheels working in his head. You never saw him nail someone, but as the winger was taking me on, this little sod would be around him like a bee. 'You need me Steve,' he would say. There was always a bit of humour in our games – it was lovely.

"In the Liverpool game we played poorly but faced them in the league three weeks later. Keith had a talk about how to play them. I said to him, 'I don't care if we get beat by ten as long as we have a go, because we didn't do that last time'. So we played 4-2-4 to stop their full backs who were usually dominant. I never saw a pair of full backs knock the ball out of play so often or be so ruffled before, they were taken by surprise. It was tactically really brave. The problem with that was that it was brave off the back of such a poor first performance – you have to be brave first time. But we beat them 2-0, deservedly."

In any successful side, as Spurs were soon to become, there are many ingredients that turn a group of individuals into a cohesive and effective unit. Primary among these is team spirit and at Tottenham that vital commodity was in abundant supply. "We used to have an honesty hour where you could say what you want and no one could take offence to it," Steve says. "There was that spirit about us. A fan spoke to me the other day and he called us a pub team. He wasn't saying we were unprofessional, but that we were so close to the supporters. 'You were like us,' he said.

"We used to play silly numbers games. After a match in Austria we were given a load of cake as a gift. Someone had a taste and it was evil, so we played a forfeit game called 'Buzz' and if you made a mistake, instead of having a drink you had to eat some of this cake. Can you imagine professional players, finely tuned athletes, doing this? Someone, I can't remember who it was, had to eat about ten pieces of this cake in a three-hour coach journey. But it was funny."

As befits the times, many clubs had a strong drinking culture and Spurs were no exception in Steve's eyes. As captain, he in-evitably made his contribution. "We were really good at knowing the rules and the rules were not so tough. One was that you never went out from a Thursday onwards before a Saturday game if drink was involved. You could go to a restaurant as long as you didn't drink. I don't know of that ever being abused.

"Keith said to me one day, 'Someone told me that you were drinking in the Coolbury Club at 2.30 the other night after the game, and I don't think it's right that you were.' I said, 'Keith, you got that wrong. It was 4am, and although there was drink involved I was there with Pat Jennings, George Graham, Frank McLintock and John Docherty, and we were talking football like you won't believe. That was the reason we were there. And actually, Keith, I've learned as much in those sessions as I have on any coaching field.' 'Well, I don't think that's right,' said Keith. But I was right: we'd just beaten Bayern Munich, I was 32 and we were off the next day, so there was no problem.

"I knew where Keith was coming from. But you hear about the likes of Liverpool and Man U and we certainly were never big drinkers like they were. I saw that when Spurs and Liverpool were on tour in Swaziland and we were nowhere near them when it came to drinking. We had a good time and enjoyed ourselves. There was no nastiness, no malice, nothing like that at all, we just had a good time. I remember the quote from Maurice Norman [veteran defender of the Double side] when we got relegated, and his reaction was, 'They don't even drink together!' A stunning comment, but back in his day they really did drink!

"We did, of course. But the truth is the players didn't need to engineer bonding sessions, we were forced together. Bus journeys, train journeys, airports. Take the 1981/82 season, the amount of time we spent in hotels we thought we owned them in the end. We were always in that environment, so what are you going to do with your time? If you don't like each other's company, you're in trouble."

What differed at Spurs was how that team spirit was fostered. In a then revolutionary move for a football club, Burkinshaw secured the services of a team of sports psychologists led by John Syer. In a dressing room environment, where close-knit privacy is fiercely protected, any intrusion is treated with suspicion – even from other 'football people', let alone an outsider from another profession. The club had retained a deep-seated doubt over the wisdom of admitting strangers ever since Hunter Davies was a fly on the wall for the 1971/72 season, chronicled in his incredible book *The Glory Game*, because it broke the golden rule of keeping what went on in the dressing room in the dressing room. So to bring in Syer and his colleagues was risky to say the least. Their arrival was understandably low key.

"For three team meetings they sat behind us all when Keith was having his normal training ground team talk. I don't even think they were introduced to us, they were making notes about how these meetings were run. Eventually they had a meeting with Keith and they then had their conversations with us, and particularly with me, about how they didn't like how our meetings were run, especially Keith's moaning that the young players didn't ever speak. The thing was, how are the youngsters going to speak after the manager has had his say, then the captain and the senior players? Keith would say, 'Micky Hazard, what do you think, you've been quiet.' Guess what? He wouldn't say anything, how could he possibly talk after what's just happened, you'd have to be incredibly brave. So meetings were then structured in a different way. The psychologists were there to improve the communication."

Once established and having earned the tentative confidence of the players, Syer and his team went to work. It was Burkinshaw who had made the bold move to bring them in, but once again, Perryman was integral to turning innovative ideas into practical benefit.

"I think the big deal in all of this was Keith's decision to bring them in. It was unbelievable, to give away a bit of his power over players, because it's another person for players to moan about the manager to. But if they are giving the moan to someone else, at least he's not getting it. At least he can do something about it, work on it or ignore it.

"I think I was the one who, as I did in other situations, said to the rest of the lads 'It's OK' and that these fellas were all right and it was worth our while to speak to them. They talked about 'muscle memory' and 'visualisation', plus some other things about relaxation. I was aged about 30 at the time and I remember thinking, 'Hey, I already do all that stuff'. So if I, with my years of experience, could see that what the sports psychologists were saying to me made sense, and confirmed it was a tried and trusted technique, then it must be OK. I hadn't got the words or methods to communicate what I'd learned through experience so was unable to pass it on to these young players, but this fella obviously had and could. Young players would benefit straight away without the need to have to wait and find it out for themselves.

"I trusted John Syer and I could place the players' trust in him on their behalf. Hopefully I didn't abuse my position. I don't think the players were aware that I would speak to John and say to him, 'Listen, I think you should say such and such to so and so.' But it was the obvious thing to do. We were employing these people to get the best out of us, so how can they do their job if they didn't know? They needed help, needed advice on what line to take.

"Previously these kinds of discussions had been done in a team situation, which was wrong as the players were all different individuals. They now had this man asking them all sorts of common sense questions from the angle of not being 'pure' football. It was about discussion and opinion and a bit of depth, explaining why you should be doing things. And that's what the players needed. The end result was we got results."

By way of example, Steve cites the case of star strikers Crooks and Archibald. Purchased for a combined £1.45 million, in their debut season of 1980/81 the pair scored 48 goals between them. For the second season the stats were less impressive, with a combination of injuries and a drop in form resulting in 27 goals. "The first year they had to justify themselves in a new team and it worked: we got to Wembley and we won it. We were all elevated to a new level and we all felt we deserved to be at this great club. It was a massive boost to your ego and confidence.

"Garth and Steve had that success by running forward. Glenn, the 'quarterback' type, made good things happen by playing balls over the top for them to run onto. But because of the success in the first year, they didn't want that any more, they wanted the ball to feet. Garth playing that way wasn't a tenth of the player he was if he was running onto the ball – we had seen what his strengths were in the Highbury semi-final of '81. Now, all of a sudden he wanted to have a touch, play people in. Garth was a runner towards goal and a finisher. Somewhere along the line, someone had got to get that message to them – 'For Christ's sake, start running forward.' That was the manager's responsibility, but if I could have helped that by suggesting to John Syer to ask them what they were doing differently and raise that issue about running forward, I said it. It worked last season – why change it?

"The John Syer contribution was a part of getting the message across. To be honest they weren't my type of people, they were softly spoken, they were gentle men. They had no place in this group of bastards that we were. But they fitted. And they fitted with my help, that's for sure.

"By the time Keith bought Syer in we were emerging anyway. It was a good team to get us up but we had to be better to win something. Keith added to it: it looked OK but not quite right and then the final piece in the jigsaw was the two strikers. Which sounds disrespectful to the people who were already there, but it was Archibald and Crooks that meant for all the good football, we scored goals as well. The signing of those two was the turning point."

Both Crooks and Archibald were perceived as different from the players already in the squad. They were signed for substantial fees and arrived with reputations to live up to rather than establish. They both needed strength of character to thrive.

"When they first arrived at Tottenham, signed for big money, Steve and Garth formed a bit of a strikers' union between themselves, thinking they've got to fight their corner. It's great if you can be inventive as an individual player, but it's easier if you can do it together as a pair, or link with your partner. They realised their combination play was vital.

"They were different characters. I really respected Archie because he was different, and anyone who's different, they leave themselves open to ridicule, so I have real respect for him. He was quiet, on certain days moody. You could walk in the dressing room one day and say 'Good morning' and he'd be 'Morning Steve!' Next morning . . . [Perryman pulls a blank face].

"Garth reminded me the other day," says Steve, "that I was instrumental in him coming to the club. Ray Evans [Perryman's ex-Spurs team-mate] was at Stoke. He phoned me about Garth and I fed this info back to Keith and it eventually happened. We signed him, a very lively character, great fun, but a bit whizz-bangish. Excitable. Northern – there weren't too many of them around in our team at the time. He was just such a different character, good for team spirit. It wasn't nailed on that he would be a good signing. We didn't think, 'We've got a great player here' – I don't think we had to fight off too many people to sign him. But he settled, he was quick, and he always fancied himself as a player. He came as a very naive, lovely young man and he learned a lot of lessons with us and he elevated himself up to where he is today. What he did best was use his pace.

"Garth had the mickey taken a lot. He fancied himself and gave you the chance to have a go at him, in a nice way, to take the rise. Socially he would make an entrance, he set himself up with it with his clothes, he stood out and wanted to stand out. When he made the comment on the Wembley pitch, 'My name's in lights', that was

typical Garth − it was theatre, more than what we w
me it was messing about in the mud but for Garth it
thing more."

The lynchpin of the team, however, was neither an exotic
Cup winner, nor even a big-money signing. It was the homegrown
genius of Glenn Hoddle that arguably played the most fundamental
part in turning a promising team into a truly great one.

"Glenn was the crux of all that was good or so-called bad about
Tottenham," says Steve. "If northern clubs wanted to have a go at
us as southern softies, then Glenn was the one they went for; if
others wanted to describe us as the best attacking team in the
country, it was Glenn who they talked about.

"It was his vision and ability on the ball. He was the main man.
I was the leader in how we did things, but Glenn was the leader
of our play. Albeit that Ossie once told me, 'I am the most intelligent player in this team. Glenn needs to think he's the best player
in the team. And I let him think that, but really I am.' Of course
there'd be periods when Glenn was off form or injured, so how
would we cope with that when we had built it all around him?
But then, of course, we had Ossie who could change his game,
Micky Hazard to come in; if it was an away game in Europe maybe
we didn't want Glenn in there. There was more to the team than
Glenn, with a lot of thought − a lot of leaders if you like. But I
think Keith and I spoke more words to each other about Glenn
then any other player, how to get the best out of him, give him
the ball, and cater for his interests. We knew he was the catalyst. If
he was right, we were right."

How to exploit this extraordinary talent to the full was a
responsibility for the whole team. "We just realised that the more
time Glenn had the ball the better we were going to be. Without
doubt, the fella could accept the ball in any situation, anywhere
on the field, and you could trust him to deliver. It didn't go right
all the time. What he did was so special it was very hard to keep

delivering it – but percentage-wise he could handle it all, under pressure with players around him. His vision was outstanding.

"We evolved this moving set piece: Clemence would take the cross, I'd get out early and he'd give me the ball. I'd look long, cut into Glenn, he would feint, let it run across his body and smash it to Tony Galvin in the corner and off we went. I liked getting it off the keeper, I was quicker than any forward in getting out. Glenn wanted the ball from me, to feet, rather than having to run for it, and Tony was a willing runner into a forward wide position. It was players doing good things together, matching each others' abilities. There would be times when I would receive the ball and there would be 50 yards of space to run into, so I might as well run into it. But we trusted each other, Glenn wouldn't complain if I didn't give it to him. That team grew up together and we all trusted each other."

It's reasonable to think that keeping company with such a stellar talent might intimidate other players, or breed resentment. But if there was any envy or tension in the squad concerning Hoddle's class, Steve is quick to disavow the notion.

"Keith accused me one day of being soft on Glenn. 'The only one you don't go for is Glenn – why's that?' I had to cajole Glenn as I didn't think he would have taken too kindly to a bollocking. I had total respect for him as a player. If you ever imagined the kind of player you wanted to be, it was Glenn; that's why I think he was such a special player for the crowd. The crowd could imagine themselves being a Maxie Miller, or me, or Robbo – I don't think they could imagine themselves being a Glenn. He was the kind of person you paid to watch. We had to elevate him to a status that Glenn was our strength, not our weakness. If we'd said, 'Glenn, get back, put your foot in', or, 'Glenn, any chance of heading that?' you may as well not have him, you may have just switched him off, which is what a lot of managers would have done. Keith was absolutely right for him.

"I've heard Glenn say about me, 'You know, that Steve Perryman was a lot more talented than you ever gave him credit for.' I know he also said that when I was playing. Well guess what, I'm gonna give him the ball more! I think we all wanted to be liked by Glenn, we wanted this great player to give us his approval. I don't think I was soft with him, but I erred on the side of respect."

If anything, the criticism of Hoddle by outsiders brought an already close-knit squad closer together. To mock 'Glenda' for his supposed lack of stomach for a tackle, or to snipe at his talent with a football was seen not just as an affront to a friend but a slur against the squad as a whole and the abiding philosophy of the club. As a result, Hoddle's successes brought a sense of pride to his colleagues, with Steve as pleased as anyone.

"When he scored on his debut for England, against Bulgaria, he came into training the next day and there was joy for him. Absolutely no jealousy, we were all just delighted for him. We truly believed in him. I've got some very good friends, football people who did not stop questioning me about Glenn. So much so it led to me saying to Keith, 'Let's stop talking about what he can't do, let's talk about and make hay out of what he can do.' Because that talent was so special, it was obvious.

"Keith said to me recently, 'Have you ever watched the '81 final?' I've seen bits of it but I don't think I've ever sat down and watched it all the way through. Keith said, 'I watched it the other night. Do you know who our best player was? Glenn Hoddle. He worked, he ran, chased, headed, he even tackled.' So we're still talking about Glenn all those years later. We all wanted to be like Glenn, if we're truthful. We all wanted his ability. We were in awe, respected him, but outside influences questioned him, which is probably why he never got to the stage he did with England as he did with Spurs. They didn't discuss him enough, think about him enough, respect him enough. And therefore when they did use him it was done out of the attitude that 'everyone's clamouring for him, we'd better play him'. Which was a waste of time.

Media cliché from the sizable anti-Hoddle faction in the press and ranks of ex-players would also have it that Hoddle was and still is an aloof figure, too enamoured with his own talents to relate to other footballers. Again, Steve dismisses the idea. "He was one of us, homegrown, fun, a bit more serious now as we probably all are, but one of us. He met Paul McCartney once on *Top of the Pops*. McCartney was in such awe of Glenn, and Glenn was wilting at the fact Paul McCartney was stood in front of him, it was unbelievable – they couldn't speak to each other. But there was always going to be conversation about Glenn. You could be sat with an MP or whatever and it would get round to Glenn, and this is in the day before blanket TV coverage and the internet. Can you imagine what it would be like now?"

Back in 1980 with the varied parts of his team now assembled, Burkinshaw set about translating promise into tangible reward. By the start of the season, Tottenham fans had endured seven trophy-less years. The promotion campaign and cup runs had reinvigorated the club, Hoddle's emergence as a world-class talent and the big signings had made Spurs headline news again, but with such relative progress there was added expectation: Burkinshaw's Spurs now needed to deliver.

In his understated way, the manager gave his players the freedom to put his purist principles into practice. "Keith trusted us to do it right. I think he just created the team, the stage and the environment for us to go and play. I suppose his main job was to keep it going right and solve any problems.

"You could disagree with Keith, no problem. He challenged you, he'd come over in his Yorkshire way and ask, 'Where are you going to be in five years' time?' That was his technique, to ask searching questions. There was freedom – I don't ever remember any strong vibe of 'must do this or that'. With Bill Nick, the instruction for midfield players was, for the first 20 minutes, you nail your opponent, you don't give him one free kick of the ball. You don't have to win it, not even block it, but let him know you're there so he can't get his head up and make the pass. With a normal type of opponent after 20 minutes you can release yourself and go and do what you can do. If it's a good opponent it might be 60 minutes, if it's a great opponent you might have to do that for 90 minutes, you nail him. There was structure there to build on. I don't ever remember Keith, to me at least, ever being quite so structured with a framework."

"Keith and Peter Shreeve worked well off each other. They were totally different characters, but made for a great partnership. He was a good man, Pete, tactically astute and very, very thorough. And when he spoke the players listened. He could absolutely hit the mark in the dressing room at half time when something needed to be said.

"Peter was a very important asset to the club, and he was good for Keith; Keith was a quite serious northerner, not a strict disciplinarian, but he could be quite blunt. Peter was very much a football man, but a bit more light-hearted, especially away from the game, and he could put something across in a 'cockney' way we could all relate and react to. That went down well with us players; there were times to be serious and times to enjoy yourself, and you could have a laugh with him. There were a lot of Londoners in the team and he could relate to that. There was a 'London humour' if you like in the dressing room, and Pete revelled in it. He believed in the team being together and bonding, and would come with us on, say, a trip to Cheltenham races to spend time together. And he made training fun; Fridays we'd have the nine-a-sides where we'd all take the rise out of each other and Pete would join in with his 'I've got a plan' catchphrase. We liked him for it. He was really, really funny, and brought a smile to the club. But when he needed to be serious, he was. Pete was a smart dresser, too, and he used to wear flash ties – all good quality stuff, some of them from Aquascutum, but Pete would wear them to make an impression, get a comment and break the tension – a little ice breaker. He had a bit of style about him and that matched our team."

Within that loose framework, the side blossomed. In the league, Spurs could not maintain the consistency needed for a title tilt and ended the 1980/81 season yet again in mid-table. But in the FA Cup it was a different story. The one-off, winner-takes-all knockout game in which moments of individual and collective brilliance could make the difference were ideally suited to how the team was set up. Commentators were tipping Spurs for a good cup run, with Manchester City manager John Bond predicting Spurs would lift the trophy, and all the portents were in the north London club's favour.

But the run nearly came to an end at the first attempt. Spurs laboured to a replay victory over QPR, but from then on there was no stopping the Lilywhites. Successive draws were kind: Spurs did not leave the capital until the semi-final on neutral territory against Wolves, but with the midfield and forward line in free-flowing, goal-scoring form, Spurs became an irresistible FA Cup force.

"We knew something was happening the season before when we beat Man U in the cup," says Steve. "We were desperate to win something then. But we were more able to accept the breaks the next year. When we had a front pair scoring like ours were, when Glenn was coming to the fore, Ossie was settling down more, it was all just building.

"At the time we weren't consciously thinking we would win a trophy, but something was happening. The first bit of success was the hardest to get, because it gave us momentum. Everyone became happy, our standing with the fans improved and we were a big club again – it was the start of the winning sequence. But we had to get that first trophy under our belts."

Home wins against Hull City, Coventry and Exeter took Spurs to the semi-final meeting with Wolves at Hillsborough. The game is remembered for two things. A frightening crush in the Leppings Lane end of the ground in which the Spurs fans were packed – the narrow avoidance of serious injuries an unheeded warning of the terrible events eight years later at the same stadium – was an incident barely reported. But the controversial way in which Spurs were denied victory by a late equalising penalty mistakenly awarded by Clive Thomas dominated the sporting headlines.

Seething with injustice, Spurs were determined to ensure there was no such travesty in the replay. That the game was to be played at Highbury gave the encounter added spice. With Spurs fans virtually commandeering the home of their fierce rivals, Tottenham were given the ideal platform to let loose their many talents.

Steve remembers, "We wore all white, that was clever, because it was the kit Bill Nick had introduced for when Spurs first played in Europe, so it had a bit of an aura about it. We came out firing; there was no way we were going to get beat in that game."

To the accompaniment of a deafening atmosphere that shook Highbury to its foundations, Spurs didn't so much beat Wolves as exact ruthless revenge for the Midlanders having the temerity to take the tie to a replay in the first place. Two first half goals from Crooks, the second an emphatic illustration of his ability to finish chances beautifully crafted by Hoddle, decided the outcome. Villa's dipping, swerving, long-range effort in the second half merely emphasised the gulf in quality between the two sides.

So the boys from White Hart Lane were on their way to Wembley. The run was so entertaining it even had its own theme tune – the Chas & Dave-penned *Ossie's Dream*. Tottenham's name really did appear to be on the cup. The problem was that no one told the players of Manchester City, whose muscular approach in the final threatened to turn the experience into a nightmare for Spurs. "We won the semi in such good style, it was almost impossible to recreate that. Man City were poor in the league, Bond had bought in half a new team, it was the workers against the skill and we didn't show any skill on the day." Thankfully, an own goal from Tommy Hutchinson took the game to a replay and the rest is FA Cup history, written in a colourful, mesmerising Argentinian style.

Perryman had become the first Spurs captain since Dave Mackay in 1967 to lift the FA Cup. It was a proud moment for this Tottenham stalwart and reward for the loyalty he had shown the club through some lean times. Ever the professional, however, Steve saw the victory as the springboard for further success, and an opportunity to further hone his leadership skills.

"I actually probably think about it more now than I did at the time, having been a coach and a manager, and later realising how important a captain is as a player – both in terms of his own job in the team, but also how he can add something to the players around him. If you find a player like that, don't let him go. Players need leading on and off the field.

"You got the clues about your team-mates from all kinds of sources. This is not my line, I picked it up from somewhere, but 'the pitch is a reflection of life'. There's good and bad, heroes and villains, all life is out there on that football pitch whether it's the parks pitch or White Hart Lane, and it's very difficult for people to be different characters on and off the field. One who was the exception was Pat Jennings. He was quiet off it, you'd struggle to hear him, but at Old Trafford in front of 60,000 people, when he wanted to tell you something, you certainly heard him. He could change his manner when it came to getting serious, he would find the venom. At that point he was serious.

"I put great importance on character and leadership. Judge me on my delivery of the ball or my fighting qualities and determination, but also what I gave to the other players. What sense of security or leadership I had I gave to them. I'm proud when I think back about the effort I put into that."

The next few years saw Spurs re-established as one of the top sides in the country. The 1981/82 campaign was another productive, trophy-winning season, but there was a nagging feeling of 'if only' by the time the campaign ended. Playing with a sense of endeavour and flair at odds with the physical English style of the time, Spurs were a joy to watch but occasionally a frustration to support. In the end the sheer volume of games caught up with them: "We played 10 games in 20 days," Steve points out. "Can you imagine? I played in all of them. I spoke to Maxie about this the other day and he said, 'Look, we played 17 games from the middle of April'. He said we played Man Utd and set a record for catching people offside, they got flagged for offside 35 times in one game. So much so I had a bad shoulder from putting my arm up. It was because we had bad snow in January, we didn't play for a while, and had to play all those games at the end.

"For the 1982 FA Cup final, five of us had injections to play the game. I had one, and I still have a lump in my thigh as a result: I never recovered from it, not that it hurts or anything, but it's still there. We didn't have any of that going into the 1981 game. But by the time 1982 and 1984 [the year of the UEFA Cup win] came along, we had that experience from all the big games we had played in."

Perhaps a lack of experience and competitive nous was what told for Spurs, however, in the game Perryman feels became pivotal for the club in that period and possibly for the years beyond. With three minutes to go in the 1982 League Cup final, Tottenham were beating Liverpool thanks to an early goal from Archibald, but a late equaliser from Ronnie Whelan exposed a tired Spurs to extra time in which they succumbed to a 3-1 defeat, thus ending the club's proud record of having never been beaten in a domestic cup final.

"I read in later years," Steve says, "that [Bob] Paisley used this tactic called 'treacle' – he would pick out a main player in the opposition and he would talk him up because it would soften them up for the day. He did it to me. He wrote a whole big thing in the *Sunday Mirror* about how good I was. I'm not saying I played particularly well or bad that game, but it showed the experience from them to know that's the sort of thing you had to do. They were battle-hardened. Liverpool, as great as they were, won many games in the last five minutes – that was part of being great, they never gave up. Our legs 'went. We sat down for the extra-time team talk; they didn't. I saw a picture where I was stood up talking to the other players who were sitting down on the turf. Maybe they were too tired, but Liverpool had this thing over us.

"We dipped away through tiredness. I don't think it affected us at all in terms of team spirit, we just moved on to the next game – the confidence of beating Man City the season before, and being in Europe made us fairly sure of ourselves. But I think if we had won the League Cup final, we would have won a lot more. If we'd overcome Liverpool in a major game, that would have been a hell of a step forward. It didn't knock us, but we could have won so much more had it gone our way."

Despite this setback, by the time of the 1982/83 season, Hoddle, Perryman and Spurs were reaching the peak of their collective powers. The skipper had been made the Football Writers' Player of the Year (with Hoddle as runner-up) and, having earlier in his career set a record 17 appearances for the England under-23 squad, Steve was finally called up into the senior national squad. He won his solitary cap coming on as a substitute against Iceland in Reykjavik, a long-overdue acknowledgement of his consistent but undervalued quality.

Though the 1982/83 season was to prove trophyless, Spurs continued to entertain, finishing fourth in the league and gaining more valuable experience in Europe. For the following season's campaign, that familiarity with continental opposition was to prompt arguably the side's competitive high watermark, in a famous home leg UEFA Cup meeting with Feyenoord in October. It was billed as a clash between the great midfield talents of successive generations. The Dutch side fielded Johan Cruyff, Spurs had Hoddle.

In the end it was no contest. Playing with a degree of outlandish skill rarely seen in an English side, Hoddle and Spurs demolished the visitors, racing into a 4-0 half-time lead. If the 1960s generation have the epic 8-1 European Cup demolition of Gornik to remember as the pinnacle of the Double side's awesome powers, Spurs supporters of a later vintage have that humbling of the Dutch side to cherish. So what did it actually feel like to play in that team?

"We were one. I'd love to see that on tape, just to see if it was as good as I thought it was. Everything we practised, everything we did on set pieces, it all came to fruition. Your 11 players feel like they are worth 13, it seems like you have so many men on the field they can't cope with you. Like Liverpool were. We never quite matched that standard again, for whatever reason. That night it just all clicked.

"That's the thing about being a player. At a certain point, the penny absolutely drops how to play. With me it did. Then it was like reading a book. I knew what was going to happen next, I knew where I should be, I was in absolute control. It didn't mean we were going to win every game or play great every time, but there were fewer and fewer surprises and that was a consequence of learning through experience. My purple patch – between when the penny dropped and my legs started to go – began at 27, and I kept going until I was about 35. I knew what I was doing, so much so that I could help others and advise them. I'm sure I had a voice before I was 27, but I had a more committed voice after that.

"But I don't think we were consistent enough. We could be sparkling – we were 4-0 up at half time against Feyenoord and then we lost the second half 2-0 which put us in jeopardy for the second leg which, thankfully, we came through, but that first half was probably the best Spurs performance I'd ever been involved in. What a display. What do you say to a team that's been playing that well at half time?

"It didn't happen that often. We played at Forest one day and beat them 3-0. Clough came in afterwards and said, 'Unbelievable. If you'd have done one more back heel I was going to fuck off home.' But for that Feyenoord game it was like we were an engine, with all the parts functioning right."

Games such as this were convincing evidence that Burkinshaw's prediction had come true – Spurs were a team again. Europe had always seemed a natural home for Tottenham and the three campaigns that the manager oversaw set the seal on the revival, culminating in yet more trophy-winning glory. The lessons in how to succeed in Europe had been hard earned; the first venture ended with a hard-to-stomach defeat against Barcelona in the 1981/82 European Cup Winners' Cup semi-final. An infamous 1-1 draw in the first leg, in which the Catalans bullied, fouled and intimidated their opponents, led to a similarly fractious encounter in the return, with a 1-0 defeat sending Spurs out.

"Their intimidation against us at home, the way we matched it and overcame it worked against us there. For the return, the ref went in both dressing rooms and said, 'If there's anything like that again, I'll call the game off.' In our naive English way we sort of believed him. The Spanish ignored him and just went at it. They weren't ever going to call it off!"

The following season, Spurs were out of the same competition by early November after a humbling 5-2 aggregate defeat to Bayern Munich. But even this stood Spurs in good stead for the victorious UEFA Cup run of 1983/84. "We were battle-hardened. If we had gone into every away league game with the same mentality as we went into in every away European game, I think we'd have been all right, we'd have been a better team. I think we used to overindulge ourselves at times. If we played well and lost we would settle for that and that's not enough – you have to have more of a winning mentality. We went to Feyenoord in the second leg in 1983 with fear. But we learned what to do."

Though suspended for the 1984 UEFA Cup final in which goal-keeper Tony Parks was the penalty shoot-out hero against Anderlecht, Perryman picked up a second European winner's medal to add to the same reward 12 years earlier. In retrospect, it might be seen as providing a tidy conclusion to his Tottenham career, complemented by the MBE he received that year for services to the game. But football was changing and Steve was caught up in the upheaval and off-the-pitch turmoil that has been a feature of Spurs virtually ever since.

Back in 1984 a new board under the commercially minded Irving Scholar and Paul Bobroff had arrived and made Spurs the first publicly listed football club. The ethos now was that, though the new brooms were genuine supporters, Spurs was going to be run like a 'proper' business. People had to pay their way; financial consid-erations were key; trust that the players would be seen right on a handshake and a promise became an outmoded, almost innocent, way of thinking. Thus, for all his long service to the club, when it came to negotiating a new deal, Steve was treated as if those years of graft and toil were by the by. Suddenly he was one of those players who might not survive the annual cull.

Steve's contract disputes with the board and Burkinshaw just before the 1983/84 season had caused serious disagreements and blazing rows that echoed through White Hart Lane's corridors, though the relationship between manager and skipper was not permanently harmed. But the disagreement reflected wider-ranging change at the club. According to legend, Burkinshaw departed from White Hart Lane in the immediate aftermath of the UEFA Cup win uttering the immortal phrase, "There used to be a football club over there." Steve is among those who isn't sure it was quite said that way, but he recognised the sentiment.

"The warning signs were there. Scholar was very difficult with us as a group of players, which I was involved in, naturally, as captain. There was an issue over bonuses for the UEFA Cup. Bill Nick had set up a scheme back in the 1970s, whereby if the club got paid well, the players got paid well. If you were to play, for example, Rejkyavik in front of 10,000 you'd get less than if you played in front of 50,000 v AC Milan. I think it was a third between all of us and it was all worked out on Bill Nick terms, very fairly – proper. If you won it [the trophy] it was kind of backdated so that instead of getting £100 for beating AC Milan, you got £500.

"All those years later, this arrangement was still on the players' contracts. We were still going to get a third of the revenue that was made from the final. But Scholar didn't want to pay. He knew there was £100,000 of TV money coming in. He didn't want to give a third of that away. The issue was whether the TV money should be counted as part of the earnings of the game or not. I suggest it should have been. I thought at the time, 'Do yourself a favour, Irving. Bill Nick's office is there, you bought him back to the club, you ask him what he meant when he put that clause in the contract.' But he wasn't interested.

"It knocked us for something like £200,000 between us when all the revenue from the cup run was taken into account. So we went into the next campaign angry. Bill Nick had realised the bonus schedule was wrong and put it right. Scholar thought differently."

Burkinshaw's decision to go was a shock at the time and a generation on it still seems an unnecessary one, but Steve's analysis places the abrupt departure in context. "Keith was discontented the moment Scholar took over. He knew what was going on, the interference. Keith said he ended up logging phone calls he got from the chairman. Once there were 36 in one day. It could be, 'Do you know so-and-so's available at Roma?' 'Er can't say I do, but in a day or two, I will.' Another call: 'Next pre-season we're going to

America.' Keith would say, 'I think you should leave that to me.' Every angle to a football club, 360 degrees, Scholar came at it. Keith got fed up and couldn't put up with it.

"Keith told me that at the after-game function when we beat Austria Vienna in 1984, Scholar called him over to meet their coach. Keith said, 'I know him, I just played against him twice.' Scholar responded, 'I've just agreed with him that you are going to visit next summer to look at his training techniques.' Keith said, 'Er, I don't think I've got a free week.'

"Scholar used to approach me. He would say, 'Steve, I've been looking for you, what do you think of that?' He showed me a pencil. 'I can get these in Spurs colours with 'Tottenham Hotspur' on them for 3p from China and sell them for 50p.' 'Great. Well done,' I thought. He was so up himself, so excited. Can you imagine the doors that opened for him being part of Tottenham? It was like a dream for him. I don't think he was a bad man – just misguided."

In the wake of Burkinshaw's resignation, with assistant Peter Shreeve taking over management duties in what appeared a fairly seamless transition and leading the team to a third-place finish in the 1984/85 season, it appeared that matters on the surface at least were relatively calm. Behind the scenes there was an undercurrent of upheaval. It is common knowledge that Alex Ferguson had been considered for the manager's role and, coupled with uncertain futures for several of the first team, there was an air of discord. "We might have thought we were ready for a change," Steve recalls. "Jack Charlton talks about five years being enough of the same voice. With Peter there was continuity, but I think the biggest shame out of all that was that we should have convinced Keith not to go, we should have turned him around.

"But the biggest problem – and I'm being selfish here – was that should have been it for the next 20 years: Keith to perhaps go upstairs, Shreevesie to be manager, me to be youth team manager or reserves or whatever. That should have been the start. Glenn's been England manager, Ossie's won titles, I've won titles, Ray Clemence, Chrissie Hughton, none of us are mugs. There was the base there of something really proper. They shouldn't have let that opportunity go."

It wasn't to be. Instead, after nearly two decades of loyal service, Perryman was deemed surplus to Spurs requirements. The unsavoury nature of the parting still has a bitter taste.

"It leads on to me being released – fine, no problem, that's what happens. But how you could possibly let someone like me out of the door over the difference between a two or one-year contract, is just . . ." Steve's voice trails off. Twenty years on he still cannot quite fathom how the club was allowed to decline and how he and others from the team weren't around to help carry the good work on. "Listen, I don't think I'd have played the second year but I would have been an influence. But obviously not the influence they [the board], and David Pleat when he arrived as new manager in 1986, would have wanted.

"As per knowing what Tottenham is about and what it should be, I could have had a role. With me involved since youth team level, I had learned lessons that would have been of benefit to the club. Liverpool were great because the lessons they learned were all in-house. If you kept bringing new people in . . . Pleat, for example, was going to have to learn the same lessons as Keith did ten years before. Some were just Tottenham lessons because you were dealing with the Tottenham style, the people etc. That's where they went wrong. By alienating Keith, it stopped what should have been a progression.

"I should not have been allowed to leave. Everyone since has been a little afraid of me and there's no need. If you're honest, if you do it right, I'm your man. The line could have carried on through me. I didn't need to be manager, I haven't got that ego. Clem could have been manager."

Perryman's final days at White Hart Lane were not the way such a long-serving player would want to end his association with a club he had joined at 15. Having played a full league programme the season before, Steve took to the field just 23 times in the 1985/86 campaign, uncomfortable with the direction the club was heading in. "It was a difficult season. I was getting old, I was disenchanted with Scholar, but Spurs was my team. I saw the Scholars of the world change things.

"I started to realise I was getting angry with myself, and I was getting moody with other players, getting frustrated when they couldn't do things. I got mad with Maxie in training once, he gave me a pass that bobbled and I smashed it over the stand and said, 'Don't ever give me that shit again.' And we had a row before it all got broken up, but before I would have just said 'That's Maxie'.

"So it was probably right in a way for me to go. But it weren't done right. I'd lost a bit of faith in Scholar, that's for sure, but it wasn't the end of the world, on to the next and all that. It was disappointing, a hell of a wrench, but I'd had 19 years of driving round that North Circular and that was enough. My legs were going: if it had been a pure footballing decision it would have been right. But can you imagine that club not being better off with me? If you said to an Arsenal supporter today, 'We're playing Spurs next week – would you prefer Steve Perryman to be in Tottenham's camp or out of it?', I think the Arsenal supporter would say, 'out of it'. That suggests I should be in that camp, in some capacity."

Spurs, perhaps, have lived to regret Perryman's absence. The collective remorse for players and supporters of that era is the failure to add a league title to the list of honours. It is a lasting frustration that, with the best team since the Double side, Tottenham could not land the big prize. Though a passionate disciple of the 'Spurs way' Perryman is no romantic when it comes to analysing why the title was not won.

"I think if you look at 1982, there were only 13 players who played a high number of games. Others just played a handful, but there was no real depth. Our style of play wasn't suited to grinding out league wins. I said to Keith after we won the cup a second time, 'Keith, for want of a better word, let's go Arsenal style, as per the league. You have got so much backing now having won two cups, let's close the doors and be a bit more ordinary, but on our bad days get draws – because when we're good we'll beat anybody. You can't stop Glenn being good, and when he's good he's great – it's carnival time when he's spraying the ball over the place. But maybe we get sucked into that way of playing out on the field.'

"Keith said, 'Steve, if you ever sit behind this desk, you'll know that's not possible.' Keith lived by the Tottenham tradition. Which is right, but it's not right we didn't have a serious go for the league either. If we'd have gone my way, maybe we'd have been nowhere near it and not enjoyable to watch, so who knows?"

Perryman's relationship with Spurs, or at least the people who now ran the club, was broken. "John Moncur rang me one day and said, 'I don't know if I've done you a favour or not, but we're obviously toiling. We had a meeting and Pleat said, 'We need someone in here who can link all the different parts of the club together. Anyone got any ideas?' John said, 'Steve Perryman.' Pleat said, 'Hmm, I thought you might say that. Anyway, anyone got any other suggestions?'"

Steve did eventually return to sit behind the manager's desk, as assistant to Ardiles when the Argentinian was installed as boss in the aftermath of new chairman Alan Sugar's ugly clash with then boss Terry Venables. Ossie and Steve may have been the right appointments at the right club, but it was the wrong time and both were dismissed when Sugar swiftly rang the changes in 1994.

For all the disappointments at the end, however, Steve still has plenty of time for his beloved Tottenham people. That relationship, with the supporters and the backroom staff he remembers so fondly, is a strong as ever. It is why, for all the regrets about how the modern Spurs has turned out, Steve can still proudly say, 'This is my club'.

"As players, we made people feel important. We would go to the leaving dos. We did one for one of the security guys, Gerry, lovely fella. It was like a *This is Your Life* theme – fantastic. The office staff were part of us; when we played they went to the game and wanted us to win. It was a family. Great people.

"People like Mickey Stockwell [Tottenham's legendary former groundsman] – bless him, he always used to walk around with this two-by-one bit of wood. One day I said to him, 'Mick what's that all about?' 'You got to have something in your hand all the time,' he answered, 'that way, no one can say you ain't working.' Real proper characters who wanted you to win. Tottenham people."

2
PAUL MILLER

"LOOK THE PART, ACT THE PART, BE THE PART"

PAUL MILLER
TOTTENHAM HOTSPUR

"I used to come into the tunnel before we played and the other team would be there and I'd say, 'Listen lads, this lot are expecting to get beat today; let's not disappoint them.' I wouldn't say that against Liverpool, obviously, but most of the sides I would. People who played for West Ham, Birmingham, all them, that I've spoke to over the years said that used to drive them mad, and wind them up. I said, 'Good, that's what it was for'."

That's Paul 'Maxie' Miller all over. Typical Cockney, always looking to get one over. But Maxie is not flash. Confident, yes; direct, street-wise, fiercely competitive – but it's all based on a knowledge that you need more than front. Miller is what Steve Perryman calls "a proper bloke", and while he rarely features in the lists of Tottenham's greatest players, he was a vital part of Keith Burkinshaw's great Spurs side because of his influence on and off the pitch.

These days, Miller is a little stockier, there's some grey hair, but the face is still instantly recognisable. There's still the twinkle of the cheeky chappie in his face, but also the flash of steel that was a key part of his game. He's well turned out: flannel blazer, quality shirt, nice pair of trousers and good shoes, blending in well in the foyer of the Lanesborough Hotel by London's Hyde Park Corner where he has asked to meet. "I use this place as an office," he says as we walk through to the drawing room, all plush furniture in reds and golds. Miller's now a businessman, a successful one, dealing in property. And we're not talking suburban semi-detached. An Italian waiter dressed in crisp black and white looks up from behind the counter as we walk in, his face opening into a beaming smile as he greets "Mr Miller" and the pair clasp hands. "Nice to see you," says Paul, "can you bring us over some tea?"

Miller is pleasant company, with a sharp wit delivered deadpan for killer effect, and a keen mind evidenced by the speed at which he delivers his thoughts. You sense that, as many a top player found in the '80s, little gets past him. A tidy fella, as they say in the East End, and one whose observations prove eye-opening.

The question that will always be asked of that team is why they didn't win the league title? Maxie's view is clear. "We would've had more chance of winning the league, and we had a good go at it for two years, if we'd have tightened up defensively in front of the back four.

"I believe in retrospect that we should have had one team for playing at home and another for playing away. I've talked to George Graham about this many times over the years, and he certainly believes that you should change two or three faces to play away. You do get more freedom at home, and obviously the other team are a bit more negative. Where we persevered with Glenn and Ossie and Ricky and Mickey Hazard when he came in, we only had one grafter – Tony Galvin. We did used to get overrun a lot. People used to criticise us as defenders sometimes, but basically Chrissie Hughton was like a flying winger so it was me, Stevie and Graham Roberts against the world – we'd have five against three all the time. It was no wonder we were getting suspended a lot, we had to belt people because we were getting overrun. I would love to have seen us be a bit more defensive, but you had no chance with Keith."

But Miller is never less than a fierce advocate of the team as a whole. This team was a tight-knit unit and Miller, as social secretary, played a key role in making sure everyone knew what was expected. "We'd sign a new boy and I would take him and his wife out to the West End for dinner," he says. "Archibald, Crooks, Ossie – you name 'em, I took 'em out to dinner. I used to take them to one of the casinos and have dinner, followed by a night out in Tramp. That was like an initiation for them and their wife. I'd tell them about London and where to live, where the best shops were, whatever. It'd be like saying, 'This is Tottenham, this is what is expected of you, who we are. Remember who you are, what you are and who you play for. It was a Bill Nick thing: smarten yourself up – haircut, clean shoes – we were very into that. The London boys made the others very aware of it and slaughtered them if they didn't do it."

At its heart, this was a London team, its confidence, swagger and grit a reflection of the capital's character. It's one of the reasons the team was so fiercely loved by supporters, and much of this character goes back to Miller and his background in Stepney Green – a background he values without romanticising it.

"If you talk of Stepney and Bethnal Green, where I was born and brought up, it wasn't just West Ham – more of an Orient, Millwall, West Ham, Arsenal and Tottenham area. I'm a Cockney. West Ham is east London, but where we were we were in the heart of it, within the sound of Bow bells. If you lived south, it would be more Millwall, or Chelsea maybe. Chelsea were very popular when I was growing up 'cause of the '60s: it was all King's Road and all that. I loved Chelsea when I was a kid because of the way they played, they were the glamour team and an exciting side. But I never really supported anyone specifically. I played for a youth club called Senrab, which is very famous, it's still turning players out now. Chelsea supplied all our kit so I went and trained at Chelsea when I was ten years old – training at Stamford Bridge first, then at Mitcham at the training ground. Hell of a journey, by the way, for two young Stepney boys, me and a lad called Jerry Murphy, who eventually played for Palace and Chelsea, getting on a train and going to Morden in Surrey. I don't think I'd let two ten and 11-year-olds get on a train like that now, but being two Cockney kids I suppose there weren't too many that were going to start on us.

"I spent three years at Chelsea, then they had a lot of financial problems that I was starting to read about, so I started doing the rounds. I went to most of the clubs. I remember speaking to Bobby Moore, who I knew through a family friend. I was about 13 and I said, 'Which club should I sign for?' and he said, 'You've got to sign for a London club because you can't leave home. And there's only two in London you should sign for anyway and that's Arsenal or Tottenham, because you get a good education.' So I went to them both. Arsenal I felt was a bit cold at the time, and I had good chats with Bill Nick, so I went with that.

"And I know it sounds strange, but I also looked at the Tottenham side and I thought, 'They're getting old: give it three or four years and I might play, it might happen for me'. And it turned out well.

"I saw a chance; financially it was quite good. It was going to get my parents out the East End, and me as well. It was a tough place, a bit of a ghetto. There was two ways out, sport or crime. Education really wasn't on the agenda. Thankfully, I had the sport side. I was given every encouragement by Mum and Dad to go and be a footballer. But it was a good place to grow up: good values, family values, and it gave you a lot of character which was important because in football you take a lot of knocks."

Signing for a side in decline in order to get into the first team quicker was an astute decision typical of Miller. The early days were rocky though. "I signed, then I had three managers in two years," he remembers.."I thought, 'Have I done the right thing here?' I joined when Peter Shreeve was the youth coach, with Ron Henry, from the Double side, and it was a fantastic experience. Along with me at that time were Glenn Hoddle, Chrissie Hughton, Mark Falco, Micky Hazard and we provided the nucleus of the youth team. We had a terrific young side coming and Keith [Burkinshaw] had to go with youngsters because the club wasn't flush with money, unlike today, and he persevered. Then we bought a couple of non-league players in Graham Roberts and Tony Galvin – I think they cost us £45,000 the pair of them, which was unbelievable – and Garry Brooke, a bit younger than us, he came through and all of a sudden half the team were homegrowns. It was a good time to grow up at Spurs."

Much of Miller's growing up came under the shrewd tutelage of Peter Shreeve, who Miller retains a huge amount of respect for. "The first two years at the club I never played centre half, I played right back or central midfield. Peter Shreeve wanted me to see other things on the pitch," he remembers. "It made me a bit more aware, a better player, improved my passing which was one of my great strengths. But eventually I settled at centre half."

The arrival of Keith Burkinshaw gave everyone at the club a fillip. Including Miller, whose reaction to relegation was typically positive. "I thought I'd get in the team even quicker!" he laughs. "I used to drive the manager mad every Friday. I'd knock on his door and say, 'Why ain't I playing?' and he'd say, 'Because you're only 17', so I'd say, 'Well, I'm good enough.' I used to drive him absolutely crackers, Burkinshaw, every week. He'd tell me to piss off and go home, but I was captain of the reserves and we were flying. We'd turn over any team. We broke the Combination record and won 29, 30 games on the trot. The Combination was a very difficult league to win back then, because half the teams against you would be first team players. And at our place at Cheshunt, first team v reserve matches were very tight affairs. On a Thursday morning we'd have a lot of people come and watch the games because they were very competitive. It became so bad that Keith wouldn't let me play against the first-team centre forwards in case I injured them. I was eating raw meat then and I couldn't wait to play."

Miller's chance eventually came – away in the north London derby in Tottenham's first season back up in the top flight. "I'd gone to Skeid FC of Oslo in Norway on loan for the summer which done me fantastically good – finished top European overseas player, qualified for Europe, became a big fish in a small sea if you like. That set me up nicely: I was always coming back to Spurs, no doubt about that, but having tasted that limelight I wasn't going to let it go. So I drove Keith absolutely potty and in the end, we'd had some bad results and he called us all together. He was thinking about bringing some of the youngsters in. I'd been in the squad a couple of times, I'd been 13th man and I'd travelled. So we had tea and toast at the ground before we left for Highbury. I remember seeing the chairman at the time, Sidney Wale, walk across the car park, and he said to me, 'Good luck tonight.' I thought, 'That's strange, I'm not even playing'. And you don't think anything of it. Bless him, Sidney wasn't the best expert on football. So we get in there and obviously there's only 13, 14 of us, so we had eggs and toast and Keith then says to everyone, 'OK, I'm going to make a couple of changes from Saturday. I think it's a chance to bring someone a bit different in and, by the way, he's driven me fucking mad for a year, so Maxie, you're going to get your chance. Let's see what you're made of.'

"So that was hardly inspiring," he laughs. "I didn't have too much time, so I phoned home to my mum and dad – they went to all the first team games – and I said, 'I'll leave you the tickets, I'm playing.'" It's no surprise that Miller relished the challenge. "It was a fantastic place to go and play. Sixty-odd thousand people, including a lot of people I went to school with, a lot of them would know me. I have to say we absolutely hammered Arsenal. Pat Jennings had a magnificent night, he saved four or five one-against-ones, and Stapleton scored in the last minute. He lost me on a cross, and maybe Barry Daines might've done better but he scored and we lost 1-0: same old Arsenal. But I think I done well and made my mark, and I stayed in the team, played the rest of the season. Then we went on tour round the world, and that was it, I was in."

What moved things onto a new level was adding some exotic ingredients to the bunch of young, hungry London boys. What does Miller think the effect of Ossie Ardiles and Ricky Villa joining the club was? He answers immediately: "It changed our club, changed our history. Wages all went up, demands went up; we stayed in better hotels, we had more sponsorship, we got invited to better places . . . It was a defining moment. I would imagine it was like winning the Double was a defining moment, or the push-and-run side in '51. It vibrated all over the country, all over the world. It was a great time to be a young player at the club. They changed our club. Forever."

The change was felt on the pitch as well as off. "We'd always had great individuals playing for the club," says Miller. "Ricky had a tough 18 months before he got it together, but Ossie was magnificent from day one. And he certainly gave youngsters like me great confidence, just by saying, 'Keep giving me the ball, you're a great player'. One of his favourite sayings was, 'It's 95 per cent confidence, five per cent ability.' That's very true.

"We had two world-class players in Hoddle and Ardiles. Ossie was the better player – he was either good, or very good. Glenn could be very average, or obviously very good. He was erratic, and the way he played he could be taken out of the game. I've spoken to people like Graeme Souness and Peter Reid over the years –

top, top midfield players – and they felt Ossie was different class. But Glenn could win games on his own and do things that were magical. Ossie was the outstanding player of our team, and we did build the team around those two. Everything we did went through them. But when you played against some of the long ball sides . . . I remember we played against an early Wimbledon team, and they were crap in those days, we said, 'Look, for half an hour we've got to miss you out because the other team are giving it a whack, hitting balls over the top to stretch us. We have to counter by hitting it long as well, that will stretch them and force them back, enabling you two to have a bit more time and freedom when you do get it, and give you more space to play, and there were *massive* arguments about that. I remember Glenn and Ossie coming in at half time and rucking us, saying we weren't giving them any balls. We'd say, 'But it's 0-0, and we'll get time to play second half', and we did, and we'd win games. Glenn always wanted to play, sometimes overplay, and so did Ossie and sometimes that was to the detriment of us."

Wedded to the talent on the pitch was a powerful team spirit, and this owed much to the social scene Miller was in charge of. "Socially, win or lose, we'd booze," he chuckles. "We'd socialise massively, and no one enjoyed it better than us, no one enjoyed it better than me. There were a lot of wealthy supporters, as well as the hardcore, so we were invited out all the time. Some of us made more of it than others! That meant we were very close, that nothing was ever bottled up. Of course there were arguments. We were a very democratic squad – we had meetings every morning – an hour, two hours. We had terrible rows. We'd all care passionately, and there were a lot of strong individuals. When we signed Clem, who was the final piece in the jigsaw, he'd come from Liverpool where he'd been extremely successful and he certainly had an opinion. Myself and Stevie, we were massive, loud characters, very strong in the team. Then you had Glenn and Ossie with their philosophical thoughts, Crooksie and Archibald always, always had something to say. So you can imagine in a team meeting on a Monday morning, a debrief – it went on for ages. And you were shouting people down. Keith as well was very passionate and Peter Shreeve had to be a big peacemaker in those days. Once or twice blows were nearly exchanged. But that was good, because we cared, and then we'd get out on the training pitch and it was all forgotten about. I think men were men then.

"Verbally we were very loud. Me and Steve used to be terrible on the pitch to other teams. It was part of the game, part of putting them off. It got us a reputation I suppose. I remember we walked into Nottingham Forest one day with our club blazers on from Aquascutum – flannels, you know. We looked smart, and there were some apprentices there looking at us wide-eyed and I said, 'That's right, the main men are in town.' And they nodded. We went out and beat them 3-0. Sometimes you could be one up before you even got out of the dressing room. Especially in away games, because of your status and your persona. That was very important – look the part, act the part, be the part."

With the character of the side being what it was, it seems even more amazing that John Syer and Christopher Connolly were embraced by the players when Keith Burkinshaw brought them on board. For Miller, it's not so surprising. "You've got to remember we were so far ahead of the game in those days," he says. "We had dietitians come in, fitness experts . . . the psychologists, we were the first team to do that. I have to be honest, I didn't need a psychologist, and they'll tell you that. Me and Clem used to laugh at it, but I think there were two or three individuals in the squad who definitely benefited. If one player benefits and plays better because of it, then it's good."

He warms to his theme. "We were one of the first teams to bring in proper physios, and they were part of the team too. Physios then were known as sponge boys. If there was anything wrong you went to the hospital and they forgot about you. So we really did lead the way in that sort of thing."

So with all this expertise on board, how did the team approach matchdays? "We didn't need too much of a talk before the game because the team picked itself and we knew how to play. We were very much into theory and tactics. We'd discuss what we'd do first 20 minutes, how Ossie and Glenn would play. As a back four it was pretty straightforward, we pushed a nice tight line, but we would talk tactically before the game about whether we'd push on, drop off, let 'em have it. Especially in Europe, we dropped off all the time, we had a lot of experience in Europe because we had a lot of internationals, and Peter Shreeve was good on that. The team talk before the game wasn't much because it'd all been done. We'd have a meeting on the morning of the game, about 20 minutes, and we'd have a big meeting on the Friday, dossier on the other side, talking about them, especially the big sides and certainly European ones, and we would know everything about them – free kicks, corners, penalties. We were very well organised, very well prepared, so team meetings before the games were short."

At the root of everything was Burkinshaw. "We got relegated and Keith was given time to have a go again. And also Keith, even with being such a hard, dour Yorkshireman, loved to play. He's the one who always wanted to buy flair players and play creatively, he loved the passing players. He was a good coach as well, he put on good practices, and we had a lot of players wanting to learn."

The team began to flower in the second season back up, embarking on an impossibly romantic run to the Centenary Cup Final. The semi-final saw Spurs leave London for the first time, to face Wolverhampton Wanderers at Sheffield's Hillsborough Stadium. Miller has a forthright view on how that game turned out. "At Hillsborough the fans were fantastic. We were very unfortunate, we'd done enough to win and then that clown and cheat [Clive] Thomas gave a penalty in the last minute against Glenn and they scored." The bitterness is still evident in the way Miller delivers the line.

But on the day, there was no alternative but to fight on. "I have to say, in extra time it was probably one of my best performances, helping to hold the team together because we were struggling, fitness-wise and mentally. But we held on and we were lucky to get a right result, defended really well last 20 minutes. At Highbury there's 60,000 people – and 52,000 of them was Spurs fans. I remember the place was jumping; you could feel the vibrations on the pitch. That's the best noise – crowd decibels – I've ever heard in my life. I've never heard a stadium louder than that, and I've played at the Bernabeu. Highbury was a great stadium and that night our fans took it over. We scored early on with Garth, and he added another before half time, then Ricky scored in the second half with 30 minutes to go; 3-0 up, it was one of the few occasions in your life when you can look around and enjoy it, and the crowd were just jumping. I think they were trying to knock the stadium down. It was just fantastic. We had a party afterwards at Garth Crooks's house, it was a memorable, special, special night – one I'll never forget."

After such a special semi-final, the danger was that the final would be an anti-climax. It wasn't, and Spurs approached it with typical swagger. "It was the centenary final, we made the record with Chas & Dave, which was one of the most successful football records ever made, and I still think one of the best; *Blue Peter*, *Top of the Pops* – a lot of the clubs hadn't done all this.

"The day of the final we didn't play particularly well, but we hung on. We all determined that in the second game we weren't going to make the mistakes we'd made in the first. It was a great game, and Glenn Hoddle, arguably, played his best ever game for Spurs that night. Especially the last 20 minutes when he kept the ball on the right, he was absolutely magnificent. He had tears in his eyes, he thought it was his last game for the club – his contract had expired and he thought he was off. But he stayed and thank God he did."

Miller also has a clear memory of 'that' goal. "I'm saying, 'Let's push up, push up,' so I miss the first bit of what Ricky did. Then I'm watching him from the other end and willing him – willing him to pass actually – and he keeps going on and on and the ball goes through the legs of the defenders and goes in. And you just want to chase up and celebrate, and then as you get there me and Stevie start saying, 'Whoa, calm down, calm down – we've got to defend now, we've got to win the game.' So it was ten seconds of absolute jubilation and then we're shouting and swearing and reminding everybody, 'Hold on, the game ain't over yet.' And that's what Keith and Peter were doing on the line as well – big time. City had a right go at us last ten minutes, Dennis Tueart came on and just missed the post."

At the whistle the Tottenham hordes in the old stadium went mad. "It was a great feeling, when you win something, especially as half of us had grown up together," Miller says. "We had the party of all parties afterwards, back at the ground at the old Chanticleer restaurant with Chas & Dave and all our families and just close friends. It was the perfect way to end the season. I came out about half five in the morning, all of us did, but you couldn't get drunk because you were already drunk when you started, you know what I mean? It was a fantastic night."

Great things were expected the following season, but the club's quest for four trophies combined with terrible winter weather that caused an enormous fixture pile-up which took its toll. "We did play 10 games in 20 days in the '82 season," says Miller, echoing Steve Perryman's memory of the period. "1982 was the last big snow and I think we lost four weeks to postponements, which was at least half a dozen league games. We had to cram those in with League Cup and Cup Winners' Cup, FA Cup – in the end it got to all of us. Four or five players had operations at the end of that year, 'cause we all had to play – everyone played 50 or 60 games. Stevie only missed three games. It was on heavier pitches, and we trained on heavier pitches, so don't say they're fitter today because they can't be."

Miller checks himself, anxious not to be seen making excuses. "But all the other teams at the time, Liverpool and Forest and Everton and Villa, they was all doing the same. But we didn't have the depth of squad that we should've had, and we got serious injuries. I felt we were a good side that year and we were unlucky not to win the league."

The first disappointment came in the Milk Cup final, when Liverpool became the first team to beat Spurs in a major Wembley final. Miller took it hard. "I walked off. I didn't do a lap of honour. I was disgusted with it. For 90 minutes we done enough and we got caught by a sucker punch, lacking a little bit of concentration, Tony Galvin got injured very early on by Graeme Souness. Liverpool regarded Tony as our best player – always. Tony was the one player in that team you could never replace – you ask anyone and they'll tell you. He very rarely got injured – fantastic player. Souness done him early on, he lasted but he wasn't really at the races. And Keith made a big decision that day. He left out Graham Roberts. Paul Price had done OK, but in those days anyone could've played in our back four we were that good. So Keith left Robbo off the bench and made Ricky sub, which was a big call. I don't think I'd have done that, but that was the romantic in Keith, having an attacking midfield player on the bench rather than a defender – against Liverpool! We got beat on a bad goal really, the equaliser. In extra time, Liverpool were always going to win."

The focus switched to Europe, but Spurs fell foul of a tough Barcelona side in the semi-final of the Cup Winners' Cup. "We were the best team in Europe that year, we should've won that competition. Barcelona kicked us out. Maybe we were a bit naive on that home leg, rising to the bait, they got us at it. Which probably stood us in good stead for when we won the UEFA a couple of years later.

"It was a bad mistake from Clem that gave them it, one of the few mistakes Clem made all year – two in the Charity Shield and one then – that was the only three rickets he made. Not bad for 60-odd games. But that gave them a lifeline. We went out there with a few injured and tired and we weren't really at the races. We tried to change our gameplan but we should've been more physical. We weren't the Spurs side that we should've been. But we were tired and the games were coming thick and fast."

With the league also slipping away, only retaining the FA Cup remained as a target to salvage the season. "We had a great semi-final against Leicester, although they were useless. They were white with shock in the tunnel: the game was over before we started. We beat them, got to the final, but by then it was patched up sides going out. There were five of us carrying injuries. I had four injections before the game, and three to play in the second game. In my groin. And Glenn had 'em, Tony Galvin had 'em, we had loads of players having injections. It was QPR in the final and I don't think they was ever going to beat us. We felt we earned something that season."

Miller felt the players learnt a lot from a tough season, but that the club's board didn't. "We grew up a lot that season as a team, and got a lot of plaudits. But the carry-over from that season left us short the next, with all the injuries. That's when we realised we've got to buy more players. And of course they didn't. That was my biggest criticism of the board in them days, they didn't invest. We had 14 or 15 in the squad, which was ridiculous. They were small-time people who were running the club – they had no personal money. Remember this was a time when you could buy Man United for three million quid. The money we must have been generating must've been a fortune. Every ground we played at was sold out and we were always going away on European trips and world trips to earn more money . . . Always, to get an earner."

The following season appears to prove Miller's point, with Spurs knocked out of both domestic cups in the fifth round and crashing out of Europe in only the second tie after a 4–1 beating at Bayern Munich. In the league, fourth place was secured. The next campaign was to be a dramatic one, culminating in a European final.

"The UEFA Cup was harder to win, because you only had eight decent countries in Europe, so the eight champions go into the European Cup and the eight cup winners go in the Cup Winners' Cup, which was probably the weakest of the trophies depending on what year you played. But the UEFA Cup you'd have three or four sides from all these eight countries, about 30 good teams. You played three extra games, another two at the start and the two-legged final, so in those days it was by far – by far – the hardest trophy to win. You had Feyenoord, Bayern Munich, Anderlecht, Hadjuk Split, who all did or would go on to win their own championships, so we were a good side to win that competition.

"In the semi-final and the final, we changed our system. We had Gary Stevens in midfield, playing with Stevie in midfield – two defensive midfield players – with Tony Galvin and Micky Hazard. We rarely looked like conceding goals. In the first leg of the final we slaughtered Anderlecht; Mark Falco and Archibald could both have had two each, and funny enough Parksie made a bad ricket for their equaliser in the last minute, dropped the ball and they were in. Bad ricket, and it just shows you how things can change in a fortnight. He became a hero. We didn't have Clem for those matches, so we're missing three big players – Clemence, Ardiles and Hoddle – for the final stages of a European competition, and we still won it."

Miller had more reason than most to relish the victory. "I got one of my rare goals in Brussels. I'd had a terrible knee injury, got injured against West Ham at the start of the season – really bad, cartilage. I went to the rehabilitation centre at RAF Headley Court in Surrey, where I spent eight weeks, living there, to build myself up, and I came back for the FA Cup replay against Fulham. I came back in, and I really struggled. I was warming up for an hour before games, having injections so I could play. It took three or four years off my career, having those injections. It was only towards the end of the season that I started getting fitter and stronger, so I didn't want the season to end.

"In the game in Brussels, I came up, met Micky Hazard's corner, and it went in. It was a great moment for me. My contract had expired, and I was getting courted by a number of clubs – including Arsenal. Don Howe had had a chat with me. Spurs weren't going to give me anything like what I wanted money-wise, what I thought I'd earned and deserved, so that was the closest I came to leaving. So that goal was a defining moment, because after I scored in the final the club wanted to hang on to me – it's funny that, ain't it? – and my loyalty to the club, which had always been there, and the promise of a testimonial in two years' time, made me sign a new contract. Not too many players get to score in a European final."

The final also marked Keith Burkinshaw's last game in charge. "We knew he was leaving. Keith had problems with Irving Scholar, who was a chairman who loved the club but never had no real finances. Well, he didn't want to put them in. You could've done with Alan Sugar and Irving Scholar together, one who had loads of money and one who had the love and passion – like Jack Walker and Steve Gibson have had in the past for their clubs.

"We knew Peter was about to take over and most of us had grown up with him so it evolved quite well really. Keith went off to make a lot of money in the Middle East; he done his bit, but it was sad really.

"Keith had his Yorkshire stubbornness. I'm sure after he'd won the UEFA Cup, if he'd said, 'Do you want to keep me or not?', I'm sure he could've got a share in dealing with the transfers. It wouldn't have gone back to how it had been before because Irving was determined to change it. I knew Irving from before he became chairman, by the way, he was a fan and he'd be around at the games. He was determined to change things and he was probably right in retrospect, but he didn't go about it in the right way, and Keith – he was very similar to Bill Nick – he walked out on principle. That was very sad for the club, and for everybody. But I suppose he said, 'I've been here eight years, done my bit, second most successful manager in your history, I'm leaving a legacy' – which he did. Unfortunately, Peter wasn't allowed enough time to take it on."

Miller makes no bones about what went wrong after Burkinshaw left. "The facts are that David Pleat was used to running a corner shop quite well. Never won anything in his life, as a player or a manager – he kept Luton up so I suppose that's something – but he was like a small-time shopkeeper who'd come to run Harrods. He couldn't handle the players, he couldn't handle the place, he couldn't handle the whole thing. And in his own negative, slimy way he sold most of the characters in the team. He broke it up entirely, and not to the benefit of the club. A couple of players he signed early on did OK for us, but it was silly to get rid of the mainstays of the side. He called myself, Graham Roberts, Mark Falco and Tony Galvin into his office pre-season and said, 'You four are leaving'. We've got 1,500 games between us, all in our prime still, between 27 and 29 years old: he was foolish to do that. He had a big row with Glenn Hoddle pre-season, big row with Ossie pre-season, he ostracised himself from the team so much we all hated him. It's a wonder we did what we did. We could've won the Treble with a decent manager."

"By then we had the best squad: 18 players, 16 internationals – me and Mark Falco were the only two non-international players. It was criminal he never won anything. Not only did he break the first team up, he sold all the underbelly to Norwich. When Terry

Venables, a great family friend of mine, took over the club years later he said, 'Where's all the players gone?' David Pleat couldn't handle big characters. I knew that from Steve Foster and Mick Harford at Luton he'd done the same thing there. It's very sad because it's the supporters, again, who suffer. When you needed a decent manager to decide tactics and selection, give a little bit of motivation, he couldn't give it."

It's no surprise that in 1987, Miller left the club he had joined 15 years before. "It got sour for most of us," he says. "I had my testimonial, played a few more games, and then left. I really should've stayed but I felt Pleat was taking us down the wrong route. I'd been there since I was a 13-year old, I was nearly 28, and I had nothing to prove. The club was only going to go into turmoil after I left. I'm not being big-headed, but I'd left, Robbo had left, Tony Galvin was on his way out, Chrissie Hughton stayed but didn't really play, Mark Falco had gone. The underbelly had been sold off. Glenn and Ossie had made it clear it was their last season, so did Clive Allen, and Clem – no one wanted to play for Pleat. The club had gone as we knew it. I think they acted too quickly with Peter [Shreeve], who had a great first year – we should've won the league in 1985 actually. Unlucky with injuries again."

Then Miller throws in a piece of information that is so typical of the infuriatingly frustrating continuous loop of 'what ifs' that dogs those cursed with following Spurs. "And we should've bought Gary Lineker in January. He wanted to come, they wouldn't pay 800 grand, so he went to Everton and the rest is history. The last few games, we played with one striker. Again, no investment. Peter, if he could've bought Gary Lineker in January – which Glenn had all settled up through the England squad, Leicester wanted to sell – we would've won the league, because he would've made that difference. Instead we wait three years, pay double, and he comes into a crap team. It's too late."

It's been an explosive discussion, utterly at odds with the genteel surroundings of the hotel tea rooms where we are sitting. Perhaps realising this, Miller says: "That's my opinions. I don't often say these things, and I'm not one for sneaking off to the papers. I got asked by Sky the other week for my comments on the Martin Jol thing and I didn't say anything, because if I give my honest opinion I wouldn't be allowed back in the club, so what's the point really? I'm still a supporter, it's still my team."

After leaving Spurs, Miller went to Charlton and proved he still had something to offer. "I took a big pay cut to go to Charlton, and the challenge appealed to me," he says. "They were adrift at the bottom of the table, only 11 games left, I helped keep them up. Lennie Lawrence has been very nice to me and said it was one of the most important signings Charlton ever made because it kept their status and kept their club alive; 11 games, won seven, drew two, lost two. As an individual, that was my greatest ever feat − keeping Charlton up."

So what was his high point at Tottenham? "Winning the FA Cup the first time," he says, without hesitation. "It's your first trophy, for the players you've come through with, for your family. FA Cup finals are always special. It was a magic moment that defines your life really. And the way we did it − the romance, the Argentinians, the record, the parade down the High Road afterwards − it was all wonderful. And knowing we were on the verge of something great. We knew it was just the start, it wasn't a one-off. With a little bit more luck, with a little bit more investment, we could've won more trophies, but it was a great time."

Despite the bitterness that provided the backdrop to his last days at Spurs, Miller still has fond memories. "We had great times, it was a proper football club, and it was a family, one of the strongest bunch of players there's ever been. With a very strong leader, Steve Perryman, very strong. He didn't stand no shit from anybody. He was a very big influence in my life. When we used to travel on the long trips, I'd sit up the front with him and we'd talk about business, which is why I went that route. It helped us. If you look at most of the team, we've all done all right after that."

Miller's strong opinions about the bigger picture beg the question of whether he ever wanted to manage. "I've never really fancied management. I think I could do it, but it's too late now and I've got my own life, which I enjoy," he says. "I still enjoy watching the football, and talking about it, but there's another life after football."

3

RICKY VILLA

"MY DREAM WAS TO SCORE A GREAT GOAL IN A GREAT PLACE"

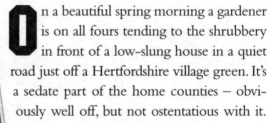

On a beautiful spring morning a gardener is on all fours tending to the shrubbery in front of a low-slung house in a quiet road just off a Hertfordshire village green. It's a sedate part of the home counties – obviously well off, but not ostentatious with it.

It's a very English scene, but a very Spanish accent that issues a soft greeting when the front door opens. A neat, petite woman indicates the way to a long living room and offers tea. The room is chintzy, tidy, with a clutter of framed photographs of family life crowding the available flat surfaces on the furniture. It looks out through sliding glass doors on to a garden that stretches away to a brick structure with a built-in barbecue.

Mrs Osvaldo Ardiles comes back into the room and sets a mug of tea down on a coaster on a polished table surface. The mug carries the logo of the Association of Teachers and Lecturers – an unexpected detail. "They are on their way," she smiles, before gliding out of the room again. There's the sound of footsteps padding across a carpet, the clink of cutlery on china, and a new, deeper Spanish voice. Then he walks into the room. He's still a big guy, still got that trademark lope, still flashes that familiar grin as he sticks out a hand. "How are you, my friend?" says Ricky Villa. There's more grey in the beard, and he's more drawn than he was when he was first introduced to an astonished British public 29 years ago. He's staying here at Ossie Ardiles's family home, as he invariably does when he pays one of his regular visits to the UK.

As we chat about the beautiful morning, Ossie pads in, clad in tracksuit bottoms and a training top with 'OA' on the left breast. His greeting is friendly, but he's less relaxed than his friend, his body language a little less open, his eyes taking in the situation and weighing it up. We agree that Ricky will talk first, and so as Ossie flits off into the depths of his home, Ricky settles his still imposing frame into a sofa and begins to speak.

We start by recalling that now distant summer of 1978 and how Ricky felt when his country won the World Cup. "We felt like the best, the happiest people in the world. And," he says, laughing, "we believed everything would be easy from now on." Room-mates Ricky and Ossie had discussed what would happen after the tournament. "We had prepared to move," Ricky says. "Always in Argentina when you play in the national team you expect a move to Europe. The big money is in Europe – it is not nice to say, but it is the truth. We are professional. In Argentina most of the time the clubs don't pay big money so you are expecting to go to Europe. We were expecting to go to Spain or Italy because the language and other things make it an easy way to come into Europe."

What makes a remarkable story all the more remarkable is that the two Argentinians, dreaming of a move to a familiar Latin climate and way of life, were persuaded to come to London by a partnership rooted in Yorkshire.

Spurs boss Keith Burkinshaw had taken a phone call from his friend Harry Haslam, manager of Sheffield United. Harry's assistant was Argentinian and knew through his contacts that some of the national team's stars would be available. Haslam knew his club didn't have the money to make a move, so he called Burkinshaw. The Spurs boss immediately called his chairman and within 20 minutes was told, "Get on with it." So he booked a flight to Buenos Aires and within 24 hours was face-to-face with Ossie and Ricky. So what did Ricky make of the straight-talking Yorkshireman who appeared suddenly in the Argentine capital?

"I was impressed with Keith, his very English style," Ricky remembers. "He is very honest, he likes discipline, he likes order. When you are a player you just think to train and play, you don't think much about other things. But now I reckon he was a very, very good English manager. I meet him every time I come here and I still appreciate that."

Burkinshaw's achievement in persuading the pair to sign is even more impressive when it is remembered that Tottenham Hotspur's star was on the wane. The club hadn't won a major trophy since 1973. The decline of the '70s ended in what had long seemed the inevitability of relegation in 1977 and, despite returning to the top flight at the first attempt, a team lacking depth looked set to struggle.

Ricky admits the north London side was off his radar. "We only hear about the big, big clubs in those days – Manchester United, Liverpool – we don't hear nothing about Spurs. When we arrived here we understood more about the history and the supporters, and that these were really great things."

But behind the scenes the situation was new and challenging for everyone. And, despite Ricky's efforts to emphasise that he was well looked after, it's clear just how tough this new life in an unfamiliar country was.

"It was very hard for us because we had very little English.

Everything was new; it was really a difficult time. Everything was very nice when we first came. We came in summertime, and I believe England in summertime is perfect really – long days, sunshine, everything we saw impressed us. But the big, big problem was the language. I like to talk with people, and now I can only talk with my wife and Ossie. It was very, very difficult. I believe if I hadn't come with Ossie I would have left the country because if you are not happy off the pitch it is no good for playing good football. We had to really fight to stay in England, and it was not easy I can tell you. Imagine if you moved to Argentina now; you have to know the people, the customs, the food, you can't watch TV, you can't read the paper. It's very hard – for at least six months you are on another planet."

Quite how isolated Ricky felt becomes clear when he talks about the day he and Ossie were paraded at White Hart Lane amid an unprecedented scrum of press and thousands of fans. "It was a very difficult day because people wanted to meet us, and say 'Hello, how are you?' and we can't answer even the simple questions," says Ricky. "I felt very sorry and really very depressed. When I arrived at my house after this happened, I said, 'Oh, I am a stupid person, I can't talk, I can't say anything.' I felt very depressed; not depressed – unhappy. Because if you can see the faces of the people but you cannot say anything to them, you feel really unhappy."

The duo, who could at least fall back on the fact that the club had found them houses next to each other a short journey from the training ground at Cheshunt, resolved to ride out the tough initial period. But the routine was dull and the efforts made to bed them in often rudimentary. "We trained, we went home – and we visited places. We were like tourists," says Ricky. "If I sit at home it is . . . boring is not the word, but me and my wife like to catch the current and move.

"We had a language tuition every week, but it was still very hard to learn because the teacher didn't speak Spanish. He would teach us, but we don't understand anything. He'd say, 'This is a spoon, this is a table' and we'd start from there. Ossie understood a little English, but not me. We struggled to improve our English and be comfortable. It was a really bad time for me – quite lonely. I joke about it now, but it was hard. I want to move quick with the chat, and people want to talk to me – but I can say nothing. In the first days I came home quick to my house to speak with the wife and the parents, which was not good for mixing."

It's clear from the way Ricky talks that this was a very dark period of his life, his natural exuberance and sociability stifled by the new surroundings. But, as he will do often during the course of our conversation, he quickly moves to put things in context, never wanting to seem ungrateful for what he maintains was a great opportunity and – eventually – one of the best times of his life. He is clearly not a man to whom negativity comes naturally.

"Everything was a surprise," he smiles. "The countryside in summer in England is perfect: it's green, everyone has flowers around the house – this is a very, very good-looking country. But we missed our families and our friends. It's not that easy to explain – we are happy here, but we are still missing all those things."

What also helped was the response of Tottenham's fans, whose attitude was a real eye-opener for Ricky. "The supporters here have more passion than in Argentina, because if you lose, people still go. In Argentina, if you lose a few games the people stop going and never come back until you are a good side and expected to win. In England we had really bad results in the first year but the people still believed in us." He leans forward to emphasise the point. "This is a great, great thing. English supporters *support* the team. Not too many countries do this." And the passion of English fans has not lost its ability to impress him. "Last year I went to see Watford, the last game of the season. They were already relegated, and yet the stadium was full! This would not happen in Argentina."

While the fans impressed, Ricky's new team-mates also gave him a warm welcome, team spirit overcoming the language and cultural barriers. "Terry Naylor, the first year we arrived, he was the most funny person. And it was good funny, you know," says Ricky. "I would arrive every morning with Ossie, someone would say something and everybody laughed – we don't know what they say. But afterwards, they explained, it was a real good atmosphere. I can imagine two English players going to Argentina . . ." He raises his eyebrows and laughs.

"And I remember Stevie as a great captain. He was always in the right places, would help you with the right position. He would say all the time to everybody, 'Get up, we can do it.' Good character as well. He would come in early to training. Stevie was great for the club – he kept everybody together."

Asked if that kind of camaraderie was a product of the time, Ricky thinks for a moment, then leans forward again to make sure he gets his point across. "Today there is big money in the game, so maybe when you have big money in your pocket you don't care about many, many things. But when you are fighting for money everyone is like a family because you are all fighting for the same thing. Maybe this brought us all together. I don't believe money makes a better footballer or better relationships within the club. Having money in your pocket makes you feel powerful, but not many players can have money and also be a good team player."

As far as football was concerned, the struggles were more familiar and easier to deal with, and Ricky again singles out Keith Burkinshaw's management style as an important factor. "Everyone had a good character and we expected every day to improve the team. Keith Burkinshaw was very important in this part, because Ossie and me, we play a different kind of football, so he had to put the English and the Argentina style together – that wasn't very easy. Of course, sometimes players were a bit upset if they didn't play, but you have to remember we only have one on the bench, so this is very hard in a squad of 25 players. It was very hard to fight for a place, but that always happens in football."

Clearly the social bonds in the team were important to Ricky, but what about the ability of his new team-mates? Did anyone stand out? Ricky answers straight back with one word. "Glenn." In fact, watching Hoddle on the training ground had a sobering effect on Ricky. "I said to Ossie, 'Why the club buy us? He is better.' I believe Glenn was a great, great player. He could do everything – long ball, short ball, go past people, attack people, good shot . . ." Ricky finishes with a sigh and a spread of the hands. It may surprise some that the pair weren't aware of Hoddle before they came. Although still young, he had been central to the successful promotion season and his talents had already attracted plaudits. But as Ricky says, "In those days the communication was not that easy. Now in Argentina every English game on TV here is live in Buenos Aires. You can watch many players now, but back then . . ." This point leads Ricky to expand on the differences between the way the game is played and approached in each country, casting more light on his own philosophy.

"All the Argentinian people liked Spanish and Italian football. My family is 50 per cent Spanish, 50 per cent Italian so we believe Europe is Italy and Spain. Now it's different. When I talk to Argentinian people they believe the English league is very entertaining to watch because it's quick, no one wastes time, no one gets injured. The only problem for me in England is sometimes when it is 10 minutes to go you say, 'How do you score a goal?' Because everyone is forward or back, there is no space, so you need special players to make a difference. You have great players in England, but not to do special things in one second.

"We play a more individual game in Buenos Aires, and in Brazil. OK, we play like a team but in the last 40 yards, you decide; you can do what you want. In England, you still play like a team all the time. It is difficult for you to find another way to score a goal. You see the Brazilian player, or Argentinian, one moment he does a special thing and you score from there. I believe that if you are attacking people and you get past, there must be one player on your team who is free."

Unfortunately for Ricky and his team–mates, it was early in that first season that Spurs found themselves on the receiving end of a football lesson. On 2nd September 1978, Tottenham Hotspur travelled to Anfield. The game was eagerly anticipated – the standard-bearers of English football fresh from consecutive European Cup triumphs against the side who were the talk of football. For Ardiles, Villa and Hoddle especially, it was the biggest test of their credentials so far.

Spurs began strongly, determined to show their skills, and this seemed almost to affront the home side, who were more used to teams coming to Anfield determined to limit the damage. Liverpool moved up several gears and overwhelmed Tottenham 7-0. Ricky remembers the day all too well, giving a rueful grin when asked if he thought he'd made a mistake coming to Spurs as he walked off the pitch. "Not really, because the club had come up from the Second Division," he says. "You need to prepare for at least six months to play in the top division. This day especially I believe Liverpool were the perfect team, very quick, very skilful, every player looked great. It was very disappointing because if you lose 7-0 you must have had a horrible game. I said to Ossie, 'This is difficult, we have to fight.' After the game we spoke, we said this is the last time – it is impossible to lose 7-0. But Liverpool was a great team."

It was a sobering defeat, one which prompted an upsurge in press speculation about whether the Argentinians would be able to handle the English game. And inevitably, questions were asked about whether the foreigners would 'fancy it' in the English winter. For Ricky, a man who is not slow to show his liking for the sun, the onset of winter was quite a culture shock. "In those days in Argentina, when it rained the game was suspended," he says. "People don't go to the stadium and the pitch is not in good condition. But in England it is prepared to be played in that position. So if it was raining Friday and then Saturday morning we'd think the game would be suspended. But in England – never!"

Despite the trials of the first season, Ricky and Ossie bedded in, and the team finished in a respectable mid-table position to consolidate their return to the top flight. "We were really happy because we finished in the middle of the table, we stayed in the top division," says Ricky. "We felt comfortable after the season finished – we had signed for three years, and we talked and said we need to prove our quality as players. The first year was the bad one. The second year was easy.

"The worst thing was the language and the weather; the good thing was that we played football. Because football, whatever the country, is the same. It is 11 against 11 with the ball in the middle."

Did Ricky feel at home at the end of that first season? "Not really, when you believe you are established at one club it is not a good thing. You have to improve all the time. Especially for me it was very difficult to play in English football. I was a very hard-working player and I never played in between – I was either bad or good. So when I play badly everybody know. Ossie all the while is moving, he's quick – even when he played badly he was not that bad."

It's true that the press at the time seemed to praise each one of the pair only at the other's expense, saying Ossie wouldn't last the winter while Ricky's strength would see him through, or that Ricky didn't have Ossie's skill or reading of the game. Ricky is philosophical about all this. "The press is a very important part of any game – you have to accept that. You can never win with them, so I just accept it. Everyone looks at football in a different way, but who is right?"

There was one other tradition in England that particularly stood out. "The surprise for us when we arrived here was how the people were drinking. In Argentina for social life, we eat, we say, 'Come to my house to have a meal.' In England it was, 'Come to my house to have a drink.' Not only the players, all the people in England drink – this is part of the culture."

But Ricky is measured when pressed on the drinking culture that was prevalent at the time. "Everybody was very responsible, not drinking three or four days before the game, but the players in those days would drink quite a lot after the match. I think in the end it was a normal situation. Maybe some players, some coaches, do drink a little bit too much, but I think this is if they can't take the pressure."

Ricky and Ossie settled in and, by the 1980/81 season, the classic Tottenham Hotspur line-up of the era was coming together. That season's FA Cup was to bring one of the club's, and Ricky Villa's, finest hours.

"We didn't believe the FA Cup was that big, or how important it was for the people," says Ricky. "Now, I understand how it is a big, big thing for English people." This prompts the question of when he realised his goal in the final had captured the imagination to the extent it has. He laughs. "Now. Only now I realise this goal has – what is the word you have for it? Immortality. I realise this only now."

But as Spurs progressed through the competition, Ricky certainly realised it was pretty important. "The semi-final I remember especially," says Ricky. "We really enjoyed playing that kind of football. I remember training every day and we would all compete between ourselves to do special things – Glenn, Garth, Stevie Archibald, Stevie P – they were all good footballers. In this game, the replay, we played really well. After the game everybody was very, very happy, and we were confident for the final too, because if we played that way no one could stop us."

Spurs were favourites to beat Manchester City in the final. All the omens were right, they had shown themselves capable of producing thrilling, flowing football – even their cup final song was riding high in the charts. The scene was set for a showpiece 100th cup final. "But that didn't happen," says Ricky. "When you are at Wembley for the first time, it is very difficult to take the pressure. I remember walking on to the pitch before the game and it was too much pressure to take. Maybe if you go into the dressing room and you pray it is easier, because you don't think too much. But when you are walking around and you see the fans and see it is a big, big party, the pressure is coming on all the time."

Is this why he played so poorly in that game? Ricky still looks pained at the memory, and for the first time seems to struggle for the right words. "Not really . . . well, maybe yes. Who knows?" The image of an utterly disconsolate figure trudging off the pitch is the defining one of that first game. What was going on in Ricky's head as he made the walk? "I was feeling very unhappy with myself. I didn't agree with Keith Burkinshaw taking me off, but I hadn't touched the ball or done anything, so you have to make change. When I walked off the pitch, we were losing 1-0, it was a horrible moment for me – the team was losing, I was going off, and I was disappointed with the manager. But he had to make a decision. Now it is easy to understand, but when I walked into the dressing room I was very, very disappointed. I felt very depressed."

Steve Perryman says he told Burkinshaw not to pick Ricky for the replay, "because I didn't think his head was right". It's not hard to see why Perryman came to what was a tough decision about his friend and team-mate, but the captain's job involves tough calls. Burkinshaw, however, had a hunch that Ricky had got his bad game out of his system, and told him almost immediately as the team gathered in the dressing room that he would be playing in the replay.

"I don't remember exactly what happened in the dressing room," says Ricky of the aftermath of the first match, "but he sat with me and said, 'You'll play the rematch' and this was a great thing for me. A very important part of managing is to decide who will play the next game. Maybe you get it wrong, but you have to make a decision quickly. A manager has to be confident, to believe in the player.

"When I talked with Keith recently, he said, 'I knew from the first touch in the first moment of a game whether you would be in good form or bad form.' Maybe I have one or two bad touches and I give up. As I said before, I am either very good or very bad. In football, the most important game is the next, and I was happy Keith gave me the chance to play again.

"We had a game on the Monday, so we came back to training, and then we started thinking about the FA Cup again," he says. This time there was a quiet confidence. "We were more confident about the second game than the first. Not many of us had played in the FA Cup final before. In the first game everybody knew we had a 50 per cent chance, but in the replay everybody looked more sure.'

So when it came to the game, what did Keith Burkinshaw say in his team talk? "The good thing for me was that Keith never talked about defensive play. All the time we were going for winning games, and this is risky sometimes, because playing Glenn, me, Ossie, Tony Galvin – it's not a very defensive team. And I agree with this kind of football. When you go onto the pitch, you must think about winning, not about losing – that is the worst part of the game. And Keith was always about that, about giving you confidence that you could win the game. We played football all the time."

So what of the game itself, and that marvellous goal? "I scored an easy goal in the first 20 minutes, which maybe gave me confidence," remembers Ricky. "I was thinking before the game, to play worse than the first game – impossible! When you have a bad game, like I did before, you can only improve. So I scored the first goal, the team started doing well, then I finished with the winning goal."

But that winning goal was football at its most mesmeric. Ricky's powerful, surging, jinking run almost half the length of the pitch through the ranks of pale blue City shirts is just a part of a rich tableau of images. Like the seven City players surrounding him as he squeezed off the final shot. Like the sight of Garth Crooks, on the edge of the box, nervously miming kicks with his right foot as Ricky goes further, and further, and further. And of Steve Archibald away to Ricky's right in acres of space, screaming for the pass.

For Ricky, of course, the memories of those moments are quite different. "When I had the ball I was thinking all the time – 'to the goal,'" he says. "I didn't see Steve Archibald [screaming for the ball] because I was concentrating on playing. I didn't have time to watch the other players. When I put my head up, the goal was really close, and I lost control before I should, but in the end it finished in the net. My dream was to score a great goal in a great place, and this happened in the '81 final."

There can be no greater contrast with the crestfallen, substituted figure of the first game than the sight of Ricky picking himself up from the turf as the stadium erupts and running, his mouth wide with the roar of success, his arms fully extended as if he is about to take off, racing along the wing towards his team-mates. "I felt like the happiest man in the world," he says. That goal was voted Wembley's Goal of the Century in 2001.

The cup was Tottenham's, and the triumph was to prove not just a single trophy victory, but the catalyst for one of the most sustained periods of success in the club's history. "When you win it is a great, great moment, and there are not many in football, not many," says Ricky. "I have two or three great moments in my career. In the World Cup I didn't play very often – I won but I didn't feel as if

I won it. This time I played, and I had played in the semi-final. For me, the big moment in football was '81. People in Argentina say, 'But you won the World Cup,' but I only played a tiny part in the games."

The following season saw Spurs challenge hard on four fronts – three domestic trophies and the European Cup Winners' Cup – and more glory for Ricky. He scored his only hat-trick for the club in the 6-1 thrashing of Wolves on the day Spurs opened the new West Stand at White Hart Lane, and was a fixture in the side that finished fourth in the league, reached two cup semi-finals and retained the FA Cup. But the season was soured for Ricky by events far beyond his control, events which meant he did not return to Wembley to help defend the Cup he'd done so much to win the season before.

On 2nd April 1982 Argentina and England went to war over sovereignty of the Falkland Islands – which left two high-profile Argentinians living in the UK in a very difficult position. Ossie was eventually to leave the country; Ricky stayed, but it was not thought appropriate for him to play in the FA Cup final.

"There were some difficult days," he remembers. "In the end I couldn't play the final the next year, but the history is there. What could I do about the Falklands? They were very unhappy days. I believe football should keep clear of the political scene, but it was impossible then. The politics sometimes come in and touch foot-ball, and there is nothing we can do about that. These days were very unhappy because I don't like war. If I have a problem with you, the best thing is to talk."

The pain still shows on Ricky's face and it's obvious he's still uneasy talking about the episode. But he does talk about how it affected relations between him and his team-mates. "The feeling was that the English people know what was going on because you had conflicts with other countries before. I talked with the players and said, 'It is nothing between you and me, it is a problem between the government of Argentina and the government in England.' I'm a normal person, a professional. I have a country here, and I have to respect that. And people treated me very well. I can imagine the other way it would be impossible for an English player to play in Buenos Aires. English people are very polite, despite what happened." In fact, despite some comments in the press and the inevitable terrace taunts, Ricky found little to prompt him to leave the country, unlike Ossie who went to Paris Saint Germain on loan. "I never thought like that," he says. "People treated me very well – why should I move? I didn't decide to have the war, I played football. It never came into my mind to leave the country."

Ricky returned to play another 33 games for Spurs the following season, but a corner had been turned. It was the final year of his contract and when it ended he decided to move to Miami to play for Fort Lauderdale Strikers in the North American Soccer League. He remembers it ruefully. "Maybe I made a wrong decision. I finished my contract. When you are a player, you are always unhappy over one little thing or another – it's silly. I believe now I made a mistake, because I went to Miami to play football and the football in America is low level."

But was he ever offered a new contract by Spurs? "I don't remember. I don't know how to explain it – America for me was another dream. Miami especially with the way the life outside the house was. When I was younger I thought I would live in Miami one day." For Ricky, the lure of the sun was too strong, but as we talk he seems uncomfortable people might think such a big decision turned on such an apparently trivial thing, and he expands on his point. "It was OK to live in Miami, but not to play football. It is a very enjoyable part of the world, because it is sunny, there's the beach . . . but not to play football. Afterwards I went to Colombia to play for Deportivo Cali but the level was still going down. And I was getting older. I have to accept I made a wrong decision –

maybe I could've played two more seasons in England – but it's too late now." He grins and gives a resigned laugh.

Throughout our chat, Ricky has been anxious to emphasise his affection for England. In many cases this would come across as someone trying perhaps too hard to say the right things to the right audience, but Ricky's feelings seem genuine. "Our children were born here, they are English, they have the passports, I'm pleased with that," he says. "The British citizen is respected around the world. The reputation of English people is good'."

And it's not just what he says, it's what he does that underlines the depth of his feelings for England and for Tottenham Hotspur, the club he still – "of course, of course" – considers his team. A few seasons ago, there was a commotion just before the game in the away section at Fulham's Craven Cottage as Spurs prepared to take on the Cottagers. People were standing, looking towards the middle rows of seats, and applauding. The chant of, "There's only one Ricky Villa" went up and in the midst of the throng on a balmy evening a bearded figure could just be made out, smiling and a little shyly acknowledging the ovation. After the game, those who'd been next to him told how Ricky had just bought a ticket and turned up to sit with the ordinary fans and watch his team. He chatted, cheered the team, signed autographs and then, as the crowds streamed home, waved goodbye, jumped on a bus and disappeared into the night. When reminded of that evening he flashes that trademark grin. "I like to go to see Spurs. It's a nice feeling for me; people still recognise me and give me a good reception. This is nice. It doesn't happen in Argentina." And Ricky seems genuinely touched, if not a little amazed, that he is still held in such regard in this country so long after he played here.

We talk a little about his brief foray into management in Argentina when he finished playing. "Yes, I managed a few teams in the second division," he says. "I didn't win anything, and if you don't win anything people say you are not a good manager. But I don't care, for me football is exactly the same. You win, or you lose. In Argentina it is all about winning, not about how you play. It's not nice."

So has his active involvement in the game finished? "People believe that I only have opinions about football, that it is my life," he replies, "but I live now like a normal person. I don't go to see a lot of matches, football is in the past. I have a ranch in Argentina that I look after; I like that. It is my business. Football is a part of my life, the reason I come back here is because I was a player. But not all the time."

Ricky is coming to the end of one of his regular visits to the UK. "I come to the UK once a year at least and spend about four or five weeks. It's a good time," he says, then laughs. "Especially in summer. Ossie is the one I am close to; also John Lacey, Mike Hazard, Stevie P; Paul Miller I see every time I come back. Garth Crooks too – he is an interviewer now, which surprised me," he chuckles. "Garth interviewed me last year. Archibald is in Spain so it is difficult to keep in touch, and I see Terry Naylor when I come back. Johnny Pratt and Mark Falco live around here, so I see them."

Despite the regrets we've discussed, about leaving too soon and about the effects of the war between the two countries he loves, it's clear Ricky is still a man who enjoys life and maintains an optimistic approach. For such a pioneering figure, he is very down to earth, and as he gets ready to leave he says, "When we made the decision to come here, I think we didn't realise how important it would be." Keith Burkinshaw underlined how important that decision was in an interview with *The Independent* in 2006. "I was lucky with them," he said. "They were good characters. I didn't have any problem with their behaviour. They were better behaved than the English lads: they weren't drinkers; they were family-orientated. I made other good signings, but in terms of turning things around, those two were vital. They made us into a world-class team."

Next door in the kitchen, there is an animated discussion in Spanish, then Ossie Ardiles pokes his head around the door. "Hey, is this a book or the Bible you're writing?" he laughs. We've reached a conclusion. Ricky says he has promised to give someone a lift and, after extending his best wishes, he leaves the room – the man who played 178 games for Spurs, wore every outfield shirt number except 2, and scored 25 goals including the greatest goal in the greatest cup final ever.

4

OSSIE ARDILES

"TO PLAY FOOTBALL IS THE BEST THING IN LIFE"

OSVALDO
ARDILES
TOTTENHAM HOTSPUR

"Come, we go into the garden," says Ossie Ardiles, leading the way through the sitting room and through a well-appointed kitchen. As we head towards the double doors that open on to a lengthy garden we pass a section of wall that is taken up entirely by a boot rack containing about 20 pairs of football boots. Ossie strides across a well-kept lawn towards a huge, brick barbecue and wooden shelter that dominates the far end. Pinned up around the shelter are club pennants from Argentina, England, Croatia, Japan – showing all the points of Ossie's career. There's an empty manager of the month magnum of champagne, and some graffiti on the pine beams which is less than complimentary about Ossie's abilities as a chef.

Ossie begins to stoke up the smaller grate in the barbecue, then leans down and asks, "Have you seen one of these before?" He is brandishing an enormous hookah pipe. The bizarre image of reeling around the garden of a boyhood hero in a drug-induced haze comes to mind, but Ossie is smoking nothing more exotic than tobacco. And so we settle down to talk about Ossie and that great Spurs team in an English country garden with the wind gently sighing through the trees, watched by Letii, the family's small, yappy dog, and with proceedings occasionally punctuated by the sound of the hubble-bubble.

In 1978, for a World Cup winner to come to England was sensational, especially to join a just-promoted club. Spurs must have worked hard to convince Ossie he was making the right move. In fact, says Ossie, "They didn't have to sell me the club. I'd done some research so I knew Spurs were a big club, it had been through some bad times but it was big, and it was London – it's good to be in the capital. And it was England." Then he reveals that history could have been very different if Burkinshaw hadn't managed to persuade his directors to fly him to Argentina in person. "There were some rumours, apparently it was Manchester City who were interested. But Keith was there." If City had bagged Ardiles and Villa, would Spurs have been on the receiving end of that cup final wonder goal three years later?

The legend goes that Ossie asked the Spurs boss, "Can my friend come too?" when Keith arrived in Argentina to sign him. The story, as it turns out, is not true. "I didn't recommend Ricky," says Ossie, shaking his head firmly. "The truth is I played the World Cup and Ricky didn't play all the World Cup, so I was more known, particularly in Europe. The World Cup finished and I had wanted to play in Europe, always. There was a lot of speculation that people from Spain and France were looking at me.

"Keith travelled over, and I got a call when I was in Córdoba that I had to be in Buenos Aires. They talked to me and then Ricky was mentioned. Would he like to move? I said 'Yes, no problem.' Somebody had already put the idea of Ricky to Keith.

"I shared a room with Ricky at the World Cup, before the World

Cup too – so we knew each other very well. We had to go and talk to our families. My wife was very, very positive, very willing to move. I was willing as well. Ricky had some doubts, he was just married and his wife had some doubts. We talked, and then we are here."

Presumably Burkinshaw had explained what role he would expect each man to play? "No," says Ossie. "Never in his life did he say to me 'Play here' or 'Go there'. He bought Ricky thinking he was a kind of midfield animal, a hard man, because in the World Cup in one game he was kicking everybody, so he had a reputation. But in fact he wouldn't kill a fly."

Ricky has told of a lonely, frustrating experience that stifled his naturally gregarious nature when the pair first arrived, and Ossie remarks on this too when describing his own feelings. "When we first arrived I found it very exciting. Of the two of us Ricky is usually the most sociable, but there were times of loneliness. We lived next to each other, which was a big help, especially at the beginning, because it was difficult to express myself with only a little English. I could understand people, and I could read the papers but I could not express myself. So we supported each other very strongly – we were a kind of family.

"Because I could speak a little English, I found it easier to just fit straight in. I wanted to carry on learning the language, to study here . . . Ricky had this strange feeling that while he was here he was not living – he was going to live when he went back to Argentina to be a farmer. I had my two sons, my family . . . We wanted to be here. The club were wonderful as well – like Stevie P says, it used to be a family club."

If English culture in general proved a challenge, how about English football's dressing room culture? "It was absolutely great," says Ossie enthusiastically. "I have to say that immediately I arrived in England I absolutely adored, I loved, the football culture. It was football, football, football from the beginning to the end. It wouldn't be politics or religion, it was football and having fun. The joking and the banter – even though we didn't understand a lot of it – it was really great and I loved it.

"The welcome from the players was wonderful. Even those who we thought would be frightened of us for their place. It was a challenge, we had to play well and there was competition – but everybody took it in a very good way. So straight away Steve Perryman was very good to us, he was the captain; Glenn Hoddle because . . . because he played like us," he says, laughing, "John Pratt was very funny, and Terry Naylor was wonderful."

Like Ricky Villa, Ossie was also impressed with English club supporters. "We come from a Latin culture so when you are winning you are a god, but when you lose you are nothing, the worst person on Earth. So we were very surprised here because the first few games did not go well. There were some catastrophes really – the 7-0 at Liverpool . . ." He grimaces at the memory. "In that game we didn't know what we were doing on the pitch – we didn't know what our marking was. And Liverpool at that time were a brilliant team, the best. But people were very quiet about it, it was, 'OK, next match, let's get on with it.'"

The modern image of a football manager is of a tactical control freak who orchestrates every aspect of the game through a series of complex instructions to each individual player. But, as a number of players in both Burkinshaw and Bill Nicholson's teams have said, this was not the style of those great managers. "Keith never said to us, 'You have to play in this way.' We would organise ourselves on the pitch," says Ossie. "Of course, we realised very early on that Glenn was special, a special kind of player. Supremely talented, I would say, so there was an immediate rapport with Ricky and me. It was difficult for him to speak with Ricky because of the English, but with me there was a big rapport, and the play developed.

"It was great to play with Glenn, all the time we were laughing and testing each other. There was competition between him and me of course to see who was the best." It's an interesting comment given Glenn's reputation for being a little difficult to approach. Ossie is keen to challenge the popular perception, eager to defend a man he still considers a great friend. "I like Glenn very, very much," he says. "I think it was a tragedy when he was sacked as England manager, for a silly comment. I understand what he meant but he didn't say it properly and the press went for him. I know exactly what Glenn tried to say because we used to talk about it a few times when he was a player."

One of Ossie's observations on the training regime he encountered also counters some popular perceptions about how the game is played in Argentina compared to England, or at least at Spurs. "In Argentina we used to run so, so much, but in England it was always with the ball. Of course, we would do the running, but we would do most with the ball, so it was very enjoyable."

Once the press hysteria had died down those who assumed the role of wise old heads began to speculate that once the English winter kicked in, these foreign boys – particularly Ossie – wouldn't fancy it. "Even in Argentina they were saying that Ricky would survive because he is big, while I was kind of small and fragile," remembers Ossie. "When the winter came, the pitches here were so much better anyway, but with the mud and the cold" – he leans back in his chair and laughs – "I *loved* it! I would fly around the mud – I didn't get stuck."

It was a tough first season as Spurs battled to establish themselves back in the top flight. The team finished 11th, and a decent run in the FA Cup had been brought to an end by Manchester United in a fifth round replay at Old Trafford. The following season saw the two sides drawn together in the third round, and after a 1-1 draw at White Hart Lane the chances of another cup run looked to have slipped from Tottenham's grasp. But the replay was to be both a memorable game and a turning point in the fortunes not only of the team, but of Ossie too.

An injury to goalkeeper Milija Aleksic during the game meant Hoddle donned the green jersey and Spurs were robbed of a creative outlet. But Hoddle performed confidently in goal and Spurs took the Reds to extra time. With their one substitute used and the clock running down, Ricky Villa danced into the penalty area and laid the ball back to where he knew Ossie would be making a run. Ossie shot, scored and sparked pandemonium in the away section. Spurs had won. "That was a very, very import-ant game," remembers Ossie. "So much happened, and remember we only had one player on the bench. It was at Old Trafford, so it was very, very difficult, and Milija Aleksic got an injury and it got worse, and then we had extra time. So Glenn went in goal; he was very brave in fact."

Although Spurs were to be knocked out again in the sixth round, once again floundering against Liverpool, that result gave the signal that Tottenham Hotspur were able to slug it out with the big boys and come through. It was fitting that the club should send this signal in a competition which has always meant so much to everyone at Spurs – the FA Cup. But was Ardiles, like Villa, oblivious to the competition's allure? He laughs. "Maybe Ricky didn't know the importance of the FA Cup, but not me. You know, I saw the cup final in 1979, we went to see the game because Alan Sunderland was our next door neighbour. Now, with all the Arsenal supporters, well . . . it was impossible," he laughs. "But that day it was great. I realised the importance of the FA Cup."

Inevitably, we spend some time talking about the 1981 FA Cup campaign that is so closely associated with Ossie. "I wasn't in the team at the start of the run, for the first game, because I was playing in a kind of mini-tournament for the national team," he remem-bers. "After that I played all the games."

In those days, the FA Cup final was the most glamorous game of the season and the build-up would go on for weeks. One of the many traditions was the production of a cup final single, and someone at the club approached a lifelong Spurs fan called Bob England about getting one of his acts to write and help perform the song. The act was Chas & Dave, the song was *Ossie's Dream* and it was to be a phenomenal success. Bob told Chas Hodges and Dave Peacock that everyone at the club was talking about Ossie, and this planted the idea for the song. But the song's star knew little about his role until he arrived at the studio.

"I didn't know anything," shrugs Ossie. "Stevie P was a very organised guy and he'd handled it all, so I didn't have a clue what would happen. I was told we'd be doing a record and there was a line for myself. And that the record was my name, which I didn't like really – I said it should be the team.

"Chas & Dave did the song for us, and we went to the studio. I heard the song, and then they said, 'This line you've got to sing yourself' – the line 'In the cup for Tott-ing-ham'. I said, 'No fucking way. No. No. No. No. No. No. Definitely no. Anyway, they give me a few drinks and I did it," says Ossie, laughing at the memory.

Ossie is now glad he did, speaking proudly of the record's success. "It was number five nationally in the week leading up to the final, and in London it was number one. I told my friends at home that my record is number one in London!"

Although aware of the importance of the FA Cup, nothing could have prepared Ossie for the frenzied interest in the centenary final. "The build-up to the match was unbelievable," he remembers. "There was a live link to Argentina for the first time, so we were talking on the day of the final at about 10am to our families in Argentina. We were talking and talking and talking. It was a big, big thing.

"The game was tough, the first one. At the end of that match we were definitely happier. We didn't celebrate like we had won, but we were the happier team. We knew how close we were to losing it. Manchester City were a very good side – very competitive, so for them they probably felt like the main opportunity had gone. We were more confident, because the semi-final had been the same – a draw, then in the second game we were better.

"I remember Ricky receiving the ball and starting to run forward," he says of the winning goal. "And I was like Garth as well, kick it, kick it . . . But typical Ricky, he did a dummy, then another dummy . . . In England usually when you do that – whack – they get you, but he kept on."

Many who watched from the old Wembley terraces didn't really appreciate just how good that goal was until they saw the TV replays afterwards. "It is the same for the players on the pitch," says Ossie. "You don't think, 'Oh what a brilliant goal' you get on with winning. After, when we saw the replay, that's when we realised."

That goal won Spurs the cup, and the victory was one of the most important in the club's history, signalling a return to the top after the fallow years. The importance of the win was not lost in the dressing room. "Everybody was going mad," grins Ossie. "Spurs had not won anything for a long time. It was a team that had been promoted three years before; we knew we played very well – it was the making of that team. That was the start. It meant a lot to us." Ossie himself played a major part in the wild celebrations, launching himself into the deep bath in the dressing room while clutching the trophy. As he flew through the air he hurled the famous cup up and it crashed against the ceiling, leaving a hefty dent in the rim. Ossie remembers taking some stick from his stunned team-mates. "People were saying, 'You've dented it' but everything was so mad – I was saying, 'Fuck off, who cares?' That night was wonderful."

Ossie's next season was to end in circumstances that were far from wonderful, putting the mere outcome of a football match into stark perspective. He takes a long drag on his pipe.

"When we won the cup in 1981 it was a turning point. Before, maybe the team had been relying too heavily on Glenn, on me,

Stevie P. The 1981/82 team was the best team I played in at Spurs. It was just brilliant, brilliant, brilliant. We played lots of games, we were competing with Liverpool, we were in Europe, we were competing right until the very end. But at the end we had far too many games. We finished third in the league, but that was misleading because we were much, much better than that.

"But that season, everything was wonderful. Playing was such a joy. The team was really settled and that means confidence runs through the side. Then suddenly the war. For me, the world was turned upside down. It took me a long, long time to recover."

It was April 1982 when it all kicked off over the Falklands. It was the month of the FA Cup semi-final, but already events further afield were playing on Ossie's mind. "We played the FA Cup semi – won 2-0. But I was starting to feel uncomfortable. I thought it could develop into something big – I never thought a war. The relationship between England and Argentina has been always . . . tricky. Particularly because of the Falklands – or Malvinas. But at the time the relationship was good.

"There was a party after the semi-final and I remember saying to the boys that I was sure the press would be saying a lot of things about me. It had been on the front page of *The Sun* that I had been saying, 'I'm going to kill the English', that I was going to fight for Argentina, that I was the number one soldier – all complete and utter bullshit. But the press in Argentina were not much better. I couldn't win – I couldn't do anything. It was a very difficult moment for me and Ricky because the two countries we love were at war. The war was done for political reasons – both governments wanted to keep on in power, the generals in Argentina and Margaret Thatcher here."

Despite Ossie's distaste for the intrusion of politics into football, and his views of the motives of the respective governments at the time, he is keen to make his position clear. "The position with the islands is that I believe Argentina have more rights to them. Colonies we don't see in the world any more in the 21st century. So I think it is living in the past to want to be a colonial power. The way the islands were taken, Argentina was a very weak country and England was very powerful. This is what it was at the beginning. Now of course, it is much more complicated, there are between 2,000 and 2,500 people who have lived there who want to be British and of course you have to respect that as well. But fundamentally I believe the islands are Argentina's."

Although at the time Ossie kept his counsel, the very presence of two players from a country the UK was at war with inevitably attracted the ire of some fans and the media. "Things started to escalate," Ossie remembers.

The atmosphere was tense, but Ossie is also keen to make clear that his departure from England in 1982 to join up with the Argentine national squad was not something that came about because of the crisis. "A lot of people say I left because I couldn't play in England any more. That's not true at all," he says. "We had a deal between Keith and [Argentina manager César Louis] Menotti that before the World Cup arrived I will go to be with Argentina. That was the deal, and we were going to stick to it. So I went – the decision was a football decision. Nothing to do with the Falklands."

Eventually, as events changed Ossie's circumstances, he did decide to leave Tottenham to ply his trade in Paris, spending a season on loan with Paris Saint Germain. "Ricky stayed but I decided to go," he says. "I thought it would be impossible to remain in England. The club understood; they said, 'You go for as long as it takes. We will keep on paying you, and when you feel it is good, you come back.' I couldn't face not playing football, so the first thing I said was 'Transfer me'. So we came to a compromise. I would go to play somewhere else for a year, on loan – no money involved and no option to buy me. One year and I come back. I was six months in Paris; I play the worst football of my life. It was too much."

It was a dark time and, as with Ricky, it still weighs heavily on Ossie's mind, especially as he lost a relative in the conflict. "It took us a long time to recover," he says. "Even when I came back afterwards, all the time at the back of your mind was the war, the war, the war."

In fact, coming back afterwards was not to prove that easy. After the World Cup, in which he had a good tournament, a hitch in the agreement between Spurs and the French club meant Ossie would have to return to London temporarily. "I was supposed to go to Paris but they hadn't come up with what they should have, so I was told we go back to London and think again. I needed a visa to come back to England, even though I was a resident here. We went to the British consulate – and they said 'No'. No visa. I said, 'But my family is there' and they said, 'Mr Ardiles – no.'

"So I said to Keith 'How can I go back to play in England now? They won't let me in.' And he talked about maybe bringing me in through Ireland, all sorts of things. So I went to Paris. After three months, I have a visa. Spurs put a lot of pressure on."

Back in his adopted home after six months in France, Ossie was soon to have more changes to deal with. His great friend Ricky announced he was leaving Spurs to go and live in Florida and play in the North American Soccer League. "We talked a lot about that decision," says Ossie, "and at the time I told him it was a very bad decision. Ricky wanted to go to the sun. I said the standard of football will be very different. After he scored the goal in the cup final, Ricky was wonderful, playing the best football of his career, but he decided to go."

With Ricky gone, Steve Perryman became Ossie's new room-mate, cementing a strong bond that lasts to this day. At the end of that 1983/84 season, Ossie was to give his UEFA Cup winners' medal to Perryman, suspension having meant the captain missed out on the final and was therefore ineligible for a medal. It was an emotional occasion for many reasons. "We won the UEFA Cup," says Ossie, "but this team was finishing its life." Not only was that great Spurs team nearing the end of its days, manager Keith Burkinshaw had announced he would be leaving the club after the final. How did this news affect Ossie and the team?

"It was a very crazy decision," says Ossie, shaking his head. "The team was settled, he was very settled with us, there were no problems whatsoever. It was perfect. But Keith didn't like the way the new chairman was doing things. He was used to a different kind of management where the manager does everything, and now they were talking about taking some things away. I can imagine he was very happy about the commercial things being taken, but some other things he was feeling very uncomfortable about. He felt he couldn't work with these people. So he took the decision, but like I said, crazy."

Ossie had been carrying a succession of leg injuries ever since he'd broken his shin in his fourth game back in England in 1983, and he almost didn't play the final at all. "I couldn't possibly play, I was only 30 per cent fit. Keith took a big gamble on Gary Mabbutt, he was 60 to 70 per cent fit, but he couldn't take a chance on me as well. But it came to the last 20 minutes and we were losing 1-0 and Keith decided I would play, so I came on." Even a below-par Ossie managed to hit the bar just before Graham Roberts scored the equaliser.

While celebrations did follow Tottenham's win, for Ossie there was little of the exuberance that had followed the 1981 FA Cup final. "We were very, very happy afterwards, but nothing like 1981," he says. "The UEFA Cup was not, as you'd say, the first cup in Europe, maybe not even the second because you had the Cup Winners' Cup. When you compare the UEFA Cup final with all the other finals . . . But still it was a beautiful European night."

With Burkinshaw gone, more change was inevitable. Was Ossie

worried about his future with the man who travelled across the globe to sign him now gone? He smiles. "Not really. I like Keith very, very much. But you know how you are as a football player – a new manager arrives and that's it, you get on with it. Peter Shreeve was put in charge, John Pratt assistant, so basically we were going to be moving on with the same team. Players are very selfish, we just say 'hey' and carry on playing."

In fact, it wasn't the new manager that caused Ossie the problems – it was the persistent leg injury. "Peter knew what the core of the team he wanted was, but it all changed because I was injured all the time," he remembers. "In 1986/87 when I had my last operation – I had my testimonial in 1986 – it was my last throw of the dice. I thought perhaps I am not going to play any more. I had the operation, and by then I had a one-month contract. And then there was a kind of miracle. We started the season and I felt great, like I'd always felt before. I could forget about the leg; it was brilliant, brilliant. All my comebacks before had been the same, play one game in the reserves, someone touch the leg, oh no . . . play one game in the reserves, someone touch the leg, oh no . . . This time I played five or six games in the reserves – fine."

You can still see the joy in Ossie's eyes as he recounts the story of his comeback. "I went to the first team in 1986 again. That was the second best team I played in, a wonderful team, with Chrissy Waddle, Richard Gough, Gary Mabbutt at the back; Clive Allen . . ." Once again, Spurs, now under the management of David Pleat, were fighting for trophies on every front domestically – playing expansive, thrilling football the Spurs way. But the team began to run out of steam as the fixtures piled up. An epic League Cup semi-final saw Spurs agonisingly lose out to the old enemy Arsenal over two legs and the league title slip away under the weight of games. But by the time the season's traditional climax, the FA Cup final, came around, Spurs were there, and hot favourites to beat Coventry City.

It was not to be. "The final in 1987 was one of the biggest let-downs in my career," says Ossie ruefully. "We were convinced we were going to beat Coventry." Much has been made of a row over shirt sponsorship that erupted in the dressing room, a row which saw some players take the field bearing the sponsor's name, and some in plain shirts with no sponsor's logo. But Ossie dismisses this explanation. "The row about the shirts was nothing," he says sharply, "It had no effect at all, we didn't even know about it until after-wards. Maybe we were a bit complacent. Because we were much, much better than them, the better team without a shadow of a doubt. But we didn't perform."

At this stage, a difficult question needs posing. Interviews with many of those who played under him and observation from afar of his two tenures at the club suggest that David Pleat is not the most popular character ever to have graced White Hart Lane. So why was this?

Ossie weighs his words. "Look. David Pleat's football intelli-gence was very, very good. Maybe the problem was to do with man management. A lot had to do with his choice of number two, Trevor Hartley. He made a lot of people very uncomfortable. He created friction. The team were fighting each other, it was not good. But David Pleat knew about football. He was very, very good."

It's clear Ossie is not going to be drawn further, so we move on, this time touching on Ossie's relationship with another Spurs manager, Terry Venables. Chairman Irving Scholar had brought Venables back to England after a successful spell with Barcelona. When Venables took stock of the team he had inherited he decided it was time for major changes. And Ossie Ardiles was not part of the future he envisioned. So how did Ossie feel after ten years at the club?

"Maybe Terry Venables felt a bit threatened by me," he says. "Whatever it was, he decided to make a new team." But Ossie recognised that things had changed for him on the pitch too. "I remember playing in one game," he says, "and someone, Dennis Wise I think, had the ball. I went to close him down and – choom! – he was gone. I remember thinking 'This can't be right, it is impossible.' So I started to feel I was not the same player, I had less quickness. I knew that something had happened that meant I could not play football for Spurs any more because Spurs' level was very, very high. So it was agreed between Terry and me that I should go."

So whose decision was it? "He suggested it," says Ossie. "Blackburn wanted me to help them go up, so we did a deal for a kind of loan for a month. With respect to Blackburn, and QPR afterwards, it was a step down and I seriously began to consider retiring. I was spending a lot of time injured, I was not the player I had been, I was not enjoying football. So that was the beginning of the end."

And so, after ten years during which he played in two of Tottenham Hotspur's finest teams, Ossie Ardiles drifted quietly out of the club he'd travelled across the globe to join. But his love affair with the game was not over. A stint at Second Division Swindon Town saw him become first a coach, then manager, in July 1989.

"I wanted to carry on being involved in the game," he says, the sadness with which he recounted his last days at Spurs gone. "To play football is the best thing in life. For a professional footballer being a manager will always be a kind of substitute when you are not able to play any more. Of course, it is wonderful when the team is playing in the way you want them to play."

Ossie's Swindon, employing a flamboyant style, won promotion to the top flight ten months after he took over, but were then demoted for making irregular payments to players. Once more, events off the field impacted on Ossie's football dreams. Spells in charge at Newcastle United and West Bromwich Albion followed, before the call came to manage Spurs. Although, once again, the circumstances were controversial – club chairman Alan Sugar having just ousted Terry Venables in acrimonious circumstances. Despite all this, Ossie had no hesitation in accepting the job.

"When I had the Spurs job, for me it was a dream come true. But like any dream, you have to be very careful. If at the time they had offered me Real Madrid or Barcelona or Spurs, I would have taken Spurs, no question. That's how much I was in love with the club. Chris Hughton was there; everything seemed to be in place." It did not take him long to see what he had inherited. "Looking back, well, the house was on fire really. There had been great animosity between Terry Venables and Alan Sugar. I didn't want to get involved at all, but somehow the press made me be involved. The players didn't want to play for Spurs, or rather they didn't want to play for Alan Sugar. All the supporters were very much against Sugar, and at the time there were only two people who could put the fire out – Glenn or me. It was Glenn first, and he said, 'No, I am going to Chelsea'. So I became the manager."

Ossie remembers "a very painful time", when even the players he knew couldn't be persuaded to put the effort in because of all the politics going on behind the scenes. On top of all this, Spurs had also been hit with a points deduction and a ban from the FA Cup as a result of allegations of illegal payments made during the split between Sugar and Venables. "It was very hard," says Ossie. "We just avoided relegation; there was no money to spend so we had to buy cheap; we had the points deducted when the FA tried to make an example of us; we couldn't play the FA Cup. It was unbelievable. And very hard to sign players."

It's clear Ossie is still angry about much of what happened during his return to Spurs, especially as he maintains he had begun to turn things around when the axe fell. "The second season, we had a decent team, but I paid the price for the first season. My biggest mistake was not resigning when I should have done. I should have resigned when there started to be a lot of interference, after he appointed Claude Littner and he started to run the club in a kind of, well, put it like this: a 'no bullshit, kick some arses' style.

"I had some differences with Littner, because it could be embarrassing at times. We talked to Alan Sugar and he said, 'Carry on', but after that he never backed me as perhaps he should have. Maybe because he trusted Littner more. At the time the club needed to be better run; I had no problem with that. But he didn't support me in the way that he had. And I should have resigned."

The popular wisdom is that, whatever the dysfunctional state of a club that had prided itself on behaving like a family when Ossie first joined as a player, it was Ossie's cavalier approach to playing the game that really did for him. Does he think this has ruined his chances of managing in England again?

"Absolutely," he says. "All this stuff about the tactics, the five attackers – it was not true. Look, in the 1981 side I played in, we had one midfielder whose job was to be a little bit defensive, but everyone else went forward when they could – that was the idea. I didn't want to compromise. And with the team I had, what could I say, 'Teddy, you stay back', 'Jurgen, you stay back' . . . We had real, real class in this team."

Whatever the cause, the results proved decisive, but since then, Ossie's management reputation has been restored thanks to three successful spells in Japan's J-League. "Japan was very good to me because it rebuilt my confidence which was shattered after Spurs. I am the second most successful manager there," he says.

Despite his bruising experiences, Ossie is bullish about his career. "I've judged myself and I think that I work very well when things are straightforward," he says. "My problems are when things become very political. The problems I had with management in England at

Newcastle were incredibly political: John Hall was taking power, many things were happening. When the political things come in I am not very happy because I am not a political person. And I would like one day to manage in England again."

5

GARRY BROOKE

"IT WASN'T WORK – IT WAS GOING TO DO WHAT YOU LOVE TO DO"

TOTTENHAM GARRY BROOKE

If Garry Brooke is bitter, it doesn't show. As a footballer who weathered more than his fair share of setbacks, he could be forgiven for harbouring resentments – there aren't many players who have had their top-flight career cut short by the consequences of a road accident that nearly killed them. Instead, Brooke retains all the chirpy humour and warmth that made him one of the most popular members of the Tottenham squad of the early 1980s. Mention the name Brooksie to any of them today and a smile invariably appears on their faces.

It is easy to see why. A conversation with Garry is full of laughs, with a fund of anecdotes spawned from a lively dressing room. He has a reputation for being one of the quieter members of the gang, and chooses his words carefully to begin with. But as he gets into his stride, he emerges as an engaging storyteller with a thoughtful take on the game and a sharp insight into the vagaries of success and failure it can provide.

"The problem is that once you've played in the first team and you go back in the reserves, it's such a let-down," he says of the aftermath of the 1983 car crash that had such an impact on his life. "It was soul-destroying, it really was. I went from the massive high of two years, of winning cups, to a feeling that I was back to square one. But I knew I wasn't going to play regularly again. I knew it."

How Brooke ended up having to face the prospect of his career being over at just 23 is one of the sadder episodes from the story of this Spurs side. As a player, he is one of the enigmas of that team. His appearances were limited by injuries and the presence of a world-class midfield that made it difficult for a fast-paced, attacking midfielder to establish himself. As it was, he was a fixture on the bench, but still has three trophy-winners' medals that prove he was much more than a mere back-up.

Even so, he must have found it frustrating to find his own chances hindered by the presence of Glenn Hoddle and two World Cup winners? "No, not really," he shrugs. "We were all too wrapped up with the job in hand. Ossie to me is the greatest player I've ever played with. He was the one I would sort of understudy for. When I made my debut in 1980, I played the next six games as Ossie was away on international duty. We beat Arsenal 2-0, and Shreevesie said afterwards, 'We won that game in the first minute, when Brooksie got Alan Sunderland by the side and put in a really good tackle. After that, everyone was on their game.' I was thinking, 'I'm the dog's bollocks now.'

"The following Wednesday, Keith Burkinshaw came up to me saying, 'Brooksie, you've done well, but you're not playing Saturday because Ossie's better than you.' What are you supposed to say? You can't argue with that; Ossie was better than me. But that was Keith's style. I could have ranted and raved, but I didn't because Keith was so honest and straight. I walked away feeling absolutely gutted, but at least Keith told you how it was."

Garry Brooke had been schooled in this no-nonsense approach from the moment he first stepped through the gates at White Hart Lane. He looks younger than his 48 years, and still bears the stocky build that made him such a powerful player. He is talking in a branch of an American-themed restaurant, built on the site of the former stadium of Enfield Town, a power in non-league circles when Brooke was winning medals at Spurs, but now fallen on fractured, hard times.

Fresh from an afternoon of coaching local schoolkids, Brooke is dressed in a tracksuit. Indeed, he's rarely been out of football kit of some description since he was a kid. Born in Bethnal Green and raised in Walthamstow, he attracted the attention of a variety of big-club scouts from the age of just ten. He had trials at Spurs, Arsenal and Derby, then one of the country's top sides, but when a decision had to be made, there was only one choice.

"I went for a trial at Spurs and a bloke called Ron Henry [from the Double team] was coach. He had this drill where you had to knock a ball with your left foot, get it back and pass it again with your left. The bloke did it to perfection and said, 'If you think that was lucky' . . . Bing, bong, he did it all again. So when I went home I said to Mum and Dad, 'I never want to go to Arsenal again because of this fella.' Just seeing him do that with his sweet left foot got me hooked. At Arsenal they never did any demonstrations. Ron did. And someone doing that is worth a million times more than someone saying this, that and the other.

"I got good advice. When I went for a two-week trial at Derby with a mate called Gary Welsh I had to tell Peter Shreeve. He said, 'What do you expect me to say, 'Good luck'?' Pete can be a bit sarcastic. But when I came back he said, 'If you're going to Derby, the only bit of advice I can give you is that they are going to see you once every six weeks; every time you train with them you are going to have to be at your very best, because the other kids they are seeing are being watched by them every day, and they'll know what makes them tick.' Gary went to Derby but didn't get taken on; I stayed at Spurs and did, so looking back it was a good piece of advice from Peter."

The young Brooke was never a Tottenham fan as such, preferring to be inspired by the individual talents of the likes of George Best on his visits to White Hart Lane with his father, a man similarly non-aligned to a particular club. But once Garry became part of the Spurs family, the inclusive atmosphere soon made him a convert.

"We were made to feel welcome. I knew Mark Falco from district football and we arrived within a week of each other. Basically we grew up together along with Chrissie Hughton – he was and is the world's most charming man, a lovely bloke – and a few others. It was quite a close bunch. But Ron made it enjoyable. He was funny, down to earth – he said things you couldn't get away with now. He would rip into people. Ron didn't give a monkeys, he told it how it was and if you didn't like it, he didn't care. Name calling, swearing, not at kids necessarily but in conversation. I appreciated it because he was honest."

That culture of blunt frankness stemmed from one man whose presence still loomed large over the club even during Garry's early days. "We used to run away from Bill Nick. He was a lovely bloke, but you didn't like to come across him. You'd bump into him and he'd say in a very suspicious tone, 'Hello Brooksie. Do you remember that game at Forest and you should have crossed it?' You'd say, 'Not really Bill' and he'd say, 'Well I fucking do' and he'd keep you there for an hour. He was the scout then and watched youth games, and he remembered everything.

"When I was at school and he was still Spurs manager he actually came to the school to ask if they would release me to play games during the week. And because it was him, they did it. He went to my first wedding as well; he was a great man.

"But the whole coaching team worked well. Shreevesie was the best coach I ever worked with, he'd make training enjoyable every single day. It was tough but it had to be – if you can't take hard work and the mickey-taking you've got no chance, no matter how good you are."

Steadily progressing under such uncompromising but experienced guidance, Garry graduated to the fringe of the first team. But before he could make the breakthrough, the club had a surprise in store. "In a reserves game against Southend we won 4-0 and I scored three. Keith called me into the office. I was thinking, 'I'm going to get involved here for the first team' until he said, 'We want you to go on loan for six months to Sweden.' I was dumbstruck. He explained that because I still lived at home and had everything done for me it would be good for me to go abroad and fend for myself. Paul Miller had done the same, and when he came back had got in the first team, but I thought it was the end of the world for me. I started to doubt myself – 'Do they want me, do they think I'm good enough?' Keith said to go home and have a think about it and within two weeks I was gone.

"Over there you are supposed to get a normal job as well, as you are, effectively, taking a footballer's place away from a Swede – I wasn't sure about the logic but that was how they worked it. My club was GAIS Goteborg, who played in the second division. We were sponsored by a ferry company. I'd been there a few months but no one had mentioned anything about the job I was supposed to have. That was fine by me, but one day I got told to go down to the ferry company at the docks. I walked out with this bloke to where all the ferries are; he gives me a big white coat and says, 'When the cars come off you point them left or right to the car parks.' I went, 'Er, no! Sorry, I ain't doing it. I've come over here to play football not be a car park attendant.' And that was it. But a week later, Shreevsie turned up at my flat and sorted things out. At the stadium they had a sports centre and they signed me on as a tennis coach – for one day. The authorities just needed to check I was doing it for tax and employment purposes. They came and saw me and that was my non-footballing career in Sweden done.

"It all went well on the pitch, I loved living there and we just missed out on promotion. I played 21 games at centre forward and scored 14 goals, but I wanted to get back and get into the Spurs first team. And sure enough, October 1980 I was back in England and made sub, versus West Brom at home. We were 3-0 down and Keith said, 'On you go.' I said, 'Thanks!'. We lost 3-2, but obviously playing regularly in Sweden had got me noticed. And there were other benefits. They sent me there to learn about life really – pay your bills, make you grow up a bit. It was a very good experience for me."

Garry's growing maturity had impressed Burkinshaw and Shreeve. As the double act that shaped the emerging Spurs team they were fundamental to Brooke's own improvement. "Keith was like Ron but didn't swear so much. Even now when we see Keith it's like the headmaster coming in at school. We're all on our best behaviour. He'll look at us and say, 'What are you lot fucking moaning about?' But Keith and Peter were very different characters, and worked well together.

"I love Peter but he could muck you about. He lived like me in Walthamstow and I'd walk down to the Crooked Billet roundabout and get the bus to the ground. Some mornings Pete would drive up, stop and give me a lift. Other mornings he'd just drive past. He could be very sarcastic. But we were sort of 'his' boys. People who know him say, 'He always speaks very highly of you.' So I've got nothing but respect for him. And he could have a laugh. We had a player called George Mazzon, but Peter put it about that his name was Giorgio – he done that for the papers because he thought it sounded Italian. His name's George; he's not Italian at all. Shreevesie changed it because it made him sound a bit more glamorous."

Garry Brooke made his full debut in December 1980, making an immediate impact with two goals in a 4-4 draw with Southampton.

"It was a very strange week. We'd had a reserve game at Southampton that was Kevin Keegan's comeback and there were 9,000 there. Keith turned up to say that Ossie would be missing on the Saturday because he was going back to South America and he said out of the midfield players whoever played the best that night would play on Saturday. Keegan scored after 20 seconds, and I thought, 'This is going to be fun.' But we won 5-4 and I'd scored three by half time, so I made my debut on the Saturday.

"Next game we had Norwich away. On the coach back Steve Perryman sat at the front as always, close to Keith. Terry Yorath – great man, Yozza – calls me over and says, 'Brooksie, you were our best player today so you should be playing next game. Go down and speak to Keith, tell him you should play.' This went on for about 20 minutes so in the end I was thinking, 'I'm the big geezer now, I'm going to have some of this.' As I'm walking down to the front, Steve's gone, 'Brooksie – piss off.' Can you imagine if I had gone through with it? Keith would have ripped me to shreds," Garry laughs at the memory of his innocence.

It was an illustration of Perryman's gift for captaincy. "He had obviously been listening. But that was Steve being smart. He was protecting me from making an idiot of myself. To me, he ran the club. We all knew Keith was in charge, but if anybody had a problem, you went to Stevie. He would talk you through the game – 'Brooksie, five yards to your right, so-and-so's on you.' He could be a horrible bastard as well: he would cut you down to pieces if you weren't doing it. But you had respect for that, it was an old-school thing. He played a vital part in bringing on my game. He was the last great captain we've had. No disrespect to those who have come after him, but I don't think we've had anyone who could match him."

Another factor in Brooke's development was that he emerged from a competitive peer group. "I'll never meet another Paul Miller. He has been like he is since the age of 16, he was never a kid, he was like a 50-year-old then. A lot of people don't know how to take him, he can overwhelm you a bit. But he was always like that. I don't think I've ever seen Paul in a pair of jeans. He is and was a really strong person, but you had to be at that time, because if you weren't, you could have gone under.

"When Tony Galvin came down, we said he looked like a tramp out of university. Me, Mark [Falco] and Paul murdered him and he hated us. But now we're the only ones he talks to. You had to play with Tony to appreciate how good he was. He was mad as a March hare. We were playing a five-a-side once, with loads of little passes. Tony went mad and said, 'Just get the ball to me – this is rubbish this is.' We were playing by the A10 at Cheshunt and he said, 'I've had enough of this' and booted the ball onto the road into a car. A lunatic!

"Micky Hazard used to get clobbered. He was the worst dresser in the world and he'd get told every day. Him and Tony always said that as soon as they finished with football they'd both be back up north – but they still live down here now, and they'll always be here.

"It's the strong bond we still have. Steve organised a do for Keith at a restaurant a couple of years back, there were about 35 players there. It was brilliant because I saw people I haven't seen for a while. We hadn't seen Garth for years. We've all put on weight, but he got annihilated for his extra pounds.

"We used to call Mark Falco 'Gripper'. At the time *Grange Hill* was on with that character Gripper Stebson. Mark's a big fella who can handle himself, and when he turned pro he went overnight from being a great bloke to the biggest c**t in the world," laughs Garry. "One day you're working with him, the next day he's saying, 'Get my fucking boots.' And he was serious.

"They call me Buddha because of that twat. We went on tour to Israel. Ossie and Ricky are really religious and were right into it, I'm not. So we're standing outside some church or temple or whatever and there are two great big statues of Buddha next to it. Mark's gone, 'Look, it's Brooksie!' and that stuck. They still call me Buddha now, the bastards."

If the Tottenham of that era sounds like a place with a sense of playground mischief, Brooke does little to counter the notion. As a former member of the Crazy Gang at Wimbledon, where Brooke spent a spell at the end of his career, he is well placed to compare the two environments. So were the Dons all they were cracked up to be? "No, crap. They never got up to the tricks that we did at Tottenham."

"There was a real hierarchy at Tottenham in terms of the piss-taking. The boys were always doing something. We used to have cold-water fights just to wind Steve up because he hated cold water. He'd go spare. Someone like Archie, he'd do it on purpose, throwing water at Steve. Stevie was like the sensible head boy at times, but he had a laugh. Ossie was a case – two glasses of wine and he was paralytic. When he first came over, the first word Stevie got him to say was 'bollocks'. Everything Ossie then said was 'bollocks'. It was a wind-up culture, but a real pleasure to go to work. Especially once you got in the first team squad. There were downsides, but it wasn't work, it was going to do what you love to do all day long.

"The day the Argentinians arrived, it was about 70 degrees and they are both standing there going 'Brrr' like it's freezing. 'Shut up,' we said, 'it's summer!' But because we were so young, we didn't really speak to them. You didn't just charge into the first team changing room then – you didn't knock exactly, but you would have got stick from people like John Pratt and Terry Naylor if you went charging in there. You'd get ripped to shreds.

"Terry and Peter Taylor pulled a caper outside the ground once. There's a bus stop opposite next to what was Tony's Café. Word went round to get in there because Spud [Taylor] and Nutter [Naylor] were going to pull a scam. Nutter was in the bus stop; we had seen Spud walk across the road, but what we didn't know is that Nutter had dropped his wallet on the floor. Spud had picked it up and done a runner, pretending he'd nicked it. Nutter could never catch Spud in a million years but, in the middle of the High Road, he chased after him and dived on top of him. All the old dears were going, 'Stop thief!' at Peter. 'He nicked it. It was him. Get him!' The traffic came to a standstill.

"Parksie [Tony Parks] was another one. He was a bastard to Colin White, the old groundsman. He used to have a little dumper truck and Tony, being mad, used to drive it up and down. One day, Colin put all these breeze blocks in one corner, it had taken him all day, and Tony got the truck and just mowed them all down. Colin went, 'You bastard, I'll do you'. So what he did was this. We used to have this silly game where we'd get these polystyrene blocks that were the same size and shape as a normal breeze block. We'd put them into a line and then see how far we could boot them. The next day Colin called me, Mark and Micky to one side. What he'd done was paint one of the actual breeze blocks to look like one of these polystyrene ones. Tone booted that and broke his fucking toe.

"We used to go back in the afternoons and play hide and seek round the ground, real kids' games. Peter Southey – we used to have a great laugh with him. He died very young, a tragedy because he would have been a great player and he was a lovely lad. I miss him now. When we started our second year of being an apprentice, he rang me up to say all nervously, 'Garry, what have we got to wear for the first day of training?' It was July. He said 'Suited and booted, yeah?' So he came in all dressed up while everyone else was in shorts and T-shirts. First game of the season, we wound him up again and while everyone was in a suit he came in flip-flops. He was so gullible.

"The apprentices really got it in the neck. We had an Irish lad called Tommy Heffernan, though he never actually played a first team game, and another called Joe Simmonds. We used to get all the kit, and Joe used to look after the kit for Tommy. All the kits were numbered, so what we did was get Tommy's socks and soak them. He unrolled his kit and went mad, saying, 'Joe, you bastard, I'll get you!' Tommy got hold of him, took him up onto the West Stand and hung him from the flag post.

"Something was always going on. It didn't matter if it was in training, a game, wherever. We went to Swansea when they came up. They came out onto the tunnel, this big monster of a team. Maxie looked round and went, 'This is a fucking shithole – my back garden is bigger than this.' Guess what – they kicked lumps out of us. In the second half, Keith held my number up to substitute me. He said, 'Not your sort of game, Brooksie?' And I went 'Nah, not really!' They murdered us, all because of Maxie.

"We were all bollocksed when we went to sing *Ossie's Dream* on *Blue Peter*. You ain't going to go on *Blue Peter* and sing if you're sober are you? Let's be fair. The whole day was a shambles. The producer, Biddy Baxter, moved me and Micky to the sidelines saying, 'You look like you've been at a funeral.'"

The larks reached a high – or perhaps a low – with the unlikely antics of goalkeeper Milija Aleksic. His public persona was one of a popular but unassuming individual seemingly happy to get on with his job and stay in the background. The Aleksic Brooke knew was different. "He was crazy. On the face of it he was quiet, but with the boys he was completely different. Really, really funny, he was always doing something stupid with John 'Blakey' Lacey – we called him Blakey because he looked like the bloke on *On the Buses*.

"Milija pulled this unbelievable stunt a few days before the League Cup final. We were at Cheshunt and we ran the bath for the players and filled it with bubble bath; you couldn't see the water there were so many bubbles. Milija was in it, I went to get in and he said hurriedly, 'No no, Garry, don't get in.' He'd only gone and done a great big fucking shit in it and left it floating around! But because of all the foam you couldn't see it. So we quickly got out and had a shower while the boys came in. We're acting innocent, 'La di da' and that. They've got in, and after a while they've started to go, 'Aagh, no, help, fucking hell!' in horror, running out in terror as this huge turd floated towards them."

Through such pranks, the bond between the players strengthened. But by Garry's frank admission there were differences. "We said some real harsh things about one another in meetings. A couple of times, people would take things personally, people would not get on. Paul Price and Garth Crooks didn't, for example. But as long as you got on on the pitch, that was what really mattered. There's bound to be disagreements. There used to be a fight every couple of weeks, but it is inevitable with 20-odd fellas together. It wasn't a bed of roses, but we had such a team spirit that that could be overcome. Grudges would very rarely be borne. Paul and Garth will probably be all right together now.

"Some people didn't like Archie; Steve was so opinionated it was unbelievable, but that was key to how good he was as a player. He had so much self-belief. Graham [Roberts] was a very good player, but he's had his problems with the club since. Things have been said and he and certain people don't get on. He doesn't get invited to dos now, which is sad. He's criticised a few people which I think is perhaps wrong. But what a player. Him and Paul Miller would probably get sent off every week now. Stevie would struggle as well, because he was hard as nails. We had four or five who could all put their foot in. We used to have days in training when Mark, Paul and Graham would be kicking lumps out of each other. But we had a ridiculous amount of quality."

As a component of that embarrassment of talent, Brooke became established in the squad. He only realised how good it was, however, when he left White Hart Lane. "It hit me when I went to Norwich. Dave Stringer was the reserve team manager; he said, 'You're getting frustrated, aren't you? You've come to Norwich, you're playing with good players, and you're getting into good positions, but they aren't Hoddle and Ardiles, they can't play balls like they can. You've got to change your game to suit.' I had never thought of it like that before, but all that great service goes out of the window. You don't realise it until later."

Perhaps Garry had been spoilt. By the age of 21 he had two FA Cup winners' medals, coming on as substitute in both finals and nearly scoring in the 1982 replay. From that game emerges a story that reveals much about Garry's modest character. "I don't know if the rest of the boys know this but at the end of the game I offered Ricky my medal, because he had played in every game and had only missed out because of the Falklands, but he wouldn't accept it. I said to Rick, 'This is yours. I haven't done nothing and hardly played any games in the cup run.' I did it in the changing room right after the game but he said no. But that's him: he's a lovely, lovely man."

Had Brooke known then what was in store for him, he might have been less willing to make such a generous gesture. His stumbling path towards the 1982 final provided a foreboding of what was to come. "I was lucky to make it, really; in September 1981 I did my cartilage. I was out for a month, went back to training but I split the scar open. They put in butterfly stitches as they couldn't do a normal re-stitch on the scar tissue. So I'm sitting at home later on, and I'm really in pain, thinking, 'This can't be right.'

"The club doctor [the late Brian Curtin] came round, opened it all up and said, 'Oh, that doesn't look too good, does it?' Dr

Curtin said, 'Take these antibiotics for the next 24 hours – they should work. If they don't, well, it's one of those things.' 'I said, 'What do you mean?' He said, 'Well, if septicaemia sets in there's not a lot we can do about it.' He was so matter of fact about it. He was basically saying, 'Your football career could be over; you could be dead!' I thought, 'Oh right, lovely, cheers!'

"Being injured is a nightmare. I didn't play for four months. I couldn't get full bend back in my knee. And the physio Mike Varney, he did his job well but he didn't half enjoy hurting people," Garry laughs. "I'd got about 90 per cent bend back and was training, but couldn't flex it properly. So one day I'm laying on the bench with my foot up and Mike is gently working on my knee. All of a sudden Mike put his whole weight through the knee and crunched it down, as that gets rid of all the internal stuff that's left behind. Oh, the pain. If I had had a gun I would have shot him. But that was the best thing he could have done."

Varney's cruel-to-be-kind work ensured Brooke returned. But just months after celebrating at Wembley, Garry's world was turned upside down. He doesn't dodge any question on the subject of his car crash: he talks with honesty and clarity about what it meant to him, and 25 years later, his recall is almost photographic. "To be truthful the day I had my accident was the day my Tottenham career finished. I made 101 appearances and 84 of them were before the crash. It was weird, that whole year. The season after we won in 1982 I was involved in every game, either playing or sub. After the crash, that was me finished. It was February the 13th, a freezing cold Sunday night. I can remember everything like it was yesterday.

"It was a strange set of events. It happened around the wedding of Lee, a big Spurs fan and the brother of my girlfriend Tracey who became my first wife. He wanted to get married on the Saturday and asked me to be his best man as he couldn't choose between his best mates. The trouble was I couldn't say, 'Keith, can

I have the day off to be best man at my future brother-in-law's wedding?' So they changed it to the Sunday.

"We went to the reception afterwards which was near Enfield Lock. Tracey's sister Lisa was there, her boyfriend Kevin came late, about half ten, so he didn't really have a drink, just a couple, and was driving us back. I wasn't even going to get in the car, but plans changed and we all got in. I was in the back in the middle. We were going along Mollison Avenue and we hit black ice. That was it. The car knocked four lamp-posts down on one side and went down a ditch. As we were going down, I could see a stream at the bottom and I thought, 'Here we go, this isn't going to be too great.' I wasn't hurt then. But as we hit the ditch we went into the ground like a dart and I got thrown all around the car.

"It's funny now but the pain was there [points to groin]. Kevin was driving and Tracey, Lisa and her mate Kay all got out. I'd actually crawled out but the pain was just above me bollocks. I said to Kay, 'Do me a favour, undo me trousers' and she's gone, 'Oh, shut up Garry!' Funny now but I was in agony. Tracey had 11 stitches and Lisa had headaches for ages but I was the only one who was really hurt, because of where I was sitting. I had no support and was just thrown around all over the place like I was in a pinball machine.

"Maybe it was the adrenalin keeping me conscious but by the time I got to hospital I was in a bad way. Mark Falco came to the hospital that night. He saw me getting the last rites. Micky [Hazard] and his wife Yvonne came. The terrible thing was one of the ambulance people didn't know the couple he was talking to were my mum and dad and said, 'He's got no chance; he won't last till the morning. He'll be dead.'

"When I woke up the next day I had nine tubes coming in and out of me. I didn't feel that bad. I had a ventilator in my throat so I couldn't talk but I was smiling. But then on the Tuesday

I came out of shock and I was in absolute fucking agony. They gave me an epidural with morphine that didn't work. Nothing worked. I was in that much pain that if they'd offered to kill me I would have taken it. That was way above any other pain I've had.

"I had nine ribs broken on my left side, but there were 12 actual fractures. Some of them had broken into my lung. I went to Chase Side Hospital but the club flew down some specialist from Manchester who wanted to operate. The surgeon at Enfield wanted to let me heal naturally. That was his job and his choice, if you open someone up there can be all sorts of complications. I realise now he made the right decision.

"I was in intensive care for eight days and on the ward for about four or five. All the boys came and saw me, Keith came with Shreevesie, Blakey brought me a great big pile of porn mags, right in front of my soon-to-be-wife – cheers John. Chrissie came in and said they'd heard about it on the radio. He said his wife Shirl had burst into tears, crying her eyes out. It's strange details like that I remember. I had thousands of cards. I sent them to a charity appeal but I should have really answered them all. Stevie came on his own. He said he could never have forgiven himself if I'd died and he hadn't come to see me. I think he had to do that alone."

It had been touch and go but Brooke survived and the prognosis was that he would still be able to play competitive football. The long and painful road to recovery, however, had only just started. "I couldn't do anything but lie at home for two months. Once I could get up the club sent me to Marbella where one of the directors had an apartment. The club were brilliant. They paid for all the taxis, for my mum and dad to get up to hospital. They were different class. Everybody was, to be honest, everything that could be done was done.

"I went back pre-season, went training on my own. Ally Dick

was there and as I was walking across the car park Ally said, 'You look well', because I'd lost a lot of weight. This was around June; it was the first time I'd done anything for four months. Mike said to go round the track and just do as much as I could.

"So I came out of the tunnel, and I ran round the edge of the pitch. I got towards the Paxton goal and collapsed, I couldn't move, couldn't get any air inside me. Colin was there on his tractor and he jumped off and came running over and said, 'Bloody hell, I thought you were dead!' I couldn't breathe, and meanwhile his tractor's going all over the place!

"I could only run a little bit. That day made a massive difference to me mentally. I thought, 'I can't run 120 yards, how the fuck am I supposed to play football?' Every day we used to train by running round the perimeter track for 12 minutes and do at least eight laps. I was never great at running, if I could do eight and a half I was pleased – but for months I couldn't get past six. It did my head in. I hate cross-country running but was going out running on my own at night to try and get as fit as possible, but I just couldn't get past that barrier. My game was all about pace, but my recovery rate after one 60-yard sprint was poor, it was like I was smoking 60 fags. It was just never ever the same.

"You never lose your ability; Martin Chivers plays for the Spurs vets at 61 and you should see his touch now. But if you ain't fit you've got no chance."

Garry managed to work his way back into first-team contention the next season, but during a game away at Watford, the one which featured Glenn Hoddle's famous pivot and chipped goal, Brooke realised that as far as he and Tottenham were concerned, the game was up. "I hit a wall and couldn't move. I had to come off. The club sent me to Edinburgh University to see a specialist to test my lung capacity. Mine was at something like 82 per cent. The fella said most people only use 80 per cent of their lung capacity. At the time Seb Coe was the best runner in the world.

The doc said, 'If you can get Coe to believe, at the stage when he thinks his lungs are going to explode, that he still has more lung capacity, he could knock a minute off the world mile record. Mentally, people can't do it, our brains close down. Your problem is that you are at 80 per cent now, so in reality you're working at only 60 per cent.'

"That was why, after 60, 70 minutes, I was gone. The club was good, the boys were great and Keith, bless him, would still involve me. Shreevsie made sure I got a UEFA Cup winners' medal in 1984 as well, even though I didn't play. They got the old groundsman-maintenance man Mickey Stockwell to present it on the pitch. It was a nice way of doing it. But what used to be so enjoyable became hard work. The people you know and have grown up with like Micky Hazard and Mark, they've made the step up, and I felt like it was passing me by.

"I wasn't depressed as such, I've never been that sort. But I knew in myself I wasn't going to play regularly again. The club never said as much, but I'm 99 per cent sure they knew as well. Keith said there had been a few offers for me and asked me what I thought. That meant they knew I was on the way out.

"When Shreevesie took over they offered me another year, but the end was near. I had a massive row with [John] Prattie when he was assistant manager, in a reserve game. I looked at the team sheet and I was sub. I lost it. I said, 'I ain't fucking being sub; you can stick it up your arse.' I was fuming then. At the time I was on a week-to-week contract and I refused to sign a deal. I ended up staying for a year, but mentally – well, I went off the rails a bit, I was coming into training just doing what I wanted."

A case of delayed reaction to the trauma of the accident? "It could have been, but my time was up. We'd signed John Chiedozie and Paul Allen, people who play in my position, so the writing was on the wall. I said to Pete, 'It ain't gonna be: we all know I'm not going to get any fitter', and that was that. So I left. It was just so frustrating."

For all his fitness problems, Brooke was coveted by several clubs. A proposed move to Southampton didn't materialise after they failed to agree terms and there were similar wage disagreements with then Oxford United owner Robert Maxwell, whom Garry met at the newspaper baron's HQ to discuss a move to the Manor Ground. "I went in to his office. It was the big chair/little chair set up, like something out of a Bond film. He's sitting there looming over me. He says, 'Yes? What are you looking for?' I said what I was after and he straight away went, 'Goodbye'. I said, 'What?', he said, 'Goodbye!' And that was it. I came out and his son and Jim Smith asked me what happened and I said, 'That's it – he just said 'Goodbye'."

Brooke eventually moved to Norwich. He played reasonably well for the Canaries but it was a difficult period. With his new partner Jackie living in Essex, Garry had a long commute to Norfolk and found the culture at Carrow Road hard to reconcile with the freedom he enjoyed at Spurs. "My friend Trevor Putney was there and he said I was my own worst enemy. Ken Brown was manager and Mel Machin was his assistant. You weren't allowed to say anything. You didn't have an opinion. At Tottenham, you could have your say; there you couldn't. And being the sort of person I was, I wasn't having that.

"Disagreements arose over anything. My biggest one was when we played Millwall. They beat us 4-2 with John Fashanu terrifying our defence. I scored but didn't play well. Right at the end, I flicked the ball past Bill Roffey, a real big lump. He slid in, knocked the ball out and I jumped over him. After the game Mel ripped into Tony Spearing, the youngest lad in our team. I said, 'For fuck's sack Mel, leave him alone. We've had a non-existent midfield out there, our two forwards didn't fancy it, Fash has terrorised us at the back and you haven't had one go at any of our experienced players. All you've done is pick on the easy one.' He said to me, 'Well you're nothing but a fucking cheat. Right at the end of the game you should have had Bill Roffey.' I looked at him and said, 'You're a fucking idiot. As if that would have made a difference to the result.' He called me a cheat again. He was waiting for a hip replacement, so I said, 'Well you're just a plastic-hipped old c**t.' And guess what, that was about the last time I played.

"He was very good coach, give him his due. But you weren't allowed to say nothing and I couldn't cope with that."

Brooke found matters much more to his liking in Holland when he moved to FC Groningen for two seasons. "They were dedicated, even the part-timers, and while the pace was slower their technique was superb. My first game was against Feyenoord who we hadn't beat for 25 years and we won 1-0. We came in on the Monday afterwards and one of the coaches said to me, 'Garry, you work too hard, we don't want to see you in our half.' Happy days! I got in their PFA team of the season. We had Frans Thijssen playing for us, a great player. It was a good time, it wasn't so physical and with none of that defending lark, I felt like a pig in shit. To be honest, if I had my way, I'd still be out there now. But Jackie was pregnant and back in England. I had four or five offers from other bigger clubs over there, but she just wanted to be back at home."

So instead Brooke embarked on a peripatetic tour of various clubs. He spent two years at Wimbledon. "Steve Perryman says I'm the most 'un-Wimbledon' player that's ever been born. I hated it to be honest. I went there for all the wrong reasons, mainly because it was in London but it was a disaster. My knee was getting worse too, a legacy of my cartilage going septic. So it was a crap two years of football, it was awful. I was going to training thinking, 'What is the point of this?' My problem was that I'd come from Spurs and wherever you go after that, you're fucked, you've got no chance.

"At Wimbledon we'd go out on a Monday morning and play

American football. The whole club, 50 people on a pitch trying to play keep-ball. I remember me, Terry Gibson and Alan Cork standing on the side saying, 'Look at these lunatics.' Bobby Gould got the squad out one morning to do some boxing. There was a young lad called Paul Miller funny enough, he was known as Windy. Gould said, 'Put these gloves on, Windy' – someone he knew wasn't really going to hit him back. So he beat fuck out of Paul. Next week he picked Gibbo – big mistake, because Tel is tiny but an absolute fireball; he beat the fuck out of Gould. Everyone was cheering."

Garry then renewed temporary acquaintances with Perryman at Brentford, where his former skipper had been made boss, but injuries had taken their toll and Brooke's gradual drift towards retirement began in earnest. "I wasn't enjoying my football because my knee was so bad. It was arthritis and an op would have been no good. If you look at my left knee now it's twice the size of my right one. I had about six months at Brentford, did about a month with Reading and that was it really as far as league football goes. I played for Worthing, then St Albans, where John Mitchell was managing – they were very good to me, they paid for an operation.

"But non-league is basically where everyone gets their anger and frustration out of their systems. The clubs I was involved in, apart from the ones run by ex-pros, there was nothing constructive. There would be too much ranting and raving from people on the side-line, some bloke whose missus has moaned at him the night before. So that was it for me, apart from when I played exhibition games and the ex-Spurs games."

Garry never fancied a move into management. "I got offered a few amateur ones but to be honest, even at that level, if you haven't got any money, you ain't going nowhere. Sad, but true." Instead he combines training youngsters with work for the Press Association. "I coach in schools every day, working with Steve Grenfell [ex-Spurs reserve and former community officer]. I also work for the

PA compiling statistics. I'll be at Orient one game, then Tottenham, then Chelsea, so it's all round the London area. It's good because I meet people I haven't seen for 20 years.

"Coaching is great but it's different now to when I started in 1993. It's harder because there are more kids from different back-gounds so there are language issues, and kids get very short lessons. Warm-ups and warm-downs cut down the actual time playing. The standard is poor because they don't play enough. When I was a kid, on a bad day I'd have got four hours of football in; kids now are lucky if they get four hours a week. It's obvious, the more touches you get the better you are going to be. Nowadays kids . . . well, it doesn't bode well for the future. There have to be centres of excellence where they can do their academic work and still play.

"I live in Woodford [Essex] now. I can't see me moving. I've got a 19-year-old daughter and a 16-year-old son who plays football with Mark [Falco]'s boy in a team Mark manages. Mark got sent off from the ground the other day, he's murder. We don't get together enough with all the boys, to be honest; I miss it big time. I make an idiot of myself at the big dos: I'm too far gone because I've been having a drink with Mickey Stockwell beforehand," Garry laughs. "I don't have much to do with the club in any case. And I don't miss games, but it's the banter and people I miss."

It's the slightly melancholic refrain common to most ex-players when they reflect on the loss of the dressing room camaraderie. But Garry Brooke wouldn't be Garry Brooke if he left a conversation on a sad note. "Oi, one more story" he says, winding his window down as he drives off. "Did you hear about when we went to Eintracht Frankfurt and I crocked a World Cup winner? The day before, me and Ossie had a play fight, I squeezed him so hard I broke his rib. He played for about 10 to 15 minutes and couldn't breathe. We needed to score to go through, Hod did and thank fuck for that, we got through. The story put out was that it was a training ground bump with Micky Hazard but it weren't. It was me. Keith was looking at me on the bench going, 'You little bastard, you.' He could have killed me."

It's a comforting and entirely appropriate thought that Brooksie, this likeable and friendly man who has experienced genuine heartache yet still emerged smiling, could hurt someone because he hugged them too hard.

6

TONY GALVIN

"WHAT A BUNCH OF WALLIES"

Tucked away at the end of a quiet road just behind St Albans town centre is a stark box of a building which is home to a government agency. Inside it's all grey office furniture, strip lights and box files, a workspace that positively embraces the concept of ordinary.

It's quiet. Most of the staff are on their way home into a bitterly cold night; someone's fixing one of the lifts in the foyer; the security guard is doing the crossword; there's the slightly deflated air that always goes with being in the office after hours.

Not so long ago, when footballers weren't millionaires after they'd played just a handful of games, even the best players had to find a proper job after they hung up their boots, hence the visit to this most unassuming of destinations. The stairwell door opens and the man described by at least three of his team-mates as the only irreplaceable player of the early '80s Spurs side walks through.

Tony Galvin has filled out a little, he's a bit thinner on top, but he still looks you in the eye with the same firm stare familiar from the official mugshots. He wears his shirt untucked, dark trousers, soft brown boots – an ordinary bloke in the office. He extends a hand, then leads the way up the stairs. We chat about changes to the agency's work and what's happening to employment training in the UK, he makes tea and we settle down to talk about the days when he ran the wing for Tottenham Hotspur.

It's days before the 2008 Carling Cup final and Galvin – still a fan – has extra reason for wanting a Spurs win. A few weeks before he had been among those present at a dinner to celebrate the induction of Ossie Ardiles and Ricky Villa into the club's Hall of Fame. "When I go back to these dinners I still feel a connection, and when you see how passionate the fans are you think, 'My God, please let them just win something then we can all move on with our lives.' Win something, then stop talking about the past and move on." Galvin, as he will tend to do during our conversation, warms to his theme and moves up a gear – just as he used to when piling up the wing in his playing days.

"To be quite honest it annoys me. I like going to things and meeting supporters, and you want your players to have their place in history, but what Tottenham need is some new heroes. In 1991 it was looking quite promising and that all went pear-shaped, and now you think, 'Let them win something and we can be consigned to history – which is where we belong.'"

It is pointed out that the '81 team's standing with the fans is a result not just of what they achieved on the pitch, but also of the fact that they are the last team the fans really identified with. Galvin looks slightly disappointed, as if a chance to relieve the burden of the history he helped make has slipped away. Does this mean he feels the pressure of being one of that great team? "No, not pressure. I just don't like it, it makes me feel a bit uncomfortable. It was OK in the '90s, but once you get to 2008 and you're

New sensation: Keith Burkinshaw parades Ricky Villa and Osvaldo Ardiles before an astonished world's press at White Hart Lane in the summer of 1978.

Captain indispensible: Tottenham through and through, Steve Perryman is still the skipper.

Stalwart defender and social secretary, Paul Miller embodied the club's confident, cockney character.

Cop that: Ricky and Ossie make like Regan and Carter for a classic promotional shoot in front of the old West Stand entrance.

Tottenham are back: Just four years after relegation, Keith Burkinshaw leads his side out for the Centenary Cup Final against Manchester City at Wembley.

The special one: Ricky Villa completes his mazy waltz
through the City defence to score what was voted The
Greatest Cup Final Goal of the 20th Century.

ACTION IMAGES/MIRRORPIX (2)

Winners: Glenn Hoddle and Paul Miller
(*left*) parade the cup in 1981. Steve Perryman
remembers, "Everyone became happy, our
standing with the fans improved and we
were a big club again."

Winners again: At the end of the 1982 season
that had promised so much, Graham Roberts,
(*above*) followed by Steve Archibald, celebrate
another FA Cup success.

Doing it like they did last year: Back at Wembley
in 1982, the squad return to the studio to record
The Spurs Medley.

Creative sparks: With Chas Hodges and Dave Peacock up front, Glenn Hoddle on bass and Ray Clemence on piano, no one could stop Tottenham.

Come on you Spurs! Football and music rarely mix well – but Chas & Dave and the Spurs team were a prolific partnership.

ACTION IMAGES/MIRRORPIX

GETTY IMAGES

Ossie Ardiles with children Pablo (left, aged 11) and Federico (8) – seemingly not sharing their dad's love for Spurs!

Natty threads: Paul Miller and glamour model Tessa Hewitt promote Miller's knitwear range. This is believed to be the only time Miller wore jeans!

MANCHESTER DAILY EXPRESS AT THE NMEM / SSPL

Enjoying the trappings of the '80s football superstar. Glenn Hoddle and his then wife Anne by their pool, January 1982.

Ay carumba!: Burkinshaw shows the strain in Barcelona in 1982
as the media scrum rages all about him. Spurs had just lost 1–0 to
Barcelona in the Cup Winners' Cup semi-final, second leg.

The Equaliser: Graham Roberts is delighted after evening up the score in the 1984 UEFA Cup Final. "I still get goosebumps when I watch that," he says.

Saver return: Tony Parks tries out the UEFA Cup for
size after keeping out two penalties, the last of which he
modestly says "my mum could've saved."

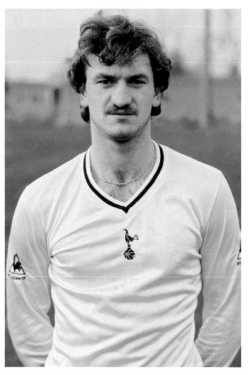

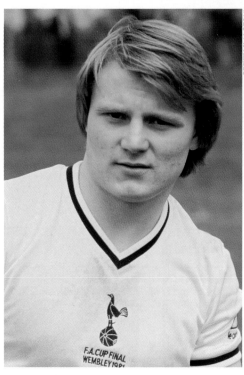

Seven up: He only made a handful of first-team appearances, but George Mazzon lived the dream.

A youthful Garry Brooke, pictured in happier days before the car accident that nearly claimed his life.

Smooth operator: Peter Shreeve; Cockney, cabbie, connoisseur of 'silky soccer.'

Tony Galvin puts into practice the style with purpose that Peter Shreeve instilled in his players.

still seeing the same old shots . . . Tottenham supporters have got a bit of a thing about looking back. Mind you, even I would say you'd never beat the Double-winning team. You'll never see a better player, a better centre forward, than Jimmy Greaves. Not ever. And I don't think you'll ever see a better footballer than George Best."

It's refreshing to sit and talk with Tony Galvin. He's outside the media circus that has become so much a part of modern football; he doesn't have to watch his words to keep anyone happy, or generate controversy to retain attention. He knows what he's talking about because he's been there and done it, but he also knows how to keep it all in perspective. There's no big talk, but no false modesty.

"I've always had massive respect for Tottenham supporters," he says. "You want them to get success because they deserve it. The club I can't stand is Chelsea; I hate them. Give Arsenal their due, they've always had the support and they play football. But Chelsea, when you look at their support, they really make me laugh because they have genuinely just come out of the woodwork in the last ten years. They are a disgrace. If they have five years with no success, they'll be back down to 15 to 20,000."

Clearly, Galvin's got no time for anything that smacks of what he later describes as a 'Billy Big Bollocks' attitude. In fact, his stripped-down style seems to contrast with the knowing swagger of the London crew at the heart of the team he joined in 1978. "Yes," he grins, "there were people like Paul Miller and Garry Brooke who were right mickey-takers, they took the mickey out of the clothes you wore, thicko student from up north, you know, uncool . . . But I did get to know the reserve lads when I joined, Paul and Garry, Mark Falco, Micky Stead was always a decent bloke. The two I've kept in touch with are Mark Falco and Garry Brooke. I don't see them all the time but we've kept in touch. I get on well with Paul Miller but I don't see him often." Galvin grins. "I don't mix in the high circles he does – and he's a great big name dropper, telling you who he's seen and where's he's been – so you have to tell him to shut up."

Did Galvin get taken on one of the dinners Miller said he always treated a new player to? Galvin raises an eyebrow. "He said that, did he? I don't remember that." You can imagine the dressing room banter.

Galvin was a northerner, but he certainly wasn't thick. One of the many facts that 1980s schoolkids managed to retain at the expense of unimportant stuff like famous dates from history or what was the main export of Denmark was, 'Tony Galvin has a degree in Russian.' It was Russian Studies, to be accurate, and when Galvin joined Spurs he was in the middle of teacher training at college in Nottingham, which made him a little older than the other lads. "I only played in reserve games initially and did a bit of training when I could," he remembers, "but I was at college most of the time. When I turned up, yes, it did feel like very much a London-based club.

"I had been playing for a club called Goole Town in the Northern Premier League. We had a game in Buxton in the Peak District. It's a lovely place, but this night it was really wild, a horrible, horrible night – typical Buxton weather really, the roads got blocked up, it hailed, and I'd been told someone was coming to watch me but I didn't have a clue who. And I thought on this night, being like it was, they probably wouldn't turn up. But Bill Nicholson was there. He just decided on the strength of that one game to sign me, and it had been an absolute mudheap; not the sort of game to show what you can do. But Bill had seen it, gone in and done the business, and buggered off and made the recommendation to Keith Burkinshaw that they should sign me.

"It was a £5,000 fee to Goole Town, with another £5,000 once I'd played some first team games. I was offered something like £50 a week. It might sound like a pittance, but I was 21 and a student, so it was useful to get the money. At Goole I was getting about £10 a week. To get that offer was great.

"Before that I'd done the usual stuff. I'd had a trial at Huddersfield and played in a youth team game at Leeds. I hated it. I didn't like the lads, thought they were a bit flash and arrogant, you know what apprentices are like. I went for two days and in the middle of the second day I just buggered off home. I didn't feel part of it. I was still at school and I thought I'd stay on and do my exams. I didn't want it, so I just played at school. Then I went to university and played a bit, got noticed and played for England under-18s, then I got a chance to play non-league and earn a bit of money. I enjoyed football, and I knew I was good enough to earn money at non-league level, but I never really envisaged being a professional footballer, it just never crossed my mind. My brother was a footballer, he was at Leeds as a kid, then he played at Hull for seven years. But I was never really obsessed with it. My dad played local amateur football and we played a lot as kids, but for me it was something I felt I just didn't want enough. And maybe that's what my mum and dad thought.

"After Bill had recommended me, Keith had me in his office for a chat and asked if I wanted to sign. It was very much like I imagine Bill Nick would've been, 'There's your offer, take it or leave it.' You didn't even think of asking for another £10 a week. And he said, 'I think the best idea is for you to finish your course, because it might not work out.' Which is very Keith, he could see the common sense in not giving everything up.

"I'd be at college all week doing my teacher-training qualification, then on a Saturday morning I'd be on a train from Nottingham to London at nine o'clock. I'd go to somebody's house, have a bit of lunch, then play the game. If I had a bit of time off I'd come down and do some training, stay with somebody down here, but it was all a bit weird. I was mixing with the reserves and youth team players, so I didn't really feel part of it at all . . . a bit of a stranger.

"I finished my teacher training that summer and two months

later I was doing full-time training, which I'd never done before in my life. The first couple of weeks full time, it was awful, your body getting used to training all the time, you feel absolutely shattered. I was in digs in Enfield, and Gerry Armstrong used to give me a lift to training. I didn't like the digs either. It was horrible; that pre-season was hard. I felt a complete outsider."

Arrangements off the pitch didn't help, either. "Living in digs in Enfield really didn't suit me. I was 21 and I wasn't a kid; I'd been at university for four years, so living in digs with a family was ridiculous. I had the girlfriend coming down, it was difficult all the way round. And they want to keep an eye on you, but I didn't need anyone to keep an eye on me, I'd been living away from home for four years. Peter Shreeve was my manager at the time, the reserves manager, and I might have mentioned it to him a few times but you never got the sense the club were trying hard. You had to get off your backside and do it yourself. I managed to get a room in a flat in Ware, so that made things a bit better because you had a little bit more freedom."

In fact, Galvin almost didn't join Spurs at all. Despite his early ambivalence about making a career in football, he knew he was being watched by scouts from several clubs. "I was thinking clubs in that area – Scunthorpe, Lincoln, Grimsby, Hull," he remembers. Then, on the day he was due to sign for Tottenham, he got an urgent phone call at his college hall of residence in Nottingham. "It was Nottingham Forest, a bloke called Ronnie Fenton who worked with Brian Clough, making this phone call. They wanted me not to go, they'd got wind of it somehow. So I had to make a decision on the day – was I going to put Spurs off and go and see what Forest had to say? But I just made the decision: 'No I'm not, I'm going to go to Tottenham.' That was when Forest were just coming good, and it would've been quite interesting because Clough's teams always had two wide players. I hadn't signed anything at that stage at Tottenham, I'd just agreed to go down. I suppose it was because I knew they'd been and seen me so I felt a bit of a commitment, but to be fair when I was younger Tottenham always had a bit of glamour about them and I had always liked them. I wasn't fanatical or anything, but I liked them. Something in the back of my mind said, 'You've got to go to Tottenham.' It didn't bother me where they were at the time – you knew they'd come back – it was just because it was Tottenham. There was a bit of an aura about them as a club, which is a bit unfair on Forest because they went on to do allright, they were magnificent in those days." Galvin reflects for a moment, then laughs. "But then again, one row with Brian Clough and you're out the door."

So in 1978, Tony Galvin joined Tottenham Hotspur, just as the club's aura was boosted further by the sensational signing of Ardiles and Villa. "I was up north in July when it happened," remembers Galvin, "It came as a surprise to me as much as anyone. There was a massive circus around it and I sneaked in unknown through the back door." And there was to be no dream start for Galvin. "I played one game for the first team that first season: Man City and we lost 3-0. It was an absolute nightmare, we didn't play well at all. The team were struggling, the first season up. We were mid-table. We'd win one, lose one – that's typical Tottenham, isn't it? So Keith decided to put some of the younger players in. Stuart Bevan played. Man City that day, their line-up was like a Who's Who? – Colin Bell, Paul Power, that Polish international they had [Kazimierz Deyna], Peter Barnes, who had a blinder. So after that it was back in the reserves."

In those days, the reserve league gave players a good grounding, and Galvin soon felt the benefit. "We had a very, very strong reserve team then. Terry Naylor played a lot of games, we had Chris Jones and Ian Moores coming out of the first team. It was very competitive, the old-fashioned Football Combination. Used to get some good crowds as well. There was me and Paul Miller and Mark Falco: we were young and because you're successful you think your chance is going to come. The first team weren't pulling up any trees and Peter Shreeve would always say, 'If you play well your chance will come.' So I was with that young group, but I was a few years older and I hadn't come up through the youth system.

"I played a couple of first team games towards the end of the 1978/79 season and I just had that feeling. When I made my debut it seemed I shouldn't be there, but when I came back in about a season later I felt ready, I felt comfortable, I had time on the ball. I'd just got up to speed with training full time: your speed and touch improves, and Spurs with Peter in particular used to do a lot of work in training with the ball, a massive amount of ball work."

It's obvious the players, particularly the younger, hungry group in the reserves, respected Peter Shreeve enormously. Galvin is no exception. "He was an absolute nightmare sometimes because he used to demand high standards," he says. "He'd make you do something again and again and again until he saw some improvement. He'd make you all go into the ball court [the recently demolished indoor pitch at White Hart Lane] and he'd say you need to get in there and work on your technique – shooting, passing, control. And it worked. Probably two afternoons a week you'd be on the ball court and it was pure technique. It used to finish with a 20 or 30 minute game for a bit of fun, but it was technique which Peter put great store by. It was a bit laborious but it was what your continental-type players had been doing for years. That's what Tottenham's all about: good technique, skill levels."

Talk of technique inevitably leads to Glenn Hoddle. What was he like to play alongside, and to deal with as a person? "I was never particularly close friends with him," says Galvin, "but I obviously had a lot of respect for him, and to me he was always quite a genuine bloke. He was honest and he'd always talk to you and help you. Even now, people see him as a bit aloof, but I don't see him as any different to what he was then; it's just how people perceive him. He's just a genuine, helpful bloke that you might not get too close to – I'm sure people have got close. But I've got to say, with my background, I wasn't a great respecter of anybody when I went on the training pitch. I was just worried about myself. So if I had to kick him I would kick him. I know he would sometimes have a moan about me being a bit over-keen in training. Ricky did, he used to moan like hell about me kicking him. I was told off once or twice for it, and Paul was the same – we were both combative in training. But it what's you had to do, and Keith would say, 'That's the way it is.'"

The tradition of the tough training games on the old White Hart Lane ball courts, forged in the days of Dave Mackay and the Double team, certainly lived on. "We'd play eight-a-side in the gym on a Friday and we'd kick the hell out of each other. The day before a match! The lads who weren't playing used to get right in there. I know Paul got banned once for being over-keen, but his argument would be my argument: if you were going to get in the first team you had to train like you were going to play. You wouldn't see that now. We had pumps on, but you couldn't half make a mess of someone's leg. Elbows were up . . . Keith sometimes had to call it a day. There were little battles with people wanting to get in the team; it could get quite nasty."

It was perhaps inevitable that things would boil over, and Galvin remembers one particular incident when it did. "I saw Neil McNab and Steve Perryman have that big fight at Cheshunt. The story appeared in the *Evening Standard*. It was a big story, especially as the press weren't really around that much, and it was a proper fight. We used to have these training games, normally the big one would be on a Thursday afternoon, reserves against first team. And it was full-blooded. It was a time when quite a few players were on the edge of the first team and asking, 'Why am I not playing?' Neil was often quite angry because he was getting left out of the first team, because we had Ricky, Glenn . . . I don't know if there was history with Steve and Neil but they went into a tackle and . . . well, there was blood: it was a proper fight, proper fight. They had to be pulled apart. I can't remember if Keith called it off but they were a mess, kicking lumps out of each other, and they would've just carried on. That was the biggest fight, that really sticks out."

After those first-team appearances in 1978/79, Galvin was eyeing a regular place, but then a groin injury struck. "I'd finished the season in the first team, but I felt like I had groin strain all the time," he says. "I got referred to a specialist. It was when people had started to diagnose it as something different, not just a groin strain. It was where your pelvis joined in the middle, a bit like arthritis, chipping away at your bone. Something had eroded and it meant you always felt you had groin strain, aches and pains all round there. Peter Taylor had it; he ended up having the same operation as me, but I had mine first. They fused the bone, took a bit of bone off my hip – I've still got the scar. It was a new operation, a bit risky. The specialist said, 'You're young enough to recover from this and come back, but there's no guarantees.' But I was in permanent pain, I couldn't sprint properly, I could only do things at 70 per cent – so I thought I might as well go for it.

"It was the summer of 1979, and it was a big operation, I couldn't move for about a week. The specialist had always said it could be anything from six months to a year to recover. And yet they had me playing a reserve game in December. Mike Varney did a lot of work. I had to take it easy for two months, but by then it had set and Mike said, 'That's it, it'll never break – not unless you take a hammer to it.' So then I had the confidence to get stuck in. I just had to strengthen my legs. First Saturday in January they had me on the bench.

"They had a problem with the left side of midfield, they didn't have any left-sided players. Ricky was playing there and he absolutely hated it, but they didn't know where else to play him. Then he got injured, I came in for him – QPR away in the cup – then played in the replay and scored: I did well, and I played right through to the cup final."

At last Galvin felt established. "After two or three games I felt like I was part of the team. It was a different team that year anyway because we had Archie and Garth, two quality centre forwards." How did the two new boys fit in? "Garth would always talk a lot, and Steve's been described as a bit arrogant . . . selfish, quite selfish. He was friendly with one or two people, but not many." So who was Galvin close to? "Graham Roberts – we used to room together a bit, I suppose because we had something in common, coming from non-league. I got quite friendly with him but then," Galvin laughs, "he changed a bit and we started going away from each other. When Gary Mabbutt came I had a room with him. I used to room with Garry Brooke as well." Galvin pauses at the mention of Brooke. "Garry was very unfortunate, because he was an outstanding player and his car crash did for him. He was always going to struggle after that. But at that stage he was an outstanding prospect. He could play right wing or middle of midfield, and he had a tremendous shot. He nearly died in that crash. One of the other lads at that time who was a really good player, Peter Southey, he died of cancer. He was a good full back. That sort of puts things in perspective."

As Galvin begins to talk about the bonds between the players, the conversation turns to the team's legendary social activities. "The time we used to go for a drink would be after the game," he says. "Occasionally we might do during the week, as lads do, but mostly it'd be after the games. We stayed together. We used to go to this pub when we got off the coach near the training ground and chat about the game, the supporters used to come in, we'd chat to them. You wouldn't believe that now, would you, playing in Leeds and getting back to Cheshunt about eight, nine o'clock and the supporters who'd been at the game coming in and having a chat about it?

"We were quite approachable. You did get a bit of abuse. If we'd got stuffed somewhere you might be a bit reluctant to go, but you'd just close ranks. Ray Clemence was very good with that, coming from Liverpool, the whole sticking-together bit. I've been in the pub when we've told people to leave us alone. If they weren't going to be civil then we wouldn't talk to them. That togetherness was the time I really used to feel part of the team. Then some people would go on somewhere, out in London. I wouldn't, unless there was a do on. But that suited me, because I like to do my own thing, get my head down and get on with it. Don't get me wrong – I did the social bit, but not all the time.

"The other thing was trips away. Trips away were very important. We'd get people together, do a bit of training. It was just the lads having a good chat. Steve was very good like that; Ray, Paul, Ossie, they all used to like to chat about football; Keith and Peter would often be there too. They were really important.

"We'd play, we'd train properly, but afterwards we'd be going out and having a good time. When people ask me about going away, some stories you just couldn't repeat. But the one that always sticks in my mind is Swaziland. They love Tottenham in South Africa and the only way we could go was to go to Swaziland: we couldn't go to South Africa because of apartheid. So we went to Swaziland two years running to play these exhibition games. We'd play Man Utd, then we'd play a mixed team against their national team. The first year was great because Man Utd were a bit like us, liked a good time. They were good lads – Bryan Robson, Arthur Albiston, Kevin Moran: we got on really well. The year after we went with Liverpool, and there was never a good feeling between Liverpool and Spurs, maybe because we would've liked to have been as successful as them, maybe because we were Londoners and they thought we were flash. But there was a very bad atmosphere between the two teams; we didn't mix.

"On this trip, some of their lads were just legless the whole time: they never sobered up. They weren't bothered about the football. Their manager wasn't bothered because they'd just won the European Cup. I've never seen people drink like it. They were only there because they'd agreed to go, whereas we were under a very strict behaviour code. It was always felt you had to represent Tottenham in a certain way.

"The first game we drew, then we played again a week later. It was boiling hot, and on the Saturday before the Sunday game we had a few drinks in the casino and started to mix a bit. As the night wore on, one by one our players went to bed – one, two, three o'clock and the nucleus of eight, nine, ten of their players were still up. At four o'clock they're still up, and there was just me and Gary O'Reilly. They were taking the mickey out of our players, calling us lightweights. They were unbelievable. It was six o'clock before they went to bed and we thought, 'We're going to stuff them when we play tomorrow.'

"But they absolutely hammered us. Kenny Dalglish played, Ian Rush, Graeme Souness . . . We lost 4-1 or 5-1. They didn't run: they were just pinging the ball around. It was one of the most embarrassing things I've ever seen, because they literally couldn't run. And that shows what a good team they were."

It's the moment to ask one of the key questions about Galvin's Spurs team – why did they never win the league? "We got close a couple of times," he says. "We had a thing about going away and trying to entertain. Mind, you'd go to Liverpool and you couldn't entertain because you couldn't get the ball. I think we did go there a couple of times and try to shut up shop, but you've got to have the right players to play that way. We could've had more of a defensive unit, and that was one of the reasons I was in the team, I could get forward or I could drop off, like a modern wing-back.

But we had other players who weren't so good at that. Glenn wasn't defensive; Ossie could do that job but his skills were elsewhere; Ricky wasn't defensive-minded at all. And when Chrissie [Hughton] would go bombing up I'd have to sit in for him. So you've got to have the players. Liverpool would get 1-0 up and they'd have this mindset; you've got to go and break them down. But you have to hold your hands up and say they were a better team. They had better individuals right through. We might've played more exciting football on our day, but to win the league you've got to do that ugly stuff."

Of course it all began with that famous 1981 FA Cup win, a significant season for both club and player, with Galvin establishing himself in a Spurs side whose self-belief was fired by the victory. "That was my first full season when I felt part of the team," he says, and he remembers well the tension during the cup run. "The pressure starts to build once you win a couple of games, especially for Tottenham who were known for winning things and hadn't done anything for quite a few years – bugger all really. So the pressure started to mount. Everyone was desperate for something to happen."

The wrong thing almost happened the first time Spurs ventured away from White Hart Lane on the cup run, at the semi-final in Sheffield against Wolves. "The team was dead on its feet, hanging on. In the end, the ploy was just get the ball to me and run it to the corner flag, because we were knackered. It could've gone then.

"In the replay, we played some wonderful football. Towards the end it was a bit of showboating, knocking the ball around, Ricky was outstanding. That night we went up to a local hotel, the Enfield Chase, had some beers, a very down-to-earth celebration – although it was mobbed, bloody hell it was mobbed. It sticks in your mind that."

What also sticks in the mind is the showbiz build-up to the final itself. "Yeah, the Ossie record was the unusual thing. That caught the imagination. We went on *Top of the Pops* – that was quite an interesting experience. I think Fun Boy Three and Bananarama were there . . . We all had a few beers at the BBC bar in Wood Lane, before, during and after. It was a good laugh. Fun Boy Three were alright, they were down to earth, and the girls were too," Galvin grins. "I remember some of the lads being quite friendly."

Three years after being a student playing non-league football, it must have seemed a bit unreal to be mixing with pop stars before the FA Cup Final. "It was a bit weird being on *Top of the Pops*, because you'd think, 'What a bunch of wallies', but it was a good laugh. Chas & Dave were great."

Mention of the duo reminds Galvin of another musical mile-stone. "Once they came up to the training ground and they made that LP, the Christmas album. We made that in a mobile recording studio next to Cheshunt and we did it in about two or three hours. It was in an afternoon after training; we had a few beers and we were away. Steve [Perryman] was a driving force, trying to generate a bit of extra money for the players." He laughs. "That was a classic: making that album; mobile studio; one take a song. And I think it's quite good fun to listen to. Quite impressive, making an album in three hours!"

But the strongest memories are of the final itself. "When you walk out, that sound, there's nothing to replicate that, ever. The first time you walk up the incline, the sound hits you. The hairs go up on the back of your neck; you never have a feeling like that again because second time you know what to expect. You go from peace and quiet to that enormous roar and you see all these people. You never ever, ever, replicate that in anything you do in football. Maybe if you play in a World Cup final. I've played at Barcelona and Real Madrid, but never ever come across anything like walking up the tunnel at the old Wembley."

And at the end? "There's an element of relief. You try and enjoy that moment and it is great, walking up the steps, getting patted on the back, then you get the chance to lift the cup, and that is very special. But there's also an element of, 'Thank God it's over, thank God we've won and a bit of the pressure's off now'. We were under a lot of pressure in those two games. And it was nice for the supporters to have something to shout about.

"We went back to the Chanticleer on the coach. Driving to the ground after the game, all singing on the coach, well, it was just mayhem on the High Road and on the North Circular – complete mayhem all the way to the ground. And the party we had then . . . It was just the players, friends, family, it was just magnificent. Sit-down buffet, plenty to drink; it was a magnificent atmosphere because it was what everybody had dreamt of. It went right through to six in the morning."

A number of the players have mentioned how important that win was, so it seems the right time to ask what difference it made to the team's mindset.

"We expected to win more often than lose, that was the difference," says Galvin. "We realised we had a good group of players, we gelled as a team and there was a real belief that we could win almost any game. So of course it was more enjoyable. We played some magnificent football that season, maybe the best we ever played."

The football was good, but despite another FA Cup win, that season will always be remembered for the ones that got away. "The Milk Cup final we were flying, really fancied on the day," says Galvin. "We were outstanding first half, we should've gone in two up. I had that awful injury when Micky played a short ball to me in the middle of midfield, and Graeme Souness – he's admitted it since – saw the opportunity to do me and he did. These days I would never have carried on: there was a great big gash down my shin – I've still got the mark. He went down the side of my shinpads. I should've come off at half-time but decided to carry on, which I should never have done. I thought we'd hang on, but typical Liverpool got the equaliser, and then we really were on our last legs that day.

"But the one that really killed us was the Barcelona game, where Ray [Clemence] let that one shot slip through his hands. We'd completely and utterly outplayed them and they'd kicked absolute shit out of us. These days they'd have had eight players sent off, they got away with murder because they were the famous club. I remember talking to Brian Glanville once and he was adamant that it was a set-up because the final was going to be in Barcelona. And the first leg, the referee was so lenient – they'd bodycheck you, kick you . . . But we outplayed them. Then we went over there, played well again, but they went 1-0 up and just shut up shop. But you've got to win your home leg. The first leg, though, it was a disgrace. That really annoyed me, it sticks with me from that season. We deserved to be in that final."

It would be another season before Tottenham tasted European glory, and that campaign holds happy memories for Tony Galvin. "The Feyenoord game was good because I scored a couple of goals. That year we played some wonderful football, especially that game. They were two great games, and going over there and winning after what had happened previously with Spurs fans was a great thing, it meant a lot to the supporters.

"The Anderlecht game away [in the final] was probably one of the best we played. But we couldn't get a second goal again. But they were a very, very good team. I watched Tottenham play them this year and I thought Anderlecht were awful. When you think when we played them back then, they had Franky Vercauteren; Morten Olsen, one of the great centre halves, they were full of internationals."

It all set up a famous, but nervy, home decider. "It was a great experience that night," he says. "We were struggling, but always felt we could nick a goal to win it. The penalties, well, it were a nightmare. They'd picked the first five to take them and I wasn't one of them. You wouldn't rely on me to take a penalty, but we were getting close – it was Chris and me being lined up so it was coming our way. We were quite nervous," says Galvin, laughing, "so when Tony pulled that save off . . . I don't think it's about taking the penalty, it's about what happens if you miss it. If you've got to take it, you've got to get up and just take it. But if you miss it they never forgive you forever and a day. It's that fear."

Galvin rates that win as the pinnacle of his time at Spurs. "That was the highlight. You were close to the supporters, it was our ground, it was nearly all Tottenham supporters, it meant something massive to win a European competition, there was the penalty shoot-out – it was all there. Afterwards we just stayed in one of the lounges upstairs – it was an impromptu thing and we just stayed the night."

Times were changing, and after the popular Peter Shreeve was deemed not to have been a success in taking over after Keith Burkinshaw left, a promising young manager called David Pleat arrived. Almost from the start, he was a controversial figure, and for Galvin – like a number of other players – Pleat's arrival was to prove the beginning of the end. "He was a very clever manager, and he played good football. He wasn't particularly close to his players, but I don't think he ever wanted to be," Galvin says. "I often wonder if that was what he wanted, almost Brian Cloughesque, to unite the team against the manager and get them working for each other. I remember once we played Wimbledon and they had been bigging it up, saying they were going to kick shit out of Tottenham. And we hammered them. Hammered them. Good football, but we physically stood up to it as well. So I often wonder if we stuck together in spite of the manager.

"He bought Steve Hodge and wanted to play a different way with a five-man midfield. So I only got a few games, and I was quite happy to be – if not playing – sub. But the killer was the semi-final against Watford [in 1987] when I was expecting to be one of the subs and I wasn't. You could sense we were going to beat Watford because they hadn't got a goalkeeper. I'd been sub in the League Cup games against Arsenal, come on as sub in every single one of those games. How we lost that I don't know. That was as down as I've ever seen that team: it hurt some of the people that had been there a while – badly. So not being picked for the FA Cup semi really killed me – it told me I was on my way out. I played a few games, the season ended with the cup final, and that cup final was a disaster. David Pleat set the team up all wrong for it. We got overrun down the right side. Mitchell Thomas had no protection. Dave Bennett was playing right wing and they ran us ragged – they looked fitter and stronger than us.

"So I'd seen the writing on the wall, and David Pleat did call me in and say, 'You're not in my plans.' I did play some games at the start of the season, but then I got injured and he made it clear that they didn't want me. I didn't want to go, but when it's made clear you're not wanted there's no point staying. It did piss me off that I felt I was being edged out when I didn't want to go. So I went to Sheffield Wednesday, which looking back probably wasn't the wisest choice, but it was a good experience. Totally different club and style of football. As it turned out, a couple of months after I went, Pleat had gone. So who knows what would've happened if I'd stuck around.

"I was due a testimonial that year, which in those days was quite important," he says. "So I had to negotiate a game when I'd left Tottenham. We arranged this game and David Pleat had been totally unhelpful. It was a disaster because Tottenham weren't doing very well. David Pleat had gone because of what had happened, Terry [Venables] had come in and the team was struggling badly. We played West Ham and it pissed down: about seven or eight thousand people turned up. I felt I'd been let down. It was a bit messy how it all finished.

"I see David now, and I'm not one for carrying things on. But at the time I wasn't very happy. I'm not one to come out and start slagging people in the press though. I was offered quite a substantial amount of money by one newspaper while I was at Sheffield Wednesday to do a story about David Pleat. But I didn't do it. I thought about it, but I didn't do it."

After helping to keep Wednesday up, Galvin negotiated a free transfer to Swindon Town after he was called by their manager – one Ossie Ardiles. "It was his first job and I think he wanted a few people he knew around him," says Galvin. By now his thoughts were turning to what to do after he stopped playing. "We had these pensions, but you were never in a position where you didn't need to work again. And you shouldn't be in your early 30s, you need to go away and do something else. I did a bit of coaching at Swindon, and went to Newcastle with Ossie as his assistant manager. I'd done my coaching badges. I applied for a few jobs, but my heart wasn't really in it. It was a difficult time to be at Newcastle because we got a fair bit of abuse, even though we were just using kids.

"So I'd had enough really. I didn't think I was particularly cut out for coaching, wasn't really in love with football. You could see it changing then in the early '90s. Players getting a bit big for their boots – players who'd achieved nothing. You had players near the bottom of the old Second Division giving it the Billy Big Bollocks, and I thought, 'I've had enough of this.'

"So I just went to work in a college, into teaching. From about 1992, for the next 14 years I taught in colleges, became a manager in a college and worked up. I always did some sport, coached teams. I managed Royston Town for a couple of years, quite low down amateur level, and really enjoyed it. And I felt there was a big gap between me and professional football – it was miles away.

"I'm at Royston Town now doing the coaching on Saturdays. I've got no interest in professional football to be honest. I get more enjoyment from what I'm doing."

A few days after the interview, Galvin answers an email sent asking for his reaction to Spurs winning the Carling Cup and, just maybe, starting to lift what he saw as the burden on his team. "They've got to build on it now," he replied. Bill Nick and Keith Burkinshaw would have been proud.

7

GRAHAM ROBERTS

"MY GAME WAS ALL ABOUT HEART"

"I love this club," says Graham Roberts. "I really love this club." Of all the clichés footballers both past and present are likely to utter, it is declarations of undying affection that supporters view with most scepticism. In the modern game a player expressing emotional ties to a club, like the maximum wage and terraces in the stands, seems to be a relic of another age, a quaint but outdated symbol of the fabled good old days.

Sitting in a west London café, over mugs of tea and the background chatter of builders, Graham Roberts is having none of it if such cynicism is aimed at him. "I love Tottenham. I actually pay now to go and watch them play, I'll always do it. Tottenham gave me my opportunity in football and I'll always love the supporters. Always."

There are plenty of fans for whom the feeling is mutual. A generation on, Roberts is still one of the most popular players from this

Spurs team. Right on cue, as he settles down to reflect on his own glory days, a passer-by bids him 'Hello', her greeting warmly reciprocated. "She's wonderful – a big, big Tottenham fan. When I went to Rangers she travelled up on the coach for my first game just to wish me luck. That's what you call a fan. Either that or she's a stalker."

Laughing along with the joke is Paul Merson, with whom Roberts has an appointment to open a new bookmakers down the road. "Is this just going to be about Spurs?" Merson asks. "In that case, I'm off." Roberts takes the opportunity to remind him about Tottenham's recent humiliation of the Gunners in the Carling Cup. "5-1, Merse." Spoken like a true Tottenham fan.

It is this bond with his supporters that marks Roberts out. Ask anyone among the generation that saw him play, and his or her favourite will probably be cited as Hoddle, Ardiles or one of the other magicians that graced that flair-packed side. Yet push them further and Roberts will invariably be mentioned as the one they really cherished most – the superstar footballer they could identify with. A rugged centre half who provided the definition of 'no-nonsense', his committed, fearless and often match-winning displays granted him enduring cult status.

For someone reared in the school of hard knocks, he's aged well. Dressed in a smart suit, he looks every inch the businessman and media performer he has become, but with the relaxed, confident demeanour of a middle-aged man in good physical nick. Twenty years on from his playing days and with a slight burr, he talks as he performed: direct, forthright and uncompromising. Matters he takes issue with are tackled head on the same way he did on the pitch: fairly, for the most part, but always firmly. It's a style that occasionally got him into trouble during his playing career and has done so since he retired, but as one of the few genuine hard men in a sport awash with pretenders, Robbo was and still is a terrace hero.

"That was the only way I could play," he says. "I couldn't go and be a Fancy Dan player. I was a 100 per center. I think my ability got better over the years, and it showed on the night of the 1984 UEFA Cup final when I think I led by example with my skill and my physical effort. But at heart I was a winner and there was no way that we were not going to win that cup; it was going to be over my dead body."

That never-say-die attitude was a feature of Roberts's career. His path to the European final was an unlikely one, punctuated with frequent moves and setbacks. Football is littered with hard-luck stories of gifted youngsters who never quite made the grade, and early on in his embryonic career it looked like Roberts was going to be one of those cruelly discarded. Yet his own determination and a chance encounter between Tottenham's most famous son and a mystery train passenger at a quiet country station enabled Roberts to get his career back on track.

Born in Southampton in 1959, Roberts had trials with his local club, but was rejected by then manager Lawrie McMenemy. "He said I would never make a football player." Brief spells at Bournemouth and Portsmouth followed until a serious injury threatened to derail his career before it had even started. "I broke my ankle. Jimmy Dickinson [Pompey's record appearance holder] had taken over. He put me in the squad to play Aldershot pre-season and they were going to give me a contract that night, but the first tackle – my ankle went. So they released me a week later."

Unlike many other aspiring youngsters experiencing demoralising rejection, Roberts at least had an alternative to fall back on. "At the time I was an apprentice ship-fitter's mate. I came out of that and got a job at Fawley refinery, then left there to go to a shipbuilding firm. I was a pipe-fitter learning the trade, but football was all that I wanted. I knew that if I got back into non-league football and played really well there might be a chance. The old Ipswich keeper Dave Best took me to Dorchester, and then I went on to Weymouth. I was only there for six months, but they were what a conference club is now, and I played really well. It was a good club, Andy Townsend came afterwards, and it provided a decent grounding for people."

By the summer of 1980, Roberts was being courted by a number of clubs and had a move lined up to West Brom, then managed by Ron Atkinson. What happened next must rank as one of the most fanciful of career developments, a switch in fortune for which Roberts owes an eternal debt of gratitude to a nameless individual he has never met.

"Bill Nicholson was the one who scouted me," Graham recalls. "He was on his way to look at a young lad at Swindon, but the game was called off. He was sitting on a train station platform and got talking to a fella there. The fella asked, 'What are you doing down here?' and Bill said he'd come to watch a midfield player at Swindon who had been recommended. This bloke said, 'Well, do yourself a favour, get down to Weymouth because they've got the best non-league player in this area.'

"I've never met this bloke but he was the man responsible for Bill Nicholson getting on a different train and coming to watch me. I was going to sign for West Brom the following week because they had made a bid of 30 grand. But Bill must have liked what he saw because Tottenham got in touch while I was actually at West Brom having talks and made the same offer.

"It was a twist of fate. I don't know who that man is, what he is, where he is. I just got a phone call from my manager at Weymouth, Stuart Morgan, to say that Tottenham had come in for me. Ron Atkinson wasn't happy and didn't want me to leave his office without signing. I then travelled to Tottenham on the Thursday; I said I would give my answer to both clubs on the following day. On the Friday I was at Spurs, training with the likes of Stevie [Perryman], Glenn, Ossie, Micky Hazard, and Ricky; I never got a kick of the ball in the gym – I ran round and round for an hour and a half, lost about a stone in weight, and came out of there wondering whether I would be good enough.

"But then I met Keith and sat in his office. He offered me £185 a week and a four-grand signing-on fee, which would go towards my house. The truth is I was on more at Weymouth. Well, I was getting £250 from my job and I was getting £150 for playing football. So I was on £400 a week and Spurs were offering me £185," Roberts laughs. "But it wasn't the money; the money never came into it. It was just about playing football.

"So the situation was that Weymouth had accepted offers both from West Brom and Tottenham. When I went into Keith's office and he offered me this enormous sum of £185 per week, the last thing he asked me was, 'What position do you play?' He'd never even seen me play. But he knew Bill Nicholson had and his recommendation was good enough – and that was also good enough for me."

It seems extraordinary now to think of a part-time, non-league player moving to a top-flight club and having to take a wage cut of more than 50 per cent, but Roberts's route to the top of professional football was as unorthodox as it was eventful. Most players never experience the 'real world' of work until their playing careers come to an end, but Roberts's time in the dockyards provided a degree of perspective, and one that perhaps strengthened his bond with the supporters, many of whom laboured in similar surroundings.

"I think it gave me more hunger and desire. I wanted to succeed. I mean, I could have lived an easy life, I could have played non-league football for ten years and earned a good living, but I just wanted something else; I wanted to be a professional footballer; I wanted to go in and train every day. When I went to Spurs I wanted to work hard at my game."

If the financial rewards were oddly inverted between league and non-league, the gap in quality of football was more predictable. "Peter Shreeve said to me, 'We'll make you a better player but your touch needs to improve.' I went back in the afternoons and trained with the reserves, which I didn't mind; I wanted to get out there and into the first team, but the only way you can do it is to work hard.

"My first proper training session was a culture shock, but I learned to do the easy things quickly. My game was all about heart. I was a tough tackler and I was a winner; that was my game. I didn't care if it was Glenn Hoddle or whoever, I was there to win the ball and win the game. It didn't matter to me. Whoever I played against and whatever team I played in, I would give 100 per cent and more, the very best that I could. If it wasn't good enough on the day then so be it, but no one could ever say of me that it was for lack of effort – that's how it was. Playing in the team and training with these players brought me on."

Coming into a club like Spurs there was little danger of Graham getting too big for his boots, even if he had had the inclination. The young defender arriving from a modest south coast back-ground was suddenly thrust in among a bunch of confident, street-wise Londoners whose jovial if merciless disdain for 'country bumpkins' could have cowed weaker characters.

"Flash cockneys? Yeah, there was bit of that," he laughs. "I got the piss taken out of me for the way I dressed. I would come in with a woolly polo neck and I would get the mickey taken out of me, because you had the likes of Paul Miller and the other Londoners and they had all the fancy dress sense. But I wasn't there to be smartly dressed: I was there to play football and win.

"I knew a bit of what to expect. I'd played against Paul and Chrissie [Hughton] before when we got to the semi-finals of the FA Youth Cup when I was at Portsmouth. We drew with them 2-2 at White Hart Lane and then at Fratton Park we lost 2-1, and I remember Maxie saying something to our lad when we had a penalty in the last minute. Maxie had a right go at him as he's about to take it, saying, 'You ain't strong enough to take this penalty', and the lad missed it. But that's what it was like, how you became in their company – not flash, necessarily – but one of the boys. I became one of them – a Tottenham player."

Given his chance Roberts soon shone. Instrumental in the way he eased into the role was skipper Steve Perryman. "What can you say about Steve?" says Roberts. "He was a fantastic influence on me. He would keep your feet on the floor; he would do everything to make sure you didn't get too big-headed.

"He taught me how to be a professional footballer, taught me how to be a captain, learned me the trade of the game. He was a superstar. People say to me, 'Who's the best player you played with? Well I played with people like Glenn and Ricky and Graeme Souness, but Stevie Perryman was the best. His distribution was fantastic and nothing was ever too much for him if it would help the team out, help his team-mates. He would bollock you – but in the right way; it was only for your needs and benefit. That's what a captain is, a leader from the front and that was Steve. I was very lucky to play under such a fantastic person.

"It's a shame he never got the opportunity to manage the club. I know he went back under Ossie, but Steve is Mr Tottenham through and through. He would be the right person because he knows how Spurs should be run. He knows what the supporters are like, and what the supporters want."

It seems an opportune moment to ask Roberts about Perryman's judgement that, of the two tough guys at the heart of the Spurs defence, Miller was the hardest. Graham grins broadly. "Maxie was Max. He didn't take any prisoners and he could be nasty. We didn't have a competition between us to see who was the hardest; we were good mates. But I would disagree with Stevie: I would say I was harder than Paul, because when I would say 'I'll do it', I'd do it, that was the difference. Maxie was more sly, but he was hard.

"To tell the truth Paul was a bit of an unsung hero. A fantastic footballer who knew what he had to do. Me and him lived in each other's pockets. He knew how to wind people up, how to put them off, which is part and parcel of the game, but he was very talented and that shouldn't go amiss; what he did for the club was superb.

"Take the '81 semi against Wolves. In the first game where we went to extra time, it was only Maxie who really kept us together. I'll always remember him that day, he was immense. Physically, vocally, everything, because we had just gone, we all looked at each other and thought, 'We've thrown this away.'

"Keith tried to buy a few other centre halves in Gary Stevens, Paul Price and Gary Mabbutt, but couldn't get a better pairing because we had a great understanding. We were good together; we'd played in the reserves and knew each other's strengths and weaknesses. Maxie would set our victims up and I would welly them."

With Miller and Roberts, it was a case of friendship allied to mutual respect, a snapshot of the bond between the players that lay at the heart of the '80s Spurs side. Much of this was forged away from the game, with the kind of socialising that would have modern day managers and tabloid editors in a frenzy. "I can remember Micky Hazard had a stag night in midweek. We went to training the next day and everyone was still paralytic. Shreevesie wouldn't have it and sent us home. He said, 'I want to see you back here tomorrow at two o'clock; we'll have an hour's training and if you don't win on Saturday then all of you will be fined.' We beat Stoke 1–0.

"That was the difference: we knew what we had to do. And that's the mentality we had in the team; we were good. Everybody went out and had a drink; everybody stuck together. After games on a Saturday night coming back from Manchester, or Leeds, we'd get back to the training ground at Cheshunt and we'd go to the Bull's Head, stay there till two o'clock in the morning and get the wives to come and pick us up. We were all very honest with each other, no one held back, and that's what made us a better team because you could speak your mind and the lads would take it."

It is abundantly clear that Roberts still retains huge affection for his friends and colleagues of that era. From Chris Hughton ("a marauding left back, and a proper Tottenham man") to Tony Galvin ("absolutely fantastic, a straight-talker who worked very, very hard for the team, another unsung hero but a big, big part of the success"), Roberts is full of praise for his team-mates. Given the similarity in their non-league backgrounds, it might be assumed that Galvin and Roberts would have a stronger affinity than with the others, but Graham is keen to emphasise the all-round friendship within the squad.

"Tony and me came at the same time and we were good friends, but that was the same with everybody; the team got on. Tony was different in that he had a degree in Russian – and you didn't find too many people like that in football – but we all just got on. We worked hard, we trained hard – we were just happy to be there. As the years went by we just gelled with everyone there.

"The young lads were very good because when we first arrived we had the likes of Garry Brooke, Mark Falco, Terry Gibson, Tony Parks, Pat Corbett, Jimmy Bolton, people like that who made you welcome. So did Peter Shreeve, and Robin Stepney – the reserve team manager – he was one of us. A down-to-earth person who just wanted you to work hard and play football the right way.

"The bond was and is very close. We had the 25th anniversary of the '81 cup final a couple of years ago and everyone turned up. How many clubs get that? If they had one for the 1991 cup-winning side I'm not sure everybody would turn up. That's the bond we've got; we're still friends, still mates. We've got different lives now, but I would think that if anybody was really struggling, everybody would pull together for him."

Not everyone, however, was quite so enamoured of the close team ethic at the time according to Roberts. "I think there was one player that didn't like it so much, and that was Stevie Archibald. He was a bit of a different character, but the fans loved him and rightly so, because he was a fantastic goalscorer. Archie was his own person; I lived literally two minutes from him and we used to travel together, roomed with him a long time and I got on all right with him."

From his vantage point, Roberts felt that Archibald found more of a bond with his attacking partner Garth Crooks. But while Archibald was comparatively reserved, Crooks was an outgoing extrovert. A case of opposites attract? "They were fantastic together. I think when you get a friendship like that, it works on the pitch. Archie was more . . . not selfish necessarily, but more single-minded, which is what all good strikers are. I've not got a bad word to say about him. Crooksie on the other hand was jolly, a Jack the Lad. Sometimes he had to be brought back to earth," says Graham, laughing at the memory, "but he was just a happy lad. He was pleased to be at Spurs. I don't think he ever wanted to go into management but he wanted to be active in the other side of it, the media work. He's got what he worked hard for and that's a great life."

Given his comfort in front of the cameras or behind the microphone, it was perhaps inevitable that Crooks was well to the fore when the 1981 Cup Final squad recorded *Ossie's Dream*. "Ah, it was a good experience," says Graham, laughing and wincing slightly at the recollection. "Well, there's not many teams that get to number five in the charts is there? It was a bit of fun; everybody enjoyed doing it we had a few beers. And then we went on *Blue Peter* – how many people get to go on that? And I got a *Blue Peter* badge! Not many people get them."

It is an unlikely yet strangely comforting image to think of the Tottenham hard man as the proud recipient of a *Blue Peter* badge, sitting side by side with the medals he won for his wholehearted football exploits. Established in the team through the 1980/81 season, time and again Roberts ran through metaphorical walls for the Spurs cause, most notably in the tense and physically demanding first game of that season's FA Cup final epic. But having suffered a gruesome injury after an accidental clash with one of his team-mates in the first half, it appeared Roberts's Wembley debut was going to be short-lived.

"I got my teeth kicked out by Chrissie. I shouted at him; he says he never heard me, but as we both challenged for a ball on the touchline I headed it and he stuck his foot in my mouth. I went into the dressing room, it was just before half time and I was a bit dazed, blood was pouring out, the doc came in and he said to Keith, 'He shouldn't go back out.' But there was no way in a million years I wasn't going to go back out on that pitch. It was a cup final, we were losing 1-0, I knew we needed everybody on the pitch to get back into the game. I said to him, 'No chance fella, I'm going' and I just walked back out on to the pitch. They'd have had to break my legs to keep me off.

"I was fine; I actually felt the fittest I had in my life until half time of extra time. One of the physios threw a bucket of water onto my head to cool me down as it was very hot and that was it – my legs went and turned to jelly. Within five minutes of the restart I was gone. I don't know if it was the water or whatever but I wish they had left me alone. That whole period became just a non-game. We all went; so many went down with cramp."

Thankfully, Roberts and his team-mates recovered for the replay. The centre half played his full part, breaking up a City attack and instigating the move that ended with Villa's piece of FA Cup immortality. "I tackled one of their players on the edge of the box and hit a pass to Tony Galvin who ran down the line, cut in to Ricky and that was it. I was thinking, 'Pass, pass!' But no one closed him down; no one tackled him and once he got in the area they were all frightened of him because he had those quick feet. We knew he could do that. When we used to train, no one wanted to go man-for-man on Ricky because you never got a kick of the ball. That's how good he was. At the end of it when he did what he did, it was like the longest 12 minutes ever. But the relief at the end of it – cor!"

In 1981 and 1982, Spurs played at Wembley a remarkable seven times in little over 15 months. For Roberts, who was playing non-league matches and grafting in a dockyard just a couple of years before, it represented a remarkable turnaround in fortunes. But the heady night of the 1981 replay provided an emotional highpoint.

"My mum and dad were the proudest people in the world. My mum's dead now, but my dad's still alive; they came to the game, and afterwards she was in tears . . ." For a split second, her son himself appears to waver, but regains his train of thought. "I'd done something I wanted to do. If you talk to older players, they know what I mean. I heard Ray Wilkins the other day get asked what the FA Cup means to him. He said, 'Getting to Wembley meant more than anything when I played, I wanted to get to that final.' And that's what I couldn't understand when Arsene Wenger played his young team [in Tottenham's 5-1 defeat of Arsenal in the 2008 Carling Cup semi-final]. You're one game away from a cup final at Wembley. Dave Kitson said this season that the FA Cup doesn't mean anything. Well, trust me, the FA Cup is the biggest cup in the world, that's what it means. Every Tottenham fan would love to see their team win the cup at Wembley. For a player to come and say the Premier League means more – yeah, money-wise it does – but getting to a final, that's what means a lot.

"I remember all of the games I played in. People say to you, 'Oh, what about this or that game?' and I remember every one because you don't forget the good times. With the Spurs players now, they are getting 30, 40 grand a week and they've only just won a trophy. I've got two FA Cups, a UEFA Cup, Scottish League, Scottish Cup, the divisional championship with Chelsea – but I wouldn't swap any of that for money. I've got all those experiences and nobody can take them away from me. You can't put a price on it."

'Price' played a significant part in one of Roberts's less happy memories, when he was dropped for the 1982 League Cup final in favour of Welsh international Paul Price. "He came in when I got injured, and I couldn't get my place back at centre-half. I was playing in the team, though. I'd been pushed into midfield and was playing well but by the time the final came round, Ricky miraculously recovered from his injury and was in the team instead of me. He wasn't fit to be honest. Keith told me I wasn't playing. I was gutted. I told Keith that, I said I didn't think it was right. He said he had to go with what he felt was right and I respected him for telling me, but I wasn't happy.

"Heading off for the final, I didn't want to be with the boys. It was the only time I didn't want to be part of it. Keith said to me, 'We'll get to the FA Cup final and you'll play in that.' My response was that, 'If I'm good enough to play in that, why aren't I good enough for the League Cup final?' We lost 3-1 so it came back to haunt him, I suppose. I thought I was a better player than Paul Price. It was a sickener for everyone, but I got back in the team and we beat QPR in the FA Cup final, so there we are. It was gut-wrenching missing out, but you have to take your knock-backs and you have to come back stronger. Stevie helped me through that; he knew because he had the experience – it was my first knock-back. But I got over it and hopefully I repaid Keith with the UEFA Cup. And the 1982 FA Cup when I fell over in the penalty area when Tony Currie brought me down. Whether we deserved it on that night I don't know, but you make your own luck."

Given his struggles to break into the professional game, it was Roberts's determination that had much more to do with his successes than luck, accidental or self-made. He has a sharp recall of individual matches and the events surrounding them, the highlights remembered as a contrast to the days when it seemed he might be destined not to make the big time. One league game in particular stands out, when he exacted a kind of revenge on one of those figures who had earlier doubted his ability. "We beat Southampton 3-2 in March '82, and I got a hat-trick. I was a Southampton boy and loved the place; my family all lived there. But that game gave me fantastic joy that day, with probably the most unexpected hat-trick ever in the way I got it – a diving header, a miskick and a volley. I spoke to Lawrie McMenemy after that game because you don't forget when someone releases you and says you'll never make a football player. I said, 'Sorry about scoring three goals'. He said, 'Well, Graham, you've proved me wrong. And that's what football's about, proving people wrong.' He congratulated me, which was good of him."

There are many other encounters that stand out for Roberts: the tumultuous 1981 FA Cup semi-final replay at Arsenal's Highbury when "we destroyed their ground and destroyed Wolves"; the bruising Cup Winners' Cup meeting with Barcelona in 1982 when Roberts scored Tottenham's equaliser and was chased behind the goal by enraged Catalan players. There is also an unforgettable league game against Everton that features prominently in Graham's mental scrapbook. In the 1984/85 season, both sides were fighting for the championship and the battle reached a crescendo on an April night in north London. The visitors won 2-1 in front of a fevered 49,000 crowd, despite the heroic efforts of Roberts and his team-mates. He scored a thunderbolt from 35 yards and nearly forced an equaliser but for the brilliance of Everton keeper Neville Southall.

"We absolutely battered them that night, I still can't believe we didn't win. The way I hit it and beat Southall, who was probably the best goalkeeper in the world at the time, was something special. It was right in the top corner, brought us back into the game, but then the save he pulled off later on was unbelievable. Devastating, really. I didn't like losing, that was my problem. I used to dig Glenn and Ossie out when I was captain, say to people, 'Come on, you've got to do more, we need you'. That's the way I was and I think the lads understood that."

Once again, Spurs were to come up short in pursuit of the league championship. Roberts agrees with the view of fellow defenders Perryman and Miller that the way the side played hamstrung any title challenge, but also shares Burkinshaw's attacking philosophy.

"I thought we should play to our strengths. I didn't think we should go defensive; we had the people who could defend but we didn't fear anyone at home, we knew with players like Crooks, Archibald and Glenn and that we were likely to score a goal. When we went to places like Liverpool, that was hard. But when we were on song there were days when we could have beaten teams 8 or 9-0. We felt that in our blood; it wasn't being big-headed. We looked at the other teams some of the time and thought, 'They haven't got any fight in them.'

"We beat Newcastle once by five and not long after Chrissie Waddle left them and joined us because they all wanted to play for Spurs. The way we played and trained, we weren't big on tactics just a lot of five and eight-a-sides. None of that ProZone stuff. Shreevesie would tell us, 'You mark him' etc, but we played off the cuff. That's the best way to be. Not now though, it's more technical. I would argue that Spurs recently have lost games because they haven't rehearsed set pieces, even with all the ProZone stuff now. You know why that is? It's laziness. That's the bottom line."

Disappointment in 1984/85 did nothing to dampen the joy of winning the UEFA Cup final the year before, however. Made captain on the night, it was Roberts's high-water mark as a footballer. Today, the happiness at recalling the memories is evident. "If you have a look at that night, we were without so many players – no Crooksie, Ossie, Ricky, no Glenn, no Stevie Perryman, no Ray Clemence. The players that came in were just fantastic and we just had it in us. We probably had the best squad of players that any team in that era through the 1980s could have wanted.

Because we had the likes of Micky Hazard, Falco, Mabbutt, Stephens and Danny Thomas in reserve – the quality of those players proved how strong the squad was.

"That night will live with me for the rest of my life. I watched a DVD of it the other day with my girlfriend and some mates, and I still get goosebumps when I see myself going through to score."

The manner in which Roberts grabbed the equaliser is perhaps the perfect illustration of what made him such a good player. Bursting through into the Anderlecht penalty area after Ardiles had struck the bar seconds earlier, Roberts didn't just blast the ball or launch a wild header, but with admirable composure chested it down, took a touch and lashed it into the net.

"That probably came from me being a centre forward earlier in my career. Mark Falco did fantastic for me; he pushed the lad in front of him. Mark was going to head it but I shouted, 'My ball' and went through. You just think to yourself then keep cool, keep cool. The noise that greeted the goal, my word, I've never heard anything like it. They said there were 50,000 in there, but it must have been 70,000."

Privy to the upheaval that followed Burkinshaw's controversial departure, Roberts views the period up to his own exit as, "A shame, a disaster for the club. All of a sudden the team started to dismantle and it was all through I think what Scholar did to Keith. I played under Peter Shreeve; I'm not sure if he was a top-class manager but he was a top-class coach, absolutely fantastic on the training pitch. He knew his tactics, and I think if he'd have been given the chance he could probably have stayed there longer. Circumstances happened and he had to leave. We had a good chance to win the league under him, but too many games caught up with us and that was the best chance we had of lifting the title."

Within two years, Shreeve was replaced by David Pleat and so began the most hurtful episode in Roberts's long association with Spurs. The wounds may have healed, but the scars are still evident as Graham surveys the sad and fractious end to his time as a Tottenham player. One individual in particular comes in for stinging criticism as tough as any of the challenges Roberts made on the pitch. "It was end of season and I was in my garden. I got a phone call from Pleat. The first words he ever said to me were, 'You're not my sort of player, you're on the [transfer] list and as soon as I get the right offer you'll be sold.' With that I just put the phone down.

"For all that, I worked really hard pre-season, but he bought Richard Gough, so I knew my days were numbered at the back, what with Gary Mabbutt playing at centre half as well. But I worked my way into midfield and played really well. As the season went on we were doing well, I was enjoying my football, but it was always in the back of my mind that Pleat didn't want me, he was just using me.

"I went and saw him as I wanted another year on my contract to get my testimonial – I still had two years left on the current deal and the extra year would have taken me up to ten years. Pleat said, 'You'll never get that.' So I thought, 'I'm just wasting my time.' One day I went up to Glasgow and watched Rangers with Gough and Chris Waddle. On the journey back I sat next to a fella who it turned out was Souness's brother-in-law. We got talking and he asked if I would be interested in going to Rangers. I said I'd go anywhere to play. Within two days a call had been made, asking if I was really interested and then it took about two-and-a-half months to negotiate the fee.

"Pleat didn't like my style of play. He liked a Fancy Dan player, so sold me and bought Steve Hodge. No disrespect to him, he was a good player. But the end of the day, Pleatie didn't like me at all. The end came when I went into training one day. I was in the team to play Chelsea, but got a phone call at 4.30 in the morning. It was David Pleat saying, 'We've sold you, you're going to Rangers, don't turn up tomorrow'. So I just put the phone down. I went up there, I just wanted to get away by then, things were miserable.

"It was great going to Rangers, they were a fantastic club. But I came back from Glasgow on the Sunday, went to Spurs to get my boots on the Monday morning and all my kit had been chucked outside in a black bag. Unbelievable. I wasn't even allowed to say goodbye to the office staff, anything. Then Pleat did a nasty article in the papers saying all I did was kick people and should have got sent off a lot more. But I still gave 150 per cent for Tottenham in the games I played.

Roberts moved from Rangers to Chelsea in 1988, but reveals that he was lined up for a dramatic return to White Hart Lane. "Rangers wanted to sell me. They'd bought other players, Graeme Souness blamed me for a goal that wasn't my fault and they wanted to get rid of me. Chelsea invited me down; they'd been relegated after losing a play-off with Middlesbrough but they still wanted me, and in the end I got a move there. At that time, in the summer, Tottenham were playing Dundee United and Chris Waddle was still at Spurs and told me, 'Venners [Terry Venables] wants to sign you.' I said, 'I'd love to come back.' Chris said, 'All right leave it with us' but then two days later they went and bought Terry Fenwick. I never got a phone call or anything; it went from them being really interested to nothing, so it made my mind up: Chelsea wanted me.

"I went there, was made captain and got them promoted. The year after, back in the First Division, we played at Tottenham. It was hard going back. I had a lot of friends there and I felt that the supporters were still my mates. And to go back and win 4-1 – we absolutely destroyed them. But it was hard, I never celebrated any of the goals, because I don't think you should milk it in front of other people and your own fans who you love. Don't get me wrong, I love winning, Chelsea were paying my wages, and if it had been any other club I would have milked it, but I couldn't do that to the fans at Tottenham."

So, for all the disappointments and the distasteful end to his association with the club, Roberts returns again to his abiding affection for the club and its fans. He's had an eventful life since retiring as a player, both in work and in his private life. "I've had two wives and I now work from five in the morning all the way through to ten o'clock at night – I do quite a lot of TV work and I've got my own memorabilia company – and I've never minded hard graft. "

But through it all there has been one constant. "I always wanted to manage Tottenham Hotspur. Always. I've done the non-league, went to Clyde, but I know I'm never going to get it because I'm not a big enough name. I'm absolutely gutted because I love the club and the club is in my heart. But that's life, you get on with it and you have to move on. But I'm always there if anybody wants anything; I'm always there for Tottenham supporters.

"The club means everything to me. My ambition in life has been to do something to help Tottenham because I came from being a 21-year-old kid, had all the knock-backs, went to Spurs and felt I gave them seven years of service, getting better every year. I know I'll never get back there but I love the supporters. I've been to Rangers; they're fantastic, Chelsea were great for me; but Tottenham is something special. When you've played there for that length of time, won the UEFA Cup, won two FA Cups, they are a big part of your life. I just hope one day that there is something for me to do.

"Do you know what? I would go back and clean the boots if they asked me. Just to be a part of the football club, that's how much it means to me. It's not about money. It's about wanting to do things in life. I never, ever played for money: we were well rewarded, but I gave up two jobs to become a pro footballer when I was earning twice as much money. These days, bad players become millionaires.

"At the end of it I've made a living out of it. I've lost it through ex-wives, but that's life, you get on with it. But I love Spurs. And

I think hopefully we've got the right manager now and we can win things if he can build on what he's done so far. We're going to go places."

There is one incident, a famous episode from recent Tottenham history, that cannot pass without comment, a legendary incident that has earned Graham Roberts immortality among the Spurs faithful – the 1986 derby when Robbo dumped Arsenal's then superstar Charlie Nicholas in Highbury's East Stand with a tackle that even has its own terrace song.

"It's why I'm well liked by Arsenal fans," Roberts laughs. "I used to enjoy those games; I hated the Arsenal and I really wanted to beat them. It was New Year's Day and freezing cold. They had undersoil heating but one of the pipes wasn't working and that part of the pitch was still icy. It was right in front of the dugout. We had a corner; it got knocked out to the dugout side and I was running after it but Charlie got there just before me. I just sort of shoved him, elbowed him, and he went flying over by the side of the dugout, over the metal bars and into the crowd. I rolled into the dirt. Everybody jumped up and their physio jumped up and said to me, 'Are you all right?' I said, 'Yeah' and then he gave me a right hook and said, 'You ain't now,'" Roberts says laughing. "But it was icy, that was my excuse."

Perhaps Roberts was just ensuring both sides of Highbury were treated to his obvious affection for the Gunners. The season before, after Spurs had scored the winning goal in a 2-1 victory in the same fixture, Roberts had given the West Stand a V-sign salute. "Did I?" he asks with unconvincing innocence. "Did we only get two points then? Ah well, that would explain it, I was just reminding them of how many points we'd won."

TONY PARKS

"YOU JUST PLAYED FOOTBALL BECAUSE YOU WANTED TO BE IN A CUP FINAL"

"Never can a man have become such a legend on the basis of just one game," writes author and Spurs fan Bob Goodwin as he introduces Tony Parks to his list of the 100 greatest ever Spurs players in *The Complete Record of Tottenham Hotspur.* Mention Parks and immediately the picture of a May night under the floodlights at White Hart Lane in 1984 is conjured up, of the keeper's two penalty saves in an extraordinarily dramatic end to the UEFA Cup final against Anderlecht, and of Parksy deliriously racing away across the pitch.

Nearly a quarter of a century later Parks is still involved in football as a goalkeeping coach with the FA. The 15-year-old Hackney boy who loved his football so much he left school early to start his apprenticeship has been back to school to get the qualifications he needed to keep working in the game he loves, now involved with the goalkeeping elite all over the world. And he talks engagingly about the game and frankly about his own career. "I think I'm a better goalkeeping coach than I ever was a goalkeeper," he says. "That comes from all the mistakes I made as a player. I never lacked ability; I always thought I was a gifted goalkeeper. But I don't think I was blessed mentally to be able to deal with life at the highest level."

We're sitting in his flat on a new-build gated estate in a north London suburb. Parks is not long divorced, and he's out of the country with FA youth teams a lot, so aside from a few family pictures and a stack of *Friends* DVDs in a rack interspersed with football discs – 'England 3 Argentina 2' stands out – it doesn't look particularly lived in. Parks is immediately warm and friendly when we meet. His build is pretty much the same, he looks relaxed in a polo shirt and training bottoms – always the football man – but there's a piercing intensity to his eyes. He's one of those guys who looks you straight in the eye when he's talking and, as we sit and chat over mugs of tea around a glass table in his front room, he is disarmingly honest when assessing his own life in football. For Parks had it all, and then . . . it just wasn't there. The 1984 UEFA Cup final man of the match, the penalty shoot-out legend, never reached those heights again, endured a long drawn out departure from the club he loved, and drifted around the fringes of the game. There's a toughness about him, something that suggests he's looked at himself in the mirror and confronted his faults – he'll admit doing as much later – but no hint of self-pity or regret. Tony Parks has had quite a journey in football, and now has the air of a man on top of his game. "I genuinely love the game," he says. "I'm a good developer of young goalkeepers, working now with the elite end – young, professional international goalkeepers – for the last six years. I absolutely love the job."

It's hard to imagine sitting for three hours over cups of tea with any of today's Spurs side. "It would've been nice to be able to retire a millionaire, but that's life," reflects Parks. "The game moves on and that money wasn't about then. But the game means more to me than I think it does to some of them nowadays. People wanted to be footballers because of the football, now they want to be footballers because of the lifestyle. I love the game."

It was that love of the game that took young Tony Parks from Homerton in East London to the park to play endless hours with his mates. "You just played football because you wanted to be in a cup final at the end of the season, you wanted to be at Wembley," he says. "When I played with my mates over the park I wanted to be Bob Wilson or Pat Jennings; you always tried to emulate those great people, and fortunately enough for me at the age of 12 I got the opportunity to train with Pat Jennings a couple of times.

"I played for a Sunday league team called Tiger FC and in that team at the time were Terry Gibson, David Boulter and three or four other lads who were already training at Tottenham. At the age of 11 I went to QPR and was really disillusioned with what I saw as professional football. It wasn't a particularly well-run club, so I made my mind up that Sunday football was for me. I enjoyed playing Sundays; we had quite a decent team, we'd been together for a while. But the manager was also a representative of Tottenham and he said, 'Why don't you come along to training on a Tuesday night?' I remember getting two buses down from Hackney, the 277 up to Dalston Junction and the 149 down to the ground. I walked in and was pretty nervous, although as I knew three or four lads there already I was OK. I walked into the training session with Ron Henry and Peter Shreeve and just fell in love with the place straight away. This was totally different from what I'd experienced at QPR. This was what a professional club was all about. The professionalism of the people, it was well organised, the coaches were qualified to coach – at QPR they had a training centre in Bethnal Green where they sent a couple of players if they could spare a few hours. At Tottenham there were people like Peter Shreeve who was really dedicated to the youth policy.

"I also knew two brothers, Pat and Steve Kavanagh, who played for Spurs, who lived not far from me in Homerton and I used to listen to them talk about Tottenham. So I had this sort of affinity with Tottenham; I half knew the place even before I'd been there. The training was very enjoyable, you got loads of encouragement. So I went there when I was 12; that was my club. This was about 1976/77."

Quite what an impression Spurs made on the young Tony Parks is underlined by another piece of information. "As a kid I would always be at Arsenal," he says. "My family were big Arsenal supporters. My dad and my older brother – who also played at a young age – were fans. My dad thought my brother had a real chance. He was offered a trial at Arsenal but he didn't take it up: he wasn't interested enough in football. I remember going to watch Arsenal in the '71 season when they won the Double. I remember being in the Clock End with my dad and my brother. My dad would stand at the back with his mates and me and my brother would have our little stools and go down the front. In those days the adults would get out of the way for you, let you stick your stool at the front and we could stand right in the corner where Pat Rice would go bombing down the wing or take corners. It was a special place, Highbury. I never lost that feeling for what was a wonderful ground. As a supporter I was an Arsenal supporter, but the day I walked into Tottenham I became a real convert. Tottenham was the club that I loved as a footballer."

Parks's arrival at Tottenham didn't come about through any particular dedication to working the system. He really did just play and got his break. "You just played football because you loved it," he says. "I wasn't the brightest of kids and I didn't like school. I went to Upton House in Homerton, an interesting place to put it mildly. It was a horrible school: seven storeys; looked like a prison block;

1,200 kids, all boys; and it was a pretty tough place. I played for the school and county teams. You thought you were the real thing when you did that. Whenever the teams were picked I was always the one they wanted. That's a real confidence booster and I played without fear.

"I think being in a school where sport was important gave me a bit of respect. It can work in your favour. And because I played in the teams for the year above me from an early age most of the kids knew who I was. And I was at Tottenham as well, so most people knew I was a decent goalkeeper, I'd been to Lilleshall for England youth trials too. Towards the end of school I didn't bother going at all, I just used to want to play football. Fortunately enough Peter Shreeve – most of the kids in my generation at Tottenham would have a lot to thank him for – realised there was no point in me bunking off to roam the streets and get in trouble, so he did a deal with the school – 'We'll take him Monday to Friday: he's off the streets, you know he's safe and he's getting a football education.' The school at the time saw it as more important for me to play and represent them in big games so they agreed to that. So the only time I ever went to school in the last 15 months or so was when there was a match to play.

"The nice thing about Tottenham at that time was that during the school holidays we would get to go to the training ground at Cheshunt as a group of schoolboys and train. We could mix with the first team players and be around the workings of a pro club from Monday to Friday, not just for a couple of evenings a week, which was a real eye-opener. It gave you a taste of where you wanted to go.

"At Cheshunt they had three pitches. The bottom pitch was for the schoolboys and the youth team, the second pitch was where the reserves played, and the top pitch was where the first team trained. There was the same structure in the dressing room too, so there was always a target, I want to get from that pitch to that pitch, from that dressing room to that dressing room. It was always, always about football. I don't think I ever once thought about becoming a millionaire.

"Being an apprentice was the happiest time I had as a footballer, and I had 20 years as a professional. It's a harsh place inside a football club, whatever age you are. You've got to be able to deal with it. But those three years were the best. On an average day we would get into the club around eight o'clock. The first-team dressing room would be looked after by Johnny Wallis, who was the first-team kit man, but the apprentices were in charge of the rest of the pros' kit and boots. There were two dressing rooms at White Hart Lane where all the kit was washed and stored, the first team and the reserves. It was an awesome place to be. We'd look after the young pros, people like Paul Miller, Tommy Heffernan, Mark Kendall. We'd need to make sure we had the right kit for them, get it packed, get the boots packed, and have a journey up in the minibus to Cheshunt and the training ground. That was always fun because Johnny Wallis was the most miserable old sod in the world and we used to love taking the mickey out of him. He would take us on long detours to try and make us late.

"Once you got to the training ground you would lay the kit out and then go and do your training. Once training was finished you'd have to do your jobs, which is something kids don't have to do today as apprentices. We'd have to scrub boots, clean toilets, make sure the first team players' requirements were looked after, and in the first year I felt there was more of an emphasis on us doing our jobs, being disciplined, making sure we'd done stuff right and being on time. It gave us a discipline and a respect for the club hierarchy and I think that was a good thing. Saturday morning was always brilliant because we'd be going to Cheshunt to play in the youth teams. You'd wait on a Friday afternoon for the team sheets to go up and in them days you'd play a corresponding fixture, like the reserves did, against whoever the first team was playing, so we had some great games against the Arsenal and people like that. That training ground was an awesome place to be. It was a brilliant place to go and just savour football."

Much of what impressed Parks came from Shreeve. "He was quite a foresighted coach. He'd batter on at us about the need to eat and drink right before people even started dealing with sports science. Peter went up with us from the youth right up to the reserves, then became assistant to Keith and then manager. We never really got on. I always felt he didn't like me, that he felt I was a little shit, but it wasn't until much later in my life that I realised what he was doing was for my own benefit. The problem as a kid is you don't see that. When I look back on it now he was a huge influence.

"One of the things that was really innovative about him was that we'd come back to training and the balls would be out first day. In those days it was almost unheard of because we'd get about eight weeks off in the summer, so normally in pre-season you were stuck in the woods doing running and that slog for weeks before you even saw a football. But Pete was really good; he wanted the balls out right from the word go, because he knew you can do all the running in the world around tracks but as soon as you start playing football it really kills you. We'd always have a ball, and we'd always go out early as well. That was the best thing about being an apprentice, we'd get all our jobs done and we'd get on the training pitch early, just playing silly games but it would be helping our technique in terms of passing, heading, catching, playing headers and crosses like you did over the park. I was 15 at the time; you signed apprentice at 16 but to all intents and purposes I was an apprentice at 15.

"Before I went full time we used to train Tuesdays and Thursdays and play at the weekend. The transition from only being there once or twice a week — every time you left you wanted the next day to hurry up — to now being able to go to this club every single day of the week was brilliant. It just felt like a great time with your mates. We had a really good team and a good laugh with each other. We'd be in at eight in the morning, then once the day was done we'd stay at White Hart Lane till six or seven, we'd get the balls and go back up in the old ball court. On the walls was all the targets and we'd play games where you'd get so many points for this, so many for that. We never wanted to go home. We'd always get a shout once the office people had gone and the security people needed to lock up – 'Get lost you lot!'. Most of us would get on the train and off at our various stops on the way to Liverpool Street; we just had a great laugh from start to finish."

It sounds an idyllic existence, and Parks confirms this when he's asked whether the contract money was a factor. "People like Terry Gibson who were England schoolboys and coveted by clubs around the country were treated slightly differently," he says. "For me it was just a two-year apprenticeship; first year I was on £16 a week, second £20 a week. They used to send £10 home to my mum for keep money, and she'd give me that back, so I had an extra tenner in me pocket but who cares? We didn't do nothing except play football. We didn't need to go down the West End and go shopping. Once you put your football kit on that was you for the rest of the day. The only time you spent money was on your train fare to and from White Hart Lane every day."

Parks's admiration for the professionalism at the club extended to the people skills employed by the management and senior pros. "It was very much a family club. People were welcomed. People like Steve Perryman made sure they knew people's names. They talk about Sir Alex Ferguson now knowing everything that goes on – Keith Burkinshaw was always at our games; he always knew who you were and would say hello to our parents. That really makes you feel part of a club. That era from '76 to '85, I don't think there's ever been a better era in a club's history."

Being a Hackney boy, Tony must have felt very at home with the corps of Londoners at the club at the time? "I went in when the apprentices were people like Mark Falco and Garry Brooke, so I got to know them. Then it was the new crop of apprentices – me, Terry Gibson, Terry Cooper, Jimmy Bolton, Ian Crook, Mark Bowen, we had our own little crew. But it was never cliquey. You got to play in games with the older guys, you trained with them, which was a good education. It was always a club that tried to integrate."

There was camaraderie, but inevitably much mickey-taking of the non-London contingent by the local lads. "One of my biggest memories of that north/south divide was when Keith Burkinshaw took over the club," laughs Parks. "He said in no uncertain terms, 'I don't like you flash Londoners and you're going to be doing it the way I want it done.' And, great man that he is, everyone respected him for that. But you'd have people like Micky Hazard for instance, who'd been at the club for a while and knew London, but still had his Mackem accent, and he'd get loads of stick, and the mick taken out of him for his dress sense – he was a shocking dresser. And Tony Galvin, who came to the game quite late. Walking into the dressing room with real mickey-takers like Paul Miller and Mark Falco and Brooksie must have been quite difficult. And he would bite, without fail, every time in his own inimitable Yorkshire way – every single time they hammered him. But he was a really dry, funny bloke too."

There was a lively social side to the club, with Paul Miller pulling the strings. "Maxie was a proper London wide boy. He always had to be the smartest dressed man; he always had a new gold chain and a shirt, and he never ever, ever wore jeans – he always wore trousers. He's always been like that. And then you'd have Micky Hazard in a polo neck jumper, a shirt with a tie done to the top of his chest and his jacket, a pair of trousers that were halfway up his ankles and a pair of pumps. He would get absolutely hammered for that. There was a guy called Joey Simmons who was Garry Brooke's age, and at the time he was the head apprentice, and he looked after Tommy Heffernan. Tommy liked to have tracksuit bottoms, long socks, long-sleeved shirt and a sweatshirt all wrapped up in a towel. What Paul Miller would do was get in extra early in the morning, undo the kit, replace the long socks with short socks which he would rinse out, take away his tracksuit bottoms and sweatshirt and give him a short-sleeved shirt – this would be on a freezing cold day in December. By the time Tom comes in to get changed Joe thinks he's got the best kit, now he hasn't.

"I remember being in the treatment room and there was Steve Perryman, Peter Taylor, Terry Naylor and Colin Lee. I was an apprentice on £16 a week. We used to have these massive ice buckets that you'd stick your ankles in if you got injured. So they filled this full of water, put all the crushed ice in and said they'd give me a fiver if I could hold my head under. So I reasoned it out, in a very Tony-like way, that I had £16, an extra fiver would come in handy. I knew it was going to be cold but it would be well worth it. So I sat with my head in this ice bucket for 30 seconds or so. When I pulled my head out, Christ, the pain was unbelievable! I could see these four players and Mike Varney just crying with laughter. I was freezing cold, holding my hand out for this money. But they did pay me so I ended up a fiver better off.

"It was also a way of connecting with first team players. We weren't allowed in the first-team dressing room unless we knocked on the door, we weren't allowed to speak when we were in there tidying kit up unless we were spoken to, and I always felt that was the right way to go. You had to earn the right to get in that dressing room. There was a lot of competition to get in there. But also I was made number two, the back-up keeper, at Tottenham from the age of 16, in and out of first-team squads, so I had the best of both worlds; I could mix with everyone at the club. It was fantastic."

While the team spirit was strong, the ambitions of the younger players sometimes led to discord. Parks remembers one such incident. "Steve Perryman and Neil McNab had a fight on the training ground.

It was to do with the fact that at the time the first team were absolutely crap, they couldn't win a game to save their lives. Every Thursday there would be a full-on reserves versus first team match in which the reserves were supposed to set up and play as the opposition would on a Saturday, to give the first team a chance to try things. The reserves were outstanding, packed with players who probably deserved to be in the first team, the likes of Neil McNab. Week in, week out the reserves beat the first team and it just boiled over one day, I think Steve's frustrations boiled over, there was a tackle and bit of a fracas. Keith decided it was all right and they could play on, and they just went at it again. That happens up and down the country every day of the training week. Even now. Because of frustration. Steve was so frustrated that the team he was the captain of wasn't performing, and the reserves were good players but they were cocky and a bit flash and so it was almost a bit disrespectful the way they were dismantling the first team, and that's how that blew up."

New arrivals at the club also needed to have strength of character, and on one of them, Tony has a different take to some of his team-mates. "Steve Archibald was different from the senior pros, a real individual; he would look after himself. He was a good pro, and one of the best centre forwards I ever played with. What a lot of people don't realise about Steve Archibald is what a good guy he was. At the time he was contracted to wear Nike boots. He went up to the Nike factory to get some boots, came back and he came into our youth-team dressing room. He gave us all a pair of studs, rubbers and training shoes which he'd brought back. He might not have connected with his contemporaries, but the lads in the youth team and the reserves, they loved him. He was someone you could go and talk to and who would give you advice. He always, always had time for the younger players. He was a fantastic bloke and a fantastic player as well.

"Garth wasn't your typical footballer. He was quite intellectual, spoke really nicely and said big words – we used to take the piss out of him. He took it in good fun. I still see him, and when I see him on *Match of the Day* he hasn't changed. He was another decent bloke who would take time and interest in young players, because he'd come up through the youth team system at Stoke City, and he knew the problems. Garth went from being a home-grown talent at Stoke to a superstar at Tottenham, because of the ability he had on the pitch."

The strong team spirit also meant lengthy sessions in the pub talking football on a Saturday night. "As a young player growing up, we all sat on the edge of that. You wanted to be part of it," says Parks. "Steve Perryman was like the orchestra leader, he would just talk football, football, football. If we played a game away and got back to White Hart Lane we'd go into the White Hart pub, now Rudolphs – we'd all go in. If we were travelling back and got dropped off at Cheshunt we'd go to a pub local to there and by the time we got in there for a beer supporters who had gone to the game were there. It was never a question of they couldn't speak to us or we were too big to speak to them. It's a bit different nowadays – players are massive celebrities surrounded by people who want to keep you away from them. We liked mixing with the supporters, although in fairness they would leave us alone most of the time – we were almost like regulars so it'd just be a quick 'All right lads' and we'd get on with it. There'd be some banter if it had been a bad game and some pats on the back if it had been good but everyone just got on with their evening. The thing about London then was . . . well, Glenn Hoddle was the superstar, but he could still walk down the street relatively unscathed. There was still that anonymity – a different era."

So, was it a particularly boozy culture? "That old adage of 'Win or lose we're on the booze and if we draw we'll have some more' was rife throughout the game. We weren't any different to that," replies Parks. "But I can honestly say, and I liked a drink, that I never went out on a Friday night. That was drilled into me by people like Steve Perryman – enjoy yourself, but when it's time to work you work. There was a respect for the professionalism of the game, and for your manager. When they said work, you worked. It has become more of a business these days, and the lads probably drink less, and there's been a good influence from the foreign players and coaches on how to look after your body. The game's moved on in terms of preparation. But then I was watching a game the other day from the '80s – Bryan Robson got a tackle in on the edge of his own box, the ball went forward and by the time it got into the other box he was there. Bryan would've been a typical top pro – he played hard and worked hard and he had the fitness levels.

"We hear a lot from foreign players and coaches about 'English players drink too much', and yet most of the foreign players I've known smoke cigarettes. Ossie Ardiles was a packet-a-day man. I find that hard to weigh up. But I don't think smoking affected Ossie as a footballer, the same as I don't think liking a drink affected Steve Perryman. So sometimes the criticism is unfair.

"I remember Sebastian Coe, when he was a world champion athlete, became friends with Garth Crooks. Coe had said to him that he didn't think footballers were very fit, they didn't work hard enough. Garth invited him in for training. We did a 15 minute warm-up, and went straight into an eight-a-side game. Within five minutes of that game starting, Coe was blown away. He couldn't cope. It's a different fitness, and footballers are extremely fit for what they do. Short sharp bursts, different pace, changing direction."

So much for the drinking. What about those other traditional off-field pursuits of cars, fashion and girls? The last subject Parks, like most of his team-mates, is not prepared to discuss. But he does provide an insight into a different era with his comments on the rest.

"There wasn't much stuff about cars or how big your house was. You knew when you pulled into a car park that Glenn Hoddle and Steve Perryman would have the best car, and in them days there was lots of club cars and sponsored cars. I went to Reading recently to do some work, and every car is the latest Merc, latest Porsche, everyone has to outdo everyone else. For us it wasn't really like that. There were a lot of sponsored cars, Fords like the guy on the street was driving.

"For me it was more of a fashion thing, and certainly Maxie would make sure it was. You were always conscious that you didn't want to go in wearing something dodgy or you'd have the piss ripped out of you. Mind you, you could just leave that to Micky Hazard – he would take the pressure off you any day. Stand next to Micky and you'd look a million dollars," says Tony, laughing. "Brooksie was a one when it came to fashion. Quiet, but he must've spent most of his wages on clothes, every month. He had a wardrobe full of suits, he was always smart. He'd go for a two-piece suit with matching shirt and tie, nice shoes; when he was casual in jeans he was always very smart, top-of-the-range stuff at the time like Kappa. There was a shop along Tottenham High Road called Mean Man, and that was his shop. There'd be Brooksie, me, Mark Falco, and we'd always be in there. At the time I wasn't on the money they were so I could afford maybe a T-shirt once a month. They'd be, 'I'll have that, that, that and that.'

"Brooksie was really into David Bowie – knew everything. He had everything Bowie had ever done. He was quite a fashionable lad. Him and Mark Falco were best mates, no doubt, but they were the biggest piss-takers of each other as well. If Garry brought something Mark would take the piss, Garry would do the same to Mark. It was almost a bit of a competition to see who could get the best gear. And where Brooksie liked David Bowie, Mark liked Bryan Ferry. There always competition, and Mark always won over him because he loved his cars and motorbikes – his dad and brother ran a garage, and he was a real petrolhead. Brooksie wasn't. So you'd always see Brooksie in Mark's passenger seat – his nickname was Buddha and you'd always say, 'There goes Buddha in the passenger seat.' They were huge pals, but there was a huge undercurrent of rivalry."

The point is ventured that Falco was a player never fully appreciated by Spurs fans. Parks nods. "Mark was a big tough bastard; he used to smash us about on the ball courts. He wasn't aggressive off the field; he could look after himself, but he wasn't aggressive. But put him on a football pitch and if it needed to be done he'd do it. He was a natural goalscorer. He was never the quickest and not the easiest on the eye in terms of being a Tottenham player from the supporters' point of view, but he scored goals at whatever level: prolific. I thought he was awesome at Tottenham and never really got the genuine respect that he deserved."

Not only was Parks loving his days at Spurs, he was moving through the ranks very quickly. "Miljia Aleksic, Barry Daines and Mark Kendall were the three senior goalkeepers at the club when I signed professional, and I'd had a battle of my own in the youth team with a guy called Paul Allies, who was older than me," he remembers. "He started the under-18s season, so the battle for me was getting him out of that place. Eventually Peter Shreeve told me I was playing – it was Watford in the FA Youth Cup – and I stayed in the team. The next day Paul went in to see Keith Burkinshaw and said he wasn't happy. Keith said, 'You can leave. I think he's a better goalie than you.' And I never forget to this day that his dad said to Keith Burkinshaw, 'You're making a big mistake; he'll come back to haunt you.' Keith just said, 'I've no problem with that.' Keith always gave me lots of confidence, always had belief in me as a goalie."

Injuries to the keepers ahead of him meant Parks was in the squad for the first FA Cup final in May 1981 – "Just to be around an FA Cup final squad in the build-up was amazing for a 16-year-old," he says – but watched from the stands as Spurs lifted the trophy in the replay. Then, in August 1981, Parks returned to the club to the news that Ray Clemence had signed. "When I first walked in and I saw

Ray Clemence there, league title winner, European Cup winner, England keeper, I thought, 'Fucking hell' – I suppose I was a little bit in awe of him. There was more to come, as Parks was informed he was now Clemence's understudy. "I didn't know the other keepers had left, I thought I'd be fifth in line. So to be told I was the number two was like, 'Bloody hell' . . ."

Clemence was to make quite an impression. "There was such a big age difference we were never going to be best pals, but he was always decent." Presumably Clemence was good to train with. "No, he was useless because he never trained in goal," laughs Parks. "He loved playing out on the pitch. Maybe on a Thursday morning he'd do about 30 minutes handling, but that was it. That was the biggest problem for me trying to learn. Make no mistake, he was a world-class goalkeeper, better than Peter Shilton. The biggest difference between Ray and Peter was that every single day Peter had to work on his game. Ray Clemence was just a natural. He was fit, strong, agile; he had natural ability – and he was the original sweeper keeper, quick across the ground – he had everything. If I was going to say to someone, 'That's what you need to be a top-class goal-keeper,' it would be Ray Clemence.

"Mentally he is the strongest person I've ever known in my life. He's a winner, he has a determination that he won't be beaten. There was a shooting practice one day and he must have stood there for 15 minutes without hardly moving. The lads were chipping him and curling it round him, slaughtering him until someone chipped him once too often and he said, 'Right, that's it. No one's going to score now.' And for the rest of that shooting practice no one scored a goal. He was making saves that were unbelievably good. There ain't many people in the game that can just switch it on and off like that. It's difficult to learn off someone like that, because I never had the ability to switch it on and off. He was fantastic. I learned loads about being a professional, what the game meant to him, what he thought made me a good or a bad keeper

– he would talk to me but he never showed me because he didn't need to practise to improve himself. In the England set-up Don Howe at the time felt that because Peter Shilton would go in and work at 100mph every day that he was the better goalkeeper. What he didn't realise was that Ray didn't need to do that. It was perceived that Ray was a little lazy which was why Peter Shilton won the battle of the number ones."

But even with such an outstanding role model alongside him, Parks recognises now that things were already going stale for him after achieving such success so early. Talking about how his working day changed once he had signed professional forms, he says: "The days were shorter because you didn't have the jobs to do. If it was the early part of the week we might pop up the road to the pub and have a beer and something to eat after training. I was living in Chigwell. Me and Ian Crook were typical snookerheads, so we'd go to the snooker hall for a couple of hours. Really, when you look back at it, it was all time when you should've been practising what it was that got you to that position. The difficult thing was that you'd have to manage your first team duties with your reserve team duties, so you'd definitely play a reserve game, you'd be in and around the first team squad – it was emotional swings and roundabouts. You'd be thinking, 'I could be playing for the first-team on Saturday' only for Ray to get fit and start training on a Friday; then you'd look at the team sheet and you're in the reserves again. I must have as many reserve team appearances as anyone that's ever played the game. I played for six years under Ray Clemence and never really got an opportunity, he was so consistent. It tends to take its toll, and you get a little bit pissed off with it really. You become resigned to the fact that you're not going to play games and you lose your edge a little bit. I probably stopped doing what I should have been doing."

But there was, of course, the 1984 UEFA Cup. As Parks is keen to point out, he played more of a role that season than is generally remembered. "I played in the quarter-finals, semi-finals and the final of the UEFA Cup, and I was in the team from January in the league. Ray was going through a poor run of form and I remember Steve Archibald saying to me, 'Make sure you stay sharp, he's not playing well and we'll have to give you a chance soon.' We played at Fulham in the FA Cup and Ray got injured. Graham Roberts went in goal and we ended up drawing. I played in the replay. I'd made my league debut against West Ham the previous season, and when I was 16 I came on as a sub in a Cup Winners' Cup game, so I'd made my debut early enough and I was thinking, 'Come on, I'll have some more of this' but it didn't come. Then suddenly Ray's injured and I'm in the team, and it carried on. I was getting quite good press, doing well. We played Austria Vienna at home in the quarter-final and I got a whack on the knee, had to have five stitches. We were playing Liverpool at Anfield on the Saturday and it was a place I'd always wanted to play, but when I got up the morning after the Vienna game the knee had swollen up, it was infected and that was it. Ray was fit, and in the build-up to the quarter-final he'd actually gone to see Keith and said, 'I'm fit, I want my place back.' Keith had told him, 'Sorry, you ain't getting it back.' So you can imagine the boost in your confidence that gives you. I was really buoyed, then I get injured and I was out of the team.

"I was still only 21 and had good experience. A lot of the supporters knew about me; the manager was happy. Ray played at Liverpool and in the second leg of the Austria Vienna game. They did a shooting practice on the Friday morning and apparently – I was training with the reserves – the last shot of the morning caught Ray on the end of his finger and broke it. So I was back in the team.

"The semi-final at White Hart Lane was a really nervy game, at one point I nearly juggled a cross into the back of my own net. I was going to punch but I changed my mind at the last minute and ended up playing pat-a-cake with the ball under the crossbar. But we went through. By the time of the final our league form had tailed off, but I was in the first team. I ended up playing about 28 games. People think Keith brought me on for the penalty shoot-out, but I played most of that season and I'd earned the right. I was really pleased.

"We knew Keith would be leaving after the final and that gave us an extra incentive. It was a difficult competition to win. Knowing Keith was leaving was a real disappointment to me because he'd always shown a lot of faith in me. Keith never really said much to us about it, it wasn't his style. He kept himself to himself, and had a real strong will. And he was a very good football man – he wasn't one for the pats on the back for himself, he always heaped the praise on the players.

"For the final I kept my place. The first game was exceptional – I don't think it gets the credit it deserves. We went into the match not really knowing European players like you do today, and they had an awesome team. Munaron in goal, he was outstanding – I've come across him recently because he works for the Belgian FA. I liked him because he was of my stature, same height. They had Franky Vercauteren, Morten Olsen the Danish captain – class all over the park. They had the lad Scifo who was 17 at the time. In that first game I thought we outplayed them. Paul Miller put us ahead, but they equalised. They got a shot, and I got a lot of criticism for this, but there was no way the goal was down to me. If I make a mistake I'll hold my hand up. The corner came in and there was a crowd of bodies, the lad hit a shot from the edge of the box and it just took a deflection and bang, it was in the back of the net. I remember feeling really hard done by with all the criticism I was getting on the telly. When we came off the pitch the feeling was that we'd done a really good job – they know we can play and we've held them at their place, now we can finish them off at ours. European nights at White Hart Lane were brilliant – when that Shelf side was packed out it was awesome.

"The weather in the build-up was warm and sunny; there were the photocalls and interviews which was a new thing for me but I was quite enjoying it. Once it started to sink in you realised the magnitude of the game. Waking up at eight in the morning when you were kicking off at eight at night was such a long day. It's the only time I've ever been nervous all day. I was still nervous when I was standing in the tunnel, but when you go on the pitch the nerves usually go. This time they didn't.

"Anderlecht turned it right round, I thought they played some superb football on the night, and probably deserved to take the lead when they did. As the second half was going by you could feel the tension in the crowd. When people say it's like an electric atmosphere it really is, you can feel the buzz around the place. You don't hear individuals screaming, you can just hear the din of the crowd. It's brilliant to play in.

"I started thinking, 'We're never going to get a goal here.' Keith did really well; he made the substitution [bringing Ardiles on to prompt an assault of the Belgians' goal] and it changed things. Munaron made three or four outstanding saves – a couple off Steve Archibald. Then we ended up with a scrambled goal, down off the bar and in the back of the net. Fantastic. Extra time it was a little bit flatter. Both teams were feeling the pace. As soon as the ref blew the whistle for the end of extra time the nerves went. I knew that I could save at least one without a doubt. It didn't phase me, because you're never going to get the blame for letting in a penalty.

"I remember the takers being organised and everything being got ready. Clem never really said anything to me; he just let me get on with it. I didn't like messing around, walking up to the ball or kicking my studs on the post. I liked to get on my line and have a look. Morten Olsen was their first taker and he was unbelievable. From about 20 yards out he just looked into the bottom corner by my left hand and I thought, 'That's it, I'm going there.' He struck it quite sweet and I thought it was a really good save because he put it low and I chucked myself at it and just got it round the post. I was really chuffed with myself. The penalties rolled on, no problem, and I'm thinking, 'We're in here.' Then Danny Thomas steps up and Munaron makes a really good save. I looked at Danny's face and it was amazing, the sadness and dejection. The crowd went quiet, then they started to roar and sing his name. A few of the lads came up to him and took him back to the centre circle – he was close to tears. I walked into the goal and Gudjohnsen [father of Eidur] came up to take his penalty. And I have to say it was the worst penalty in the world; it was just a shocker, my mum could've saved it. It was so predictable. His run-up was poor, it was short, he wrapped his foot round it, it was a beautiful height to dive at. I got me hands on it, did a couple of rolls and got up and I was off. I genuinely did not know what to do so I just ran. If that gate in the corner had been open I would've been down at Seven Sisters in seconds. I remember Ray Clemence just clothes-lining me across the throat and I was under a pile of bodies. I looked up and saw Danny Thomas's face – the biggest thing for me in the penalty shoot-out was the two faces of Danny Thomas. The despair when he missed and the absolute ecstasy just seconds later.

"I remember the satisfaction on Keith's face too. Everyone was so happy because if you look at the team that started that second leg you'd have to say, if everyone was fit it probably wouldn't have started that way. Glenn was out, Ray wasn't fit, Ossie was on the bench, Steve was suspended – people forget we were missing top, top players. The lads that came in, and I include myself, people like Alistair Dick, Ian Crook, Mark Falco, Micky Hazard . . . there was a really home-grown feel to that side. I look at Tottenham now and they've got no home-grown talent – apart from Ledley King. They don't have that strength in depth.

"After the match my biggest memory of that night was trying

to steal the replica trophy. It's about a third of the size of the UEFA Cup and the guy gave it to me so I thought it was the man of the match award. We got back in the dressing room and it dawned on me that maybe it wasn't, but I thought it would look really nice at home, so I put it inside my bag and thought if no one asks I'm going to take it and bring it back another time. When I come out of the shower someone had raided my bag and given the trophy to Irving Scholar who was sitting by the door in his wheelchair – he had a broken leg at the time – and it was on his lap. He'd come in and said, 'Where's that replica cup for the boardroom?' and they'd gone, 'Parksy had it, check his bag'. A lad from Hackney was going to nick the replica cup," says Parks, laughing. "I did get presented with a really beautiful man of the match award which for me wasn't quite right. The two saves stick in the memory, but I certainly didn't do enough to deserve a man of the match award. For me that night it would've been Munaron. We didn't have one individual that night who was outstanding; it was a really good team effort and we had a real belief.

"Afterwards we all went upstairs into the West Stand. All our family and friends were there, it was a fantastic night. People were shaking hands and wishing Keith all the best, although he wasn't leaving immediately – there was a testimonial the following week. We went down to where the old office building was to the fans and managed to say 'Hello' to them, then it was back to the party and just, relief. We were in one of the lounges, all the bars were open and we flitted around, we knew people in different bits and we worked our way round. At the time Maurice Hope was the middle-weight world champion and he was there. I like my boxing. He came out of one of the lounges and he shook my hand and said, 'Well done'. I thought, 'Blimey, Maurice Hope's shook my hand – that's awesome.'

"I left about six the following morning, and I had to be on breakfast telly at seven. The car came to pick me up and I was in no fit state whatsoever. Anne Diamond was absolutely disgusted in me. I remember her giving me the filthiest of looks. In the end they couldn't do the interview, so they stuck me in the canteen, gave me some breakfast, put me in a car and sent me home.

"That's pretty much how the next couple of weeks went. People knew you wherever you went. I remember going to a pub opposite the Blind Beggar in Whitechapel, a place called The Murphyhouse where I knew some people. It was a proper old spit-and-sawdust boozer and I thought, 'I'll get away from it a bit in here.' I walked in and ordered a pint and someone said, 'I'll get that'. I looked over and I said, 'I don't know you mate, but thanks.' He said, 'You're the lad that saved that penalty the other night. Well done, even though I'm a West Ham supporter.' I must've spent about ten days totally out of it. And why not, you never know when it'll come round again. Well, for me it didn't as it turned out. It was great, and then it all went downhill."

Parks laughs. But why did his career go into a downward trajectory? What went wrong? "It was too much too early," he says. "I always thought I played well for Tottenham but I don't think I handled playing for Tottenham very well. I was a poor pro for a couple of years. Shreevsie took over, rated Clem number one which pissed me off, sitting in stands watching games pissed me off. There was a group of us, probably half a dozen; me, Garry Brooke, Mark Bowen . . . We used to call ourselves the Mushroom Squad, we got into bad habits, felt the world owed us a living. 'Why are we being so hard done by?' We'd all massage each others egos and say, 'Yeah, you should be in the team,' when the truth was that we didn't deserve to be anywhere near the team because we weren't doing our jobs properly. That's probably where it went – I maybe should've left Tottenham a little bit sooner. But then David Pleat came in, I played a few games, went out on loan, then Venners came in and I played the first 16 games but I was never really going to be a Terry Venables man, he never really fancied me as a goalie.

It was a sad end really. I left the club in 1987. At the end my contract was up, I didn't get an offer, they didn't ask if I wanted to stay – so I went. Steve Perryman was manager at Brentford at the time and that provided an escape for me.

"I was given every opportunity by Tottenham. The club and the coaches working there never denied me the opportunity to become a success as a player. The only person that did was me. There comes a point, especially now I'm coaching and I can judge the game from both sides, I can look in the mirror and say, 'You can blame who you want, but it was down to you.' Tottenham gave me the platform and it was up to me.

"When I first started coaching I was player-coach at Halifax for three or four years and I remember ringing Steve Perryman up. Me and Steve fell out a bit when he was manager and I was his player because I was such a tit. I then realised what dealing with people like me was all about for managers and coaches. I thought, 'Bloody hell, I must have been a real difficult person to deal with.' So I made a few phone calls to apologise and Steve was one of them. Steve being the man he is accepted that and we're back in touch now."

Parks has obviously completed a tough personal journey, but facing up to his past has strengthened his enthusiasm for the game. We spend some time discussing the state of English football and English talent, his dismay at the lack of recognition of and support for young goalkeepers in this country, and his satisfaction at being able to make some input. "I get down in the dumps at times, like most jobs," he says, "but I love the game and I love helping young goalkeepers. I've worked with Scott Carson and Joe Hart in their younger days. Tottenham now have a young lad, David Button, who is going to be a fantastic goalie; Middlesbrough and Man United have some good young 'uns. I hope I've helped them in some way."

There's still much of the boyish enthusiasm of the park football player despite the ups and downs of his career, and that genuine love of the game for its own sake shines through when Tony Parks answers the question about his best experience at Spurs. It's not, surprisingly, the penalty saves in 1984. "My best experience ever playing football was making my debut in a north London derby at Highbury, by a mile," he says. "My family were Arsenal supporters and I grew up watching football at Highbury, and I loved that stadium. Making my debut in that game; my dad phoning me up saying, 'I hope you play well but I hope we beat you', all the little family things. That would've been '83/'84; we got beat 3-2 and Steve Archibald scored our two goals. Charlie Nicholas got their winner. It was an amazing day; red hot; Highbury was packed; the atmosphere was brilliant. There were a few of us young ones playing: Ian Crook, Micky Hazard. I'd always wanted to play in a north London derby – that was my best ever memory of playing for Tottenham."

GEORGE MAZZON

"FOOTBALL CAN'T LAST FOREVER.
ENJOY IT WHILE IT LASTS"

GEORGE MAZZON
TOTTENHAM HOTSPUR

I f it is every football fan's fantasy to play for a major club in a packed stadium, then George Mazzon can relate how it actually feels. His spell at Tottenham may have been brief, amounting to just seven senior appearances in a four-year period, but he was able to achieve what millions aspire to and only a privileged elite ever realise. This is a man who really did live the dream.

Few fans around at the time may remember his fleeting top-flight career, and younger supporters will probably ask "George who?" but he was a contemporary of Tottenham legends and held his own among such vaunted company. Not that the modest and likeable former defender is one to brag. Now 48, and a pugnacious-looking construction site manager for Bovis Lend Lease, with £60 million contracts and a 400-strong workforce depending on him, he concentrates on his job today and is in no rush to let people know about his former life of football stardom.

"In the industry I work in now, people know who I am and what I did, but I never tell them – they find out." Sitting in his company's offices in the heart of the City close to the Bank of England, George points to the partition window. "I'm surprised there aren't a load of faces peering in now taking the mickey. I've been out of football for nearly 20 years and at this company since I left. I've never told anyone directly what I used to be and do. But I can guarantee that within two weeks of getting on to a site, somebody will have been on the internet, found a photo of me in a Tottenham shirt, printed it out and pinned it on the wall.

"From Spurs supporters, the reaction is 'Wow!' and a pat on the back. Where my office is next door, Scott the administrator is an avid Tottenham fan and he had my photo stuck on the wall behind his desk. But fans of other clubs don't really give me any stick. They just want to talk about football. 'What do you think of this player, George? What did you think of that game?' They want my opinion. I don't mind talking about it, though I think my knowledge of the game is terrible. But the banter is good-natured.

"I've never tried to gain from being an ex-pro. But in the industry I'm in, I can't hide it. I'm now in a position where I have directors of companies recognising me and talking about games I played in – good and bad things. I can't for the life of me remember them. And I can't say to these people, 'Yeah, I remember you – seat 15, row G, West Stand – you're the one that called me that so-and-so!'"

Friendly and amenable, George is self-effacement personified. With his hard hat and work clothes, he is like any other worker on site: an ordinary bloke getting on with doing his job. The story of his sporting career, however, is far from ordinary.

To begin with, he came to the game from an unlikely background. Rather than being just another stereotypical street-playing urchin of football folklore, George Mazzon grew up in quiet and comfortable surroundings in the borderlands between Hertfordshire and London and was privately educated.

"I was born and raised in Waltham Cross and went to boarding school in Cuffley. The hotel Spurs stayed in for the cup final in 1981 was actually my old boarding school. It was called St Dominics, but is now the Ponsbourne Hotel; the golf course at the bottom of the hill is where I learned to play football. One of the bedrooms would have been the dormitory I slept in as a boarder.

"It was run by nuns, though I can't say it was particularly strict. I had Italian parentage and being Catholics, naturally, I went to a Catholic school. My parents ran a grocery business. I had an older brother, Gianni, and two sisters followed, so it was hard for my mum and dad trying to develop a business and raise a family. They must have felt it was easier to find a school of a relatively good standard and not have the day-to-day worries of looking after children."

That mention of his Italian lineage prompts a reminder of Garry Brooke's comment that Mazzon was as English as anyone in the club, and that 'Giorgio' was just a whimsical invention of Peter Shreeve. George can now set the record straight once and for all.

"My Christian name really is Giorgio. My father is Italian, my mother is Swiss. But having been born in England and lived here all my life, I've always been called George. It was before the cup final in 1981 that I had one of my first interviews. A reporter asked what my name was, to which I said 'George Mazzon', only for Peter to jump in and say, 'George? No, put a bit of sparkle behind it, it's Giorgio!' To which I said 'OK' because, after all, it *is* my name. Peter said, 'Give it a bit of glamour. We've got an Osvaldo, a Ricardo, how about a Giorgio?' To which Gary O'Reilly immediately piped up with, 'And don't forget Gario?'

"Growing up most people called me George and they do in my workplace now; very few people know what my real name is. I don't try to hide it. 'Giorgio' didn't stick after Peter's intervention, though Ossie and Ricky would use the Italian version perhaps because it rolled off the Latin tongue a little easier for them."

George played football whenever he could as a kid but, coming from a family with a distinctly non-footballing pedigree, he received little encouragement at home. "There was no football in my family. My father had greater interests in his business; He would ask, 'Why is it that I can never get Giorgio to help me out on a Saturday afternoon?' Outside of football I would work in the business, doing a bread round or whatever. He couldn't understand why I was always busy on Saturdays – and later it was as if he never realised that I played football for a living. He didn't take it on board – playing football to him was something you played over the park.

"My dad assumed I was going to go into the family business – it was called G Mazzon and Sons, after all. His expectation was that his sons were going to help his growing business. Unfortunately, my brother went into the British Army and I became a footballer, so his dream wasn't fulfilled.

"His friends would say to him, 'Your son plays for Spurs!' and he would ask me, 'Why do all these people keep talking about you and football?' He just didn't comprehend it. He never saw me play; my mum probably only saw me a couple of times, and even that was when I was under 15. They never saw me play for Tottenham."

Putting this lack of parental interest alongside the restricted opportunities to play at school, it's a wonder how George ever did make it to Tottenham in the first place – and when he did, he faced rejection at the first hurdle. "St Dominics was not a football school. I learned how to play there but I certainly wasn't *taught*. At playtime we played football, but there was no tuition, no games teacher to steer me. The nearest thing I got to coaching was when I was 12. My brother started playing for a local Sunday team and I started the next year. It was an all-Catholic team that was based around St Joseph's church at Waltham Cross. This was the era of a priest getting nine ten-year-olds in his Fiat 500 and driving us round to games. It was hysterical, really. But that's where I learned because we were trained and told how to play.

"That's how it all started for me. Gianni was a big influence; he was three years older and very talented at most sports and I followed suit. I became captain of the school team, played for the district, then Hertfordshire county at various age groups and I played against Garry Brooke in some of those games."

Having been entranced by the 1970 FA Cup final, George was a Chelsea fan through his early teens, but went to White Hart Lane for his first experience of playing at a proper club. "I was 16 and turning out for Waltham New Town, and our manager managed to get me and our goalkeeper six training sessions at Tottenham. The pair of us went down for the midweek evening sessions run by Ron Henry in the indoor gyms at White Hart Lane.

"We never played a game – just trained. Peter Shreeve pulled us to one side, said we were very good but felt we weren't quite the type of players they were looking for. I felt gutted, terrible. I was over the moon to have been training at a big club like Spurs. Despite not getting a game, I felt I was getting in with them. I had my heart set on becoming a pro. That was all I ever wanted to be.

"So the rejection was hurtful, painful. But I went to Hertford Town in the Isthmian League. I wasn't motivated as such to prove people wrong; I just wanted to play. What my plan was I wasn't certain. But the manager at Hertford knew Ralph Coates; he watched me, obviously thought I was good enough and got me another round of training sessions at Spurs. I went down, trained and this time actually started playing games – I played one, then another and before I knew it I was a member of the youth team.

"I had other options. When I was in the Spurs youth team and still playing for Hertford as well, I got a call from David Pleat who was then Luton manager. He suggested I come down for a trial. I actually played a non-first team game for Luton against an Arsenal side. We lost 1-0, and Pleat said afterwards he was very happy with the way I had played and thought I was a great prospect. However, he said I was a bit young and I should go away and play for

Wealdstone, a club Luton had an association with, I presume, for a year and then he would take another look. I couldn't help thinking 'I'm already at Tottenham – why would I want to play for Wealdstone?' When he said that, it hurt a lot more than when Peter Shreeve said I wasn't good enough for Spurs at 16. But it didn't mean anything as I ended up playing for Tottenham.

"At 18 I went straight from the youth team into a two-year professional contract at Spurs. By that time I had a job with a steel fabricating business in Enfield. I was earning £36 a week there. One of the first jobs I got was to buy all the metal for the balustrades at Wembley Stadium. So even then it was football-related. For my first Spurs contract I got, I think, £12,000 – substantially more than what I was on at my other job. I walked into Keith Burkinshaw's office and he simply said, 'The season's finished, we've looked at you and we're keen to offer you a contract, what do you think?' I said, 'It's all I ever wanted.' Keith asked me to take it away and think about it but I said no and signed it on the spot.

"The rest of that day I floated home. I caught the bus and it was just going through my head, 'I'm a professional footballer, I'm a professional footballer with Tottenham Hotspur.' I couldn't wait to tell my mum. I skipped down the street. I thought my chance had gone two years before.

"Peter never said anything about rejecting me previously. I just got the usual normal motivation stuff that was used to get people to perform – 'C'mon Mazzon, you bastard!' Nothing was said. Whether he remembered it or not I have no idea, they must have had hundreds of boys coming through the system. Maybe it was good fortune; maybe the first time I'd been unlucky in that there were better players at those first training sessions, I don't know, but playing games enabled me to settle and cement a position, to show them that I had some ability and what it takes.

"From there I progressed, along with people like Micky Hazard, Garry and Mark Falco, Kerry Dixon and Terry Gibson. It was a step up from non-league; the most noticeable thing was that everyone was of a good ability – they kicked with purpose. On a Sunday team there are always one or two who are sons of the manager or know someone and can get a game. You could tell by the scores. We'd win games 15-0 – that sort of thing doesn't happen in the youth teams at professional clubs. There was more strength, speed and skill and purpose in what you did.

"There was finesse at Tottenham. It was instilled in us. All through the training process, Shreeve and Ron were guiding us. The one thing Peter wanted was a bit of class. Everything that you did, Peter would encourage you to do it with a bit of style and charisma. It was skill 'plus' – always do things with a little bit extra. You had that talent within you, but what the coaching was designed to do was make you think that little bit more. Make you more mentally active in controlling what you are doing.

"Take passing the ball. Anybody can do it but not everyone can do it with style. Jimmy Holmes was a natural left-footer. Every time he kicked the ball his body shape and stance was very natural. It just looked so sweet the way he made contact. For some reason, all left-footers look good and Shreevesie wanted that in all his players. 'When you pass the ball,' he'd say, 'Push your arm out so it looks good, get your arm out as your foot swings through.' There was method to it, it served a purpose but had to look right as well. Peter could observe your stance, your technique, and make you think about the game.

"Peter was a character. He wasn't the fulcrum for everything but he was respected for his intelligence, very good in involving people, getting them to react and respond. He was a good man manager and knew how to get the best out of people. But also a fine coach and tactician.

"Training was hard but fair. You never went in to hurt anybody, there was no malice. You had to have the fitness and stamina. But we played with a will to impress and succeed. You wanted the ball

– playing for Spurs has always been about wanting to play, but with a recognition that you can't play if you don't get the ball.

"The crux of it was that you had to work hard and get your attitude right, with a keenness to work and run off the ball. From that foundation you could develop your skills to play as a team and carry players; not everybody was going to be on top form or not make mistakes. But ultimately it was 11 guys out on a pitch who would live and die for each other."

That element of rugged determination sits at odds with Shreeve's ethos of looking good and the reputation for Spurs being perceived as being a 'flash' club. For George, the opposite was true. "I can remember playing derbies against Crystal Palace, Chelsea, Arsenal and our feeling would be 'This lot are flash gits. They think they're class; they think they're better than us but we'll show 'em'. We never recognised it in ourselves. Playing Arsenal our attitude was, 'This is blood and guts; we've got to beat them.' We felt all the other London clubs were flashy teams full of flashy characters while we were just, well, normal."

Within that atmosphere of normality, Mazzon and his colleagues behaved like any other group of young men working together. They had their laughs, socialised and enjoyed themselves, but George points out that the players were aware of their responsibilities to their job.

"We used to give the staff the runaround: Johnny Wallis the kit man would be screaming at us all the time about cleaning the older pros' boots. Johnny had been there since the year dot, and we were always digging him out, giving him gip for not having the orange squash ready for after training, but in a good-natured way. It was a close atmosphere where most, if not everybody, got on.

"Outside of the club, it was a bit different. I was friends with Kerry Dixon, for example, but when he wasn't awarded a contract, we went our separate ways. Few of us actually lived local to each other; I lived near Cheshunt, Kerry was in Luton, and the others scattered all over. We didn't really socialise outside of football. At White Hart Lane we would have a drink in the club bar and maybe go onto the Chanticleer restaurant that was on Paxton Road, perhaps the Coolbury Club on the High Road. After training we might go to a pub near Cheshunt; if it was a weekday I'd go out round Broxbourne and Hoddesdon and occasionally bump into Ossie or Ricky or Glenn and Ray Clemence because that's where we lived. But we weren't in each other's pockets. When I was there, there was no drinking in and around the games or training. Outside of that there would be a few beers but nothing major by way of a drinking culture like at some clubs you heard about.

"I suppose I was a bit of a drinker and clubber, but I was sensible. There was the so-called rule you should never go out on Thursday night or 48 hours before a match. There's nothing stopping you having a drink at home within that time so you would exercise your own judgement. I made the decision to make Thursday night the last night of the week for me and if I did go out, make sure I wasn't going to do anything silly. Friday night I'd be in, preparing myself in the right way.

"Saturday night it depended on whether you'd had a tough game or not. If you'd been kicked around, picked up a knock or a few bruises, sometimes you'd be so stiff and knackered that you just wanted to go home and put your feet up and watch *Match of the Day*. That left you with the early part of the week to socialise, but this was a time when very little was happening unless you went into central London.

"If we did go into town it would be Saturday, but dependent on how the game went. Were we in a good mood, or in a very good mood? That would determine how keen we were to party. After the 1981 celebrations, which went on very late at the Chanticleer, I drove home. I can't remember how. But that was the thing you did in those days. Driving out of there at three in the morning, the street down to Edmonton was choc-a-bloc with people and police trying to keep the crowds back. I must have drunk myself silly. How on earth did I manage to get home?"

Like the rest of his team-mates of that era, George emphasises how strong the team spirit was at White Hart Lane, helped in no small part by strong individuals who stamped their personalities on the club.

"There were plenty of characters at Tottenham then. In my early days, Peter Taylor wasn't a drinker or party animal as such, but a bit of a comedian. He'd burst into his Norman Wisdom impressions and entertain us. Terry Naylor was another joke teller; Paul Miller was a strong character in his own right, as was Graham Roberts. Paul was a smart dresser and would always be talking about what clothes to buy. Garth Crooks was similar but had a knack for bringing you back down to earth. He was smart, sensible and educated. Garth had a dry wit and a sarcastic side. If you were getting carried away about anything, success on the pitch for example, he would keep your feet on the ground and not let you get too big for your boots.

"He once said that us defenders were the 'labourers'! But he scored goals so we could let him get away with it. Of course I had no idea he was going to go on to be a presenter, but you always felt he had an opinion, a statement to make about most things. He looked at things in a different light, an individual character different to everyone else. He was always very opinionated but his view was respected because he communicated it well and intelligently. Working in the media is ideal for him.

"Chris Hughton was a perfect gentleman, a nice person to talk to who didn't hold airs or graces against anybody and would give his heart for the game and the team. A lovely man – but then most of them were: John Lacey and Paul Price, Barry Daines – all of them wonderful people, characters and individuals with no chips on their shoulders. Just nice genuine people."

By 1978, having become a professional, George was ready to try to break into the first team. With such experienced and capable players like Miller and Roberts ahead of him, chances were to be strictly limited. But 30 years on he still recalls this period in his life with excitement and his usual modesty.

"When I broke into the first team squad I was welcomed but felt in awe of them as well. Suddenly I'm getting changed with Glenn, Steve Perryman – I still couldn't believe that I was a pro footballer. I was very, very lucky to be made a pro in that year when those kind of players were around. When Ossie and Ricky came, I was in awe of their ability as World Cup winners but I actually probably got closer to those two because of my Italian links. When Ricky arrived his English was very poor; albeit that I never actually spoke to him in Italian – or Spanish come to that – but I could understand him.

"Ossie was a cheeky chappie, a lovely person who was always smiling, always talking to you and trying to get you involved, bearing in mind that his English was poor to begin with but it improved day by day – though his pronunciation would make you giggle. Ricky was slightly more reserved but nevertheless always smiling and joking. I really do think they were tremendous people. But it was amazing to be around them. All the time I was at Spurs I was still floating on air."

Established within the group, George was privy to that most self-contained of football team environments, the club coach. Spending hours in each other's company on long drives up and down the motorways, players observed each other and their habits in intimate and inescapable detail.

"We travelled up for an away game the night before and would stay in a hotel. Depending on where you were, you might have a brief training session, a light lunch and relax. The emphasis was on being in the right frame of mind for the game. So most of your time on an away trip was spent sitting on that coach.

"It was a lot of time to kill. If you were travelling up to Newcastle, it's four or five hours on the coach there and back. What were you going to do? You listened to music, watched films, played cards, looked out of the window, read, did whatever. Tony Galvin and Chrissie would be reading a book but they also liked a game of cards, with a couple of games going on. Other people were interested in racing: Graham, for instance, would be looking at the form. There was and is a betting culture in football but it was less about the betting and more a case of filling free time if you had long coach journeys every couple of weeks.

"Ossie and Ricky were smokers. They'd have a fag at the back of the coach; there was no attempt to hide it. They'd have their fags on the table while they were playing cards. But their smoking didn't affect their performances.

"There was a lot of card playing, everybody would have been involved. We played hearts, penny a time or penny a point, possibly brag, and poker. But there was nothing to excess, no big stakes. We played for pennies because the journey could go on for hours and if you were playing for big stakes it could end up with people owing a lot of money which would not have been good for team spirit. At most, the stakes would go up to a pound. It was kept sensible so there would be no antagonism.

"Garry Brooke was a bit of a card sharp; so were Micky and Graham. Ossie was keen on playing chess; Ricky would have headphones on listening to music. We'd have music, and the latest films on the video. Glenn was a bit of an influence on what tunes we played, as he was a bit of a music buff, and Mike Varney would occasionally have his say; I remember him opening his car boot once at White Hart Lane and he had a bag of albums that we had a chat about.

"But after the game we'd always talk about football, a constant conversation about the way we played. It was a way of learning about what went right and wrong, with Keith, Peter and the players. We'd praise the good and identify the bad things or what could be done better. It was part of a learning culture at a club. Nowadays everyone's got a DVD to look at; back then we played the game, got on the coach and talked about it. Coming back we had the opportunity to have a meal, a drink and relax. But we'd be totally shattered. We'd be honest with each other – blunt even."

Back at the Lane after a long journey, players would jump into their cars for the final leg home. Despite the inevitable gap in income between the young players and the star names, George recalls an absence of explicit envy for what material signs of wealth others might display.

"There was no real competition. When I got my first contract I had an old Ford Cortina Mk II and progressed from that to a second-hand three-litre Capri. Terry Gibson, a real character, had a beach buggy and the bloody thing broke down first day! I had to get jump leads to help him get it started.

"Glenn had a black Volkswagen Sirocco. Later on some had sponsored cars. People started to get Saabs, BMWs, and Mercedes' as the team's fortunes improved. Chris, John Lacey, Paul Miller, all these types had good but understated cars. Their cars reflected their characters. No one had a Ferrari or Lamborghini. Towards the end of my time there, Garth told me that he had been asked by a sponsor to drive a different sports car every day. My reaction was 'Wow!' He ummed and aahed and said he wasn't particularly fussed. So I said, 'Well, send it my way then!'

"This was the era when football was starting to become more lucrative. There were agents but they were few and far between; they were beginning to get into the big clubs and gain a foothold in the industry. Now they are dominant, but I never had an agent. Nothing came my way, but then I was a young player trying to establish myself."

And what of that other modern phenomenon, the celebrity footballer pictured in the gossip mags with assorted hangers-on and female admirers. Did George and his team-mates enjoy that kind of attention in their day?

"Where I lived, everybody – I shouldn't say everybody, because that sounds big-headed – but they all knew I was George Mazzon and played for Tottenham. It happened as it does now – footballers are a catch. I can recall going to places like the Epping Forest Country Club, but not with recognised players; I would go with my mates or some of the younger, less well-known players like me. The recognition was not immediate. I never used 'I'm a footballer' as a chat-up line. Hmm, well, maybe I did. But as a young person I didn't benefit more than anyone else in going on the pull because I was a footballer.

"When players were out together, either in this country or abroad, we would go out as people exuding confidence. Yes we would try and pull, but in that situation I can't ever remember being successful. I don't think me saying 'I'm a pro' or playing for Tottenham ever benefited me in trying to chat up girls, or to be more accurate, got me an immediate attraction.

"When I was 17 and in the youth team, there was a police-woman who I think was attracted to the young players at Tottenham. That was the rumour – true or not, I don't know – but she was always there with a big smile on her face. I think she always volunteered for matchday duty. You'd either find her in the car park outside the West Stand with her uniform on, or in the Chanticleer with her civvies on. She was young, quite attractive – but you'd think why does she spend her life, as it appeared to be, in and around the club? It actually became off-putting for the players, albeit that she was attractive; the story was, 'Oh she's a bit of a goer'. But did anyone actually try and find out? I'm not sure. She was always there, on your doorstep. The problem is if you did the deed, she would always be around and what if something went wrong? It might be a notch on your bedpost, but . . ."

To the outsider, the lifestyle of a footballer in the late 1970s and early 1980s seems far removed from the everyday norm. "It never felt like hard graft," says George. "Training and playing required considerable physical effort, but away from the club with my non-football mates we did our ordinary socialising. We'd travel in my car (I graduated to a BMW) into London, go to a restaurant, club, or a cocktail bar but without me making it known I was a footballer. They had their own careers, I had mine and I didn't like to promote mine as being 'glamorous'."

But even for someone as reluctant to play the fame game as George, there were less savoury consequences. "Once at the Country Club there was a fight. I didn't get involved, but my mates did and it sparked up because of my connection with Spurs. I decided then that, 'This is not the place to go.' It was probably supporters of other clubs. I was on the verge of leaving Tottenham by then. I don't know the details to be honest, but it was something I didn't want and I never went back there. I wanted to avoid trouble and not put my mates in that situation if I was the cause of it.

"I tried to play things low key: if I was talking to people I wouldn't want to advertise I was a footballer. Unfortunately I had a flat, broken nose which meant they thought I was a boxer. The conversation would lead to how I got it and then it would come out that I'm a footballer. Eventually I'd say I played for Spurs. 'Who with?' I'd be asked. 'Glenn Hoddle, Ossie Ardiles . . .' I'd answer. 'Ooh, what are they like?!' would be the next question.

"I kept quiet not as a defence strategy, but because of my character. I am what I am; I didn't want to deny or advertise that I was a professional footballer at a big successful club. I wanted to talk one-to-one – as soon as it was known what I did, the balance of the conversation may have altered."

Away from the nightclubs and on the pitch, George's career proceeded in fits and starts. After a handful of brief substitute appearances, his most involved contribution came in October 1981. "I played a League Cup game at home against Man Utd. I was substitute that day. Mark Falco was playing at centre forward and got injured after five minutes, so I had to come on as a striker. I was a fish out of water and I barely touched the ball. At half time Keith switched things around with Ossie and Ricky pushed forward and me put into central midfield. We won 1-0 and I was grateful that I just felt more at home.

"I'm trying to remember the games I played in: Sunderland away, Man U at home, Everton at home, West Ham away; I played at Dundalk in an early-round European game, Exeter in the quarter-final of the 1981 run . . ."

He trails off, lost in thought. It's typical of Mazzon that his recall of the matches is hazy, as if the basic details are less memorable than the experience itself. As someone who admits he was floating on air during his time at Spurs, it is the sights, sounds and feelings of those games that have stayed with him.

"It was amazing to go out on to that pitch. I felt like saying, 'Shit! I'm out there in front of all these people – wow.' I can't adequately describe it. It was incredible to be there but the game started and you just wanted to get on with it and do your best. The crowd noise was always there. You had to scream and shout at the other players just to communicate, to make yourself heard above the din. Compared to other players I wasn't that vocal; some would dictate games, and one of their assets would be that they could not stop talking or guiding their team-mates. Graham was a great communicator; he would scream and shout non-stop. But being a defender, there has to be an element of being vocal and I was. I had to communicate with my colleagues. If you played the offside rule, you had to make sure you worked as a unit.

"There was also fear. You had to have the temperament. I was playing in front of big crowds. That affects people in different ways. But through experience players developed an understanding: we were there to play football. I'm sure I heard comments and perhaps insults from the crowd. But – and I don't mean this unkindly – they went in one ear and out the other. It was an intense experience. People like Terry Naylor could engage with the crowd at the same time as concentrating on his game – he was a showman who wanted to entertain. I was shocked to play in the first team but it felt fantastic."

The vivid memory of playing in those games, however, could have been rendered redundant had manager Keith Burkinshaw been less forgiving the first time he picked George. "How it came about is comical. The West Stand was being redeveloped, but we were still using the areas underneath and behind to change. Before the whole stand was demolished, they used to put the team sheet up on a noticeboard. The understanding was that after you'd trained, washed and got dressed to go home, on the way out you would check the noticeboard to see what team or squad you were playing for that weekend – reserves or first team.

"It got to the point for me that I wasn't in the first team, the stadium was being redeveloped and building work was going on so I didn't walk past to check the noticeboard all the time. One particular Thursday I didn't check it and went home. I came in at 8am on Friday morning to catch a coach away to Plymouth on the Saturday for the reserves. I got on with the rest of the players, the coach left, and we headed off down the M4.

"*En route* we were talking about the first team and who was playing. We got to Reading and Robin Stepney, the reserve manager, looked up and said, 'George, what are you doing on this coach?' I said, 'Well, I'm going with the reserves down to Plymouth.' He said, 'No you're not – you should be with the first team!'

"So they stopped the coach, dropped me off at Reading Station to get a train into Paddington, I got a taxi from there to White Hart Lane and arrived back at five o'clock. I went in to see Burkinshaw. He gave me the biggest bollocking I've ever had. 'Do you realise if you hadn't got back tonight you might not have made it? I'm even considering not making you sub tomorrow!'

"He gave me a going over. I felt it was a bit unjustified. Yes, it was my fault but surely someone could have said something to me before we were halfway down the M4. But anyway, because of that Keith said, 'You're sub tomorrow.' He may have given the impression he would have picked me for the actual team but I think he always intended to make me sub. It was just to wind me up. Word got around, and I got a bit of piss-taking."

For George, getting into the first team set-up meant he had arrived. He retains a sharp memory of the physical environment and day-to-day routine he was now plying his trade in.

"The stadium made you realise you were at a major club. Going abroad and seeing other stadiums in places like Spain and Turkey was an eye-opener. But I recall the height of the Shelf stand, looking at that and thinking it was really impressive. The dressing room facilities were pretty functional before the West Stand changed. It was basic, like any other changing room – square, plain, a notice-board beside the door as you went out – the one that I didn't look at! When the stand was rebuilt all of a sudden we got these new plush facilities – top-quality benches, wooden panelling, a much wider changing area with two benches in the middle, a large communal bath and showers round the back. It was a complete progression from what it had been previously.

"The facilities at Cheshunt training ground were just the standard stuff – textured tile floors, creamy tiles on the walls, with slatted benches all the way round; everyone shared a very large communal bath you could probably get 15 people in.

"They were good facilities for that time. I'm sure nowadays they wouldn't compare, with their saunas, treatment rooms and high-tech facilities with all the medical services and hygienists associated with it. We didn't have that. But then they were fit for purpose.

"Tea was always on tap from a tea urn. In the canteen at Cheshunt at pre-season training we had salads. Not the good solid stuff you'd expect for those days. Chips were on offer – it was a bit like school dinners – but the majority of us had salads. You'd run yourself ragged, trying to improve your stamina and even though we weren't so hot on nutrition in those days we ate quite sensibly. Apart from Micky Hazard who could eat anything and everything, including all the Mars Bars he wanted, and not put on an ounce.

"This was only during pre-season; during the winter months, you'd finish earlier at Cheshunt at lunchtime and go home or out to eat. Some of us might go back to White Hart Lane to look at videos of opponents, or do a bit of weight training. Come Christmas there was no necessity to have lunch at Cheshunt or the ground. There was a little cafe as you came out of the stadium and a lot of the youngsters would go there and have their fry-ups. I recall being in there as a kid and Chris Hughton coming in and ordering lamb chops and two veg – setting a healthy example!"

Mazzon's high point came with the 1981 final. Even though he didn't play at Wembley, he felt like an important part of the winning squad. "It's there in black and white – my name in the cup final programme. I was part of the 16 at Wembley with a suit made like all the rest and all that went with it. I didn't get a medal, but I was entitled to a Paddington Bear. I sat in the stands and I didn't get on to the pitch or in the dressing room. George McAlister, one of the physios, told me that in the changing rooms all the players had been left a little ceramic Paddington Bear with their name on it. He saw mine, put it in his bag and said he'd give it to me, but I never got it. I assume that it did exist. But just being part of it, doing the record and everything was great."

It was to prove short-lived, however. Starved of opportunities, George couldn't establish himself in the side. By the end of the 1982/83 season he was heading for the exit and in time towards a far more serious setback.

"I felt that I could have got a regular place, that I had the ability. The problem I had was that I needed to get confidence and experience in games to sustain a place, plus I perhaps didn't have that self-belief and confidence. It was a Catch-22 situation – to get games I needed to be playing games.

"Keith said he felt I was one of the better defenders. In his opinion I was an excellent defender with good all-round ability. But it was at a point at Tottenham when he had to start reducing the numbers. I left at the same time as John Lacey and Ricky Villa – and that was it, the end of my career at Tottenham.

"I was disappointed, but hopeful that I had enough experience and quality to be attractive to other clubs. Four years at Spurs means you have a certain ability and I was confident I could continue my career elsewhere.

"Things didn't work out as well as I would have liked; it wasn't only Spurs who were reducing their squads – most clubs were. I hoped to get in somewhere like Crystal Palace or another London club a division below, but I found they were cutting back as well. So I ended up at Aldershot Town. The jump down from First to Fourth Division wasn't where I wanted to be, but nevertheless I was there six years.

"I enjoyed my football at Aldershot. I was there with Teddy Sheringham when he was on loan from Millwall. Up until last year when he retired, I could always claim that there was one player I had played with who was still playing. But my time in football came to an end with the car crash."

It is a bombshell of a statement. Few Tottenham fans know the extra-ordinary coincidence that two of the younger veterans of the Tottenham team of the early 1980s were to have their careers cruelly ended by road accidents. Garry Brooke nearly lost his life, but while George's crash was not quite as severe, its consequences for his life as a footballer were equally devastating.

"It happened early on 26th May 1987. We were in the play-offs against Wolves to see who would be promoted to Division three at the time. We'd won at home and then 1-0 at Molineux so we went up. The night of the game at Wolves, we got a coach back to Aldershot, arriving about midnight. We had a sponsored car shared around the squad and it was my turn to have it that week.

"My team-mates Glenn Burvill and Darren Anderson drove home with me. I lived in Kingston at the time; Darren lived local to me, but Glenn lived in Sussex. Because we had got back late it was decided we would drive him to Worthing and sleep at his house, then Darren and I would drive back to Kingston the next day.

"We left Aldershot with me driving. I drove to just outside Worthing. I was the only one who had played in the game; I was getting very tired and was aching so asked one of the others to take over. Darren volunteered, so I sat in the back in the middle, put the seatbelt on and we set off.

"There was thick fog. As the car turned a corner, it just didn't respond and carried on going straight forward and into a tree. I saw it coming; I ducked down but the belt I was wearing just went across my midriff. As we impacted, my body twisted round, my head and legs went forward. Glenn had broken his forearm and Darren had cut his eye; I, as I later found out, had broken my back.

"I actually got out of the car and said to Darren, 'I'm not well, I think I'm seriously hurt; see if you can get an ambulance.' I was in tremendous pain but we managed to walk to a house in the middle of nowhere, knock on the door and get this guy inside to call an ambulance. He didn't have a phone but thankfully he took us to hospital. They found I had some internal damage but the worst thing was that I'd pulled my spine apart. I was operated on and put back together but was out of football for a year.

"I remember waking up from the operation on my internal injuries, with a drip hanging out of me. I didn't actually find out the extent of my back injury until a week later. I was continually complaining about the pain. The nurse said, 'Let's keep you alive. Have your morphine jabs every four hours and worry about recovering from your op and then we'll look at the pains.'

"After a few days they let me get onto my feet and walk around with a drip. A few days later, the Derby was on – I'd pulled a horse called Sharistani out of the sweepstake bag in the hospital. I actually pulled it out twice; the nurses knew I was a footballer and teased me saying I couldn't have the favourite, but when they redid the draw I pulled it out of the bag again! I went for an X-ray that morning, and settled down in the afternoon for the race. Just as it started, with the horses at the gate, three doctors came down. They picked me up, carried me carefully back to the bed, and put straps over me to keep me from moving. 'We've just seen your X-rays' they said. 'What job do you do?' I told them I was a footballer. 'Well, you won't be doing that again,' one of them said.

"It transpired that I'd pulled my vertebrae apart. They explained that if you look at each bone as being a plug and socket that interlock, with tendons that hold them, I'd pulled the plug out of the socket but fortunately not separated any tendons. They had to put the plug back in the socket, and put chicken wire around it to hold it together. I had to wear a body cast for six months with other bits of metal inside me. Most of it has come out now, but I'm left with a bit of chicken wire holding part of my back together.

"I had been very fortunate that there was no damage to the spinal cord but it had been exposed, which was why they were very careful about lifting me and strapping me up. I guess I shouldn't have been walking around. I had contact with one person at Spurs in the shape of a get-well-soon card from Ossie while I was in hospital. I didn't expect anything more; to be honest I didn't expect anything and Ossie's card was a nice touch.

"I got a few visits from team-mates at Aldershot and the club sent me up to Harley Street and I was put back together again at University College Hospital in London. I was out of football for a year. When I'd recovered I trained, got fit, but my problem was half time – the moment I stopped I would freeze, my whole body would go rigid. Seize up. While everyone else went in for a cup of tea, I had to run round the pitch just to keep going.

"I ended up playing about four games the next season, 1988/89, but I was sub for the last game of the season against Sheffield United in 1989 and didn't get on. At that point Aldershot said they were going to release me. OK, I had to make a decision. I had to be realistic. I couldn't run, half time killed me, so I made the bold decision to leave football. I was 29, no kids but a girlfriend and I needed to earn an income. The plan was to get employment outside of football first and then see if I could get into non-league. I tried, but I was advised by various people that the moment I left football I was never going to get back.

"Which proved correct. I wasn't going to realise my dream of climbing the ladder, aspiring to be an international, whatever it was going to be. I'd had a good ten years in this game but I had to face facts and live a life outside of it."

Faced with such a terrible personal blow, many players might be expected to have reacted with anger and a 'Why me?' sense of resentment. Yet, like Brooke, George found a way to rebuild his life, has prospered and found contentment, without a hint of bitterness.

"I had to get a job. I joined Bovis and I've been with them ever since. I worked my way up to the position I am in now. Good, bad or indifferent, that's where I am now. It's not my chosen career, football always was. But I had my chance, my time in football and they were the best years of my life. I'd recommend to anyone who has the opportunity to seize it. I accept that's a lifetime ago. I have a wonderful family, married to Karen with two children, Ellie and Tom, a career with a lot of responsibility, things of other and greater importance. But it's amazing to think what I experienced. I got a call the other day from Steve Perryman; I haven't spoken to him for years, nor any of the others. In 25 years I've been back to White Hart Lane once, to see a game against Newcastle with my brother-in-law who's a Geordie and avid Newcastle fan.

"The keenness to get back into football had always been there but I had to concentrate on building a career away from it. I needed regular work and a regular income, and I never did return to football in the end."

It seems sad that George lost contact with his old pals; does it suggest that when players go their separate ways, football can be an unforgiving game? "Possibly – you develop relationships and friendships but they can fade. The first time I saw Garry since I left Spurs was two years ago when he walked past a site I was working at on Liverpool Street. We have never talked about our shared experiences in having bad car crashes. But then a couple of months later we all met up at the 25th anniversary of the 1981 cup win at the Dorchester. It was great to see them. What is silly, though, is that Bovis have a charity match against a Tottenham XI every season and they keep asking me to play. What I should do is play for Bovis one half and Tottenham the next. But I know I'm going to hurt myself; since quitting I've played three times and each time it's agony. Mentally I want to do it but the body won't take it. A shame, but there you go.

"Football has helped me in my career now, for certain. There are a lot of similarities with construction and football: you have to look at strengths and weaknesses. Everybody's aim is to succeed, you have to communicate, work as a team, compensate for any individual shortfalls. If nothing else, football has allowed me to understand how to make the best of what you can in the situation you are in and to your greatest benefit. You could be 3-0 down to Man United, but if there's five minutes left do you give up or try and draw, maybe even win? It's the same here. If things are going against you, do you give up? No, you keep going, keep striving. Keep making the best of it. Football provides lessons for life generally.

"All of us in football had lovely careers, particularly those at Tottenham, experiencing the best days of our lives. Football can't last for ever. Enjoy it while it lasts."

It's a typically philosophical approach from a man who has got what really matters in life fully in perspective. But it's not just the memories of Spurs that he holds dear, for George Mazzon, or 'Giorgio', also has some physical mementos of his time as one of the boys from White Hart Lane – a couple of facial scars and that broken nose, for starters.

"The scar above my eye was because of Glenn Hoddle. We were playing in a friendly. Glenn played a ball up in the air and in trying to challenge for it I had a clash of heads with another player. I blacked out and can't remember it, but was told that I ran around like the Incredible Hulk, I charged into the stand, went mad, and Graham and Mike Varney had to jump on me to calm me down. All I remember was waking up in hospital. I had to rest for a week because it was a bash against the temple.

"As for the nose? I don't know, it's been busted four or five times. I got a boot on the face when a player tried an overhead kick in a game. One I got at Aldershot when Ron 'Chopper' Harris was manager. He used me as an example of the type who would put my head in where people wouldn't put their feet – and I guess my nose proves it!"

10
PETER SHREEVE

"THE JOB WAS MADE FOR ME – AND I WAS MADE FOR THE JOB"

As someone who was one of the principal architects of the second most successful side in Tottenham Hotspur's illustrious history, it's a small but curious detail that many people still get his name wrong. "It's Shreeve without an 's' on the end", says the man commonly known as Peter Shreeves.

"Because some people wrongly called us 'Tottenham Hotspurs', perhaps they thought they ought to add an 's' to mine," he says. "My real name is Shreeve, but over the years I've had so many people getting it wrong that in the end I thought, 'Why not – it's Shreeves.' I've looked in the club handbooks and I see that one year my name is spelt with an 's' at the end, the next year it's 'Shreeve'.

Whether he is known as Shreeve, Shreeves or Shreevesie, there is no doubting the importance of this widely admired coach and manager who played a key role in taking Spurs to cup-winning glory. Chatting amiably in the reception of a hotel close to the M25 just a few miles from White Hart Lane, Shreeve cuts an unmistakable figure and there are various glances of acknowledgment from passers-by. Looking supremely fit and well for a 67-year-old, dressed in a smart but not showy suit befitting his standing as a respected football professional, Shreeve has a voice that prompts instant recognition. It's that familiar chirpy accent that found such a natural home at White Hart Lane. "I was a cockney at a cockney club; I knew how it worked, understood its culture. We were a good fit."

His conversation is strewn with shrewd observations and neat little phrases: 'silky soccer' is the most common – succinctly conveying in a nutshell Shreeve's overriding football philosophy, and providing further indication of what a good match he and the club were. In the modern era of repetitive sound bites it might be mistaken for just another bit of football lingo, but 'silky soccer' encapsulates what Tottenham were about during Shreeve's time at the club.

It was management speak with a purpose. "My nickname at Spurs was Smooth, everybody knew me as that. The reason was twofold: I was a smart dresser; secondly, I liked silky soccer. I used to say all the time, 'Are we going to play kick and rush, or are we going to play silky soccer?' When you're at Tottenham, you *had* to play silky soccer; the fans would not have stood for it or accepted crash bang wallop football. Every day we were working with the ball, improving technical skills.

"We used to come back to White Hart Lane after training three afternoons a week, from Tuesday to Thursday, and religiously work at our skills. Everyone did, not just the young players but the established stars as well, including Glenn Hoddle. We'd go up in the ball courts for two hours and longer. Sometimes you'd have the ground staff knocking on the door saying, 'Come on, is anyone going home today?' This constant willingness to improve was a passion.

"The respective philosophies of the club and myself were a good match. I was right for the club at that particular time."

Shreeve spent a total of 13 years at Spurs in two spells, progressing from youth team coach through to manager, returning for one season at the helm in 1991. He's seen it all at Spurs, from relegation to European glory. Intimate with what happened both on the training ground and in the corridors of power, his insights are unique and he casts a sober and perceptive eye on the saga from the vantage point of someone who played a key role in influencing affairs.

The journey to White Hart Lane began in 1940 in Neath, where the Shreeve family were evacuated during the Blitz. He was born in South Wales, but soon went to live in Islington when the family returned to London. Unsurprisingly, Arsenal were his team – "Being a scallywag along with all the other kids from my area, I used to go to Highbury because it was local and we could bunk in for free" – but a trip to White Hart Lane soon changed his allegiances.

"Supporters might find it strange now but in those days, there wasn't such an intense rivalry – people used to go to Spurs one week, Arsenal the next. I had a feeling for Arsenal, my dad took me to my first game and that's a feeling you never lose, but one Friday night someone took me to White Hart Lane for a floodlit game. They used to have a pen for the kids where you got in for a reduced fee. Spurs won the game 5-2 and this was a whole new adventure for me. I was about 12. I thought, 'Cor, I like what I see here.' That turned my head a bit – this refreshing team playing lovely football. From then onwards, I followed the fortunes of both clubs but became a Spurs fan, if you like."

Like most kids of his generation, football was an all-consuming interest. "I played all the time. I was captain of Islington and I played for London Boys and Middlesex, but the making of me was the Boys Brigade. Islington then was a very tough district, and plenty of kids went to borstal. But I avoided all that because I was in the BB just around the corner from Upper Street where I lived.

I was there every night doing gymnastics or swimming; I used to run the football section. It gave me an ability to talk in front of people and learn about discipline. The BB gave me a very, very good start in life.

"I got picked to go to an international BB camp in Jamaica when I was 17. I captained the football team that beat Jamaica 3-1, and was captain of the cricket team that got absolutely mullered!"

Spotted playing for non-league Finchley by scouts from Reading as an inside left – "number 10 in the old money" – Shreeve moved to the Berkshire side for what promised to be a rewarding professional career. But at 18, and on the verge of a call-up to the Welsh national team, his chances were ruined by a serious injury. "It was a really bad leg break, broken in two places. I had to have a bone graft taken from my hip. I thought I might get back playing, as I was only young, but I decided to give myself something to fall back on."

Showing an intelligence and resourcefulness that marked him out from many of his contemporaries, Shreeve completed 'the Knowledge', the notoriously rigorous and demanding test to become a qualified London taxi driver. It became one of the famous facts about Spurs during the 1980s – 'Peter Shreeve is a licensed cabbie.' "That was mentioned in every newspaper, every article and every report about me when I became Spurs manager. But at 18 it seemed a pretty good idea to me. I knew then that I was probably going to live until 60 – I've got beyond that and I'm still going – but I was courting a young lady, having a family was likely and I was going to have to put food on the table, so I gave myself two options: football and taxi driving. The latter is hard work, but it did pay. I also took all my coaching badges. I was a fully qualified coach at 21. Without wanting to blow my own trumpet, I had a natural flair for it – it was just something I could do. The BB had given me the grounding to be able to manage and teach people so I didn't have to think about it. It came naturally."

With his playing career over, Peter gained experience coaching anywhere and everywhere, from non-league clubs to the England women's team, before his early Arsenal associations were rekindled when he was invited to join Bertie Mee's set up, training the likes of Graham Rix, Frank Stapleton and Liam Brady. Mee wanted to offer Shreeve a full-time job but didn't have an opening so instead recommended him as youth team coach to lowly Charlton, then managed by Theo Foley. Success there brought him to the attention of Terry Neill. "When Terry got the manager's job at Spurs in 1974 he headhunted me to become Tottenham's youth team coach; I knew Terry from the BB in Ireland so once again I had the Brigade to thank. And that was the start of the most wonderful years of my career.

"Wilf Dixon, a lovely man, was at Spurs as assistant to Terry. Wilf was the heartbeat of the club, an experienced fella who had coached at Everton when they won the title and I learned an awful lot from him. He did most of the daily work on the training ground, which was my strength as well. I couldn't be doing with all the managerial side of things like contracts, media and non-footballing matters. I wanted to be out there on the field, working with and improving players. That was my forte. I was totally involved in what I did. At the start it wasn't all about winning; it was about playing the correct way for the team we all worshipped."

Shreeve's early years at Spurs coincided with the emergence of a crop of good youngsters like Paul Miller, Mark Falco and Garry Brooke. They and many more all pay tribute to Shreeve and his excellence as a coach, not least because he put his 'silky soccer' manifesto into practice at a club committed to improving its players' skills and techniques. Reflecting on George Mazzon's comment that Shreeve demanded his players 'looked good' in what they did, Peter says: "The style had to be right as well. Most boys don't know that if you do something with your left foot you have to do something with your right arm to counter it and keep your balance, otherwise you fall arse over tit. The top half of your body has to be in tune with what the bottom half is doing. That kind of thing was drilled into everybody at Tottenham – technique, style, preparation. There was always method to what I did.

"When Ralph Coates came to the club with Terry Yorath, they were senior internationals; Terry was captain of Wales. I said to them, 'Look, rather than sit in your digs until your families can join you, come along to the ball court after training and do a few skills with us.' They've both told me since that they had a look at what we were doing with the youth team and they thought, 'We can't live with this. We're going to embarrass ourselves playing with the kids because they are so good.' I had Brooksie playing the ball off the wall and Bilko [Mark Falco] coming in and scoring with a header; I had Glenn chipping it off the wall, chesting it, turning and volleying it into a little square painted on the wall – all sorts of tricks and skills that were technically difficult. They were brought up in that environment and learned those skills. Senior, experienced pros, top players, were terrified.

"Ron Henry used to come in on a Tuesday and Thursday evening, and he was a wonderful character, the boys loved him. He used to give amazing team talks; we'd worked all week on silky soccer skills and Ron would be more old school, 'Put your foot in' and all that!

"Together, the coaching team brought through these players but it would be fair to say I did help develop the likes of Mark, Paul, Garry and others. I knew them well – I got to know their mums and dads. Mark was a big old lumberjack of a boy playing for Hackney at 15; he had a good left foot, but we thought, 'We've got to work on him, get his movement going' and he became a big star. He was perhaps underrated at the time but I think people recognise now how good he was. And he was genuinely one of those who, when he kissed the badge, it meant something to him: that was his club."

Shreeve was similarly committed to the cause. "I scouted all over the place. At that time I got to the ground at eight o'clock in the morning and left at eight o'clock at night. And the day used to absolutely fly by. I never cared about how much I was getting paid; it didn't bother me because I was doing something that I loved. When I talk to players now, I'm disappointed that they don't love the game as they used to. It's a generational change."

Shreeve was charged with bringing through young players who were technically equipped for life at the top level but also able to cope with the other requirements the professional game demanded. "What I looked for in a player changed over the years. When I first went to Tottenham it was all about technique. I've always kept that as my foremost judgement of a player – can he play, can he kick with both feet, can he receive it properly? But, when you join the big league, there are 11 other boys on the other team who want to stop you doing that.

"When Glenn made his debut at Stoke, he came in on the Monday after and I said to him, 'How'd you find it?'. He said, 'You never told me about the short arm jab!' I reminded him that I had when I told the players to go into the ball court on a Friday in the gym; I used to say, 'Kick the what-have-you out of each other, because that's how it's going to be when you make it in the first team.'

"Glenn would say that I taught him all these lovely skills, but come on, he had them – all I did was just help tease them out of him. But they all had to come to terms with the power and the pace of football at the top level. It's like standing on a railway station platform and a train flies by at 100mph. You think to yourself, 'I can't get on it, I can't make it stop.' When a young boy goes into the first team for the first time, that's how it is. Every one of the players I helped develop said that. 'I couldn't get hold of the ball, Pete.' The step up was severe and is even more so today.

"I had to ready them for that. I was firm with them – I wouldn't stand for any backchat because I had to have that discipline. They didn't answer back then, and I taught them how to conduct themselves. I sussed people out. I would know, for instance, that a boy who came over from Ireland was likely to get homesick pretty quick.

"I used to get all the boys on the bus up to the training ground and sometimes I used to drive it. I used to say to them, 'Any of you got any girlfriends yet?' 'Girlfriends? Don't have time for girlfriends, Pete,' they'd say. 'Oh right' I'd reply. 'Let me tell you. There's about 14 of you on this bus. About five of you – and I don't know which five – will go away from the game because you'll find out about girls and drink.' 'No!' they'd all say. 'I'm telling you, in 12 years time I'll bump into some of you and you'll be saying, 'You used to be my coach'.

"My role was therefore all-encompassing: coach, mentor, stand-in parent, babysitter. I got a close bond with them. There was an element of psychology involved. You had to make sure they could cope mentally with professional football. Everybody's different, but basically they were all working class kids, none of them were posh. At the start of every season 40 triallists would turn up. I'd sit them down and go through the names. 'Paul Miller. Where you from Maxie?' 'Bethnal Green,' he would say. 'Bethnal Green,' I'd reply, 'Lovely, I like Bethnal Green.' I'd say to the next boy 'Tommy. Where you from Tommy?' He answered 'Hampstead.' 'Hampstead? Let me tell you Tommy – I have never signed a kid that comes from Hampstead. So you prove me wrong, but I don't think you will.' And I still have never signed a kid from Hampstead," says Shreeve, laughing. "The reason is obvious – kids from Bethnal Green look around them and think 'What am I going to do here?' Football gives working class kids an opportunity in life to move forward. They have that hunger and desire.

"They make silly mistakes, of course. I got a phone call once from the police. 'Sorry to trouble you Mr Shreeves, but there's a boy in our cells who says he's a youth team player at Tottenham.' They gave his name and I confirmed it was true. I said, 'You look after him for now and I'll get down there and sort things out.' It would happen with kids not from London who came to Spurs and would be living away from home for the first time. All of sudden they had this freedom and would go over the pub when they'd finished training, come out and fall over drunk and get arrested on Tottenham High Road. There were three or four instances when that happened. I would have to say to them, 'Do you want to be a boozer or do you want to be a footballer?'" Asked to mention names, Peter declines. All these years on and he's still protective of his lads.

So, as someone who learned the cruel lesson of how transient a career in football can be when he was forced out of the game through injury, did Shreeve find it difficult to tell a youngster he wasn't going to make it? "I think it was a social skill I acquired over a period of time. I had a son and daughters and I knew how disappointment could hit a family, so I knew how to respond to young people.

"Letting them go was part of the job. I knew when I had to make that difficult phone call, or have that difficult conversation. I took on that responsibility because it's on your mind and you have to get it out of the way. I'd sit the boy down and say, 'I'm sorry, but we've had you for a year, you've enjoyed it, but I, along with the management and other coaches, have to make a decision and we don't feel we can offer you an apprenticeship. What I can do is help to find you a club somewhere else.' Because I've had this conversation with lots of boys and half of them proved me wrong – they go somewhere else and make a name for themselves. Basically, you are telling these young men the worst news of their lives and trying to do it in such a way that it won't destroy them.

"The hardest one was Carl Hoddle, Glenn's brother. Everyone turned up for his funeral when he died this year. It was a very sad day. That's when you see what a club is about. Everyone who was in his youth team turned up at Harlow for the ceremony.

"It was hard to let him go. I pulled Glenn to one side and said, 'Look, I'm sorry, but I'm going to have to tell your brother we're not keeping him on.' 'He'll take it hard,' he said. I knew he would, but I had to do it. They would bubble up and cry; that's natural, but they got over it. We found them other clubs; Carl went to Leyton Orient and Barnet, so he had a career. It was more difficult for him because of his name."

But amid the hard decisions there were also laughs to be had and Shreeve was one of many jokers at the club. Reminded of Brooke's story of the day his taxi-driving coach left him standing at the bus stop on the way into training, Shreeve laughs at the memory. "I think you have to have banter with the players and that was part of it, a little wind up. Sometimes I would do that because I knew that Garry would be moaning saying, 'That Shreevesie, do you know what, he drove straight past me!' Garry was a lovely lad. I saw him playing for Walthamstow schools and recognised this great prospect."

Shreeve's nurturing of young players like Brooke and his success with the youth and then reserve teams made people at the club sit up and take notice. Keith Burkinshaw had arrived at Spurs around the same time as Shreeve and, as the successor to Neil, chose to make the popular coach his right-hand man in 1980.

"What happened was that I'd had these boys on a daily basis in the youth team and a fair few had progressed to the reserve team group. Some of them asked if they could stay with me as their coach as they liked what I did. They were told no, but they still said they wanted to work with me. Keith eventually recognised that; I'd become reserve team coach as people moved on and Pat Welton, someone I had a lot of respect for, was then head coach; Keith decided to make a change and I joined the first team set-up.

"I hadn't had much involvement with the first team before then.

Keith first arrived when Wilf was still there, and Keith told me early on, 'I can't get a feel of this club. They brought me in as first team coach, I've got the experience, but I'm not doing what I should'. I said to him that he would have to have a word with Terry and ask, 'Am I first team coach or not?' Keith from then on got more involved.

"As a Londoner it had been easier for me to settle. Keith was a straight-backed Yorkshireman who took a bit longer to get to grips with what the club was like. He didn't get involved in many pranks, but there was some wind-up or trick being played every day and you had to take that in your stride.

"Keith got caught out once when we went on tour to Japan in 1979. Terry Naylor was still at the club. Terry was the funniest cockney I ever met in my life. We got invited to the British embassy in Tokyo for a very esteemed and formal function; Terry gave me the wink. He said, 'Do you know what, Keith, I was here before in Japan. Everywhere you go you have to take your shoes and socks off.' Keith didn't say a word, but we went down to this function at the embassy and he took his shoes and socks off. The master of ceremonies announced our entrance saying, 'Mr Keith Burkinshaw and members of the Tottenham Hotspurs football squad!' – and Keith walked in barefooted. The only one there without shoes and socks! Terry goes, 'You all right, Keith?' Keith had to learn to take all that.

"Nutter was up to that kind of thing all the time. When we signed Don McAllister from Bolton, he arrived as a full back. On his first day at Spurs, Don was naturally worried and nervous. Terry came in to the dressing room and said, acting dead serious, 'You're Don McAllister, ain't you?' Don said 'Yes'. Nutter said, 'You've come to take my place in the team, haven't you?' Don said, 'Er well, no, I mean, I can play centre half?' Terry said, 'No, you're a right back, I'm a right back; you've come to take my living away from me. You're very quick, ain't you?' Don said, 'Yes.' Terry said,

'Right, here's half a quid, now eff off to the bakers and get me some jam tarts and make it quick.' And Don took the money!

"On another occasion we went down to Plymouth and the weather was boiling hot. Terry walked bare-chested into the five-star hotel where we were staying. Not out of disrespect but because it was hot and he'd forgot to put his shirt on. The manager at the hotel said, 'Excuse me, are you a member of the Tottenham Hotspur football club?' Terry, without batting an eyelid said, 'Yes – and are you the manager of this hotel? Because when I walked into your hotel, I had a shirt on my back. Somebody's nicked it!' The manager fell for it straight away and asked, straight-faced, 'What colour was it?'

Away from all the laughter and banter, Shreeve and Burkinshaw and the rest of the coaching staff got down to the more serious business of assembling and developing a side that would restore Tottenham's reputation. Even before his promotion, Shreeve was privy to the team's rebuilding. "We survived relegation. The supporters gave us a standing ovation the day we went down. I couldn't believe what I saw, because I thought they would be throwing tomatoes at us. And the directors kept faith with the management team, which wouldn't happen now – it would be 'Goodnight, vicar.'

"The Argentinians coming was special. I went to meet them at Gatwick because the team was playing up north somewhere. The first thing Ossie did was walk me over to the London Underground map. He said, 'Where is Totten-ham?' He saw Tottenham Hale and thought that was it. I said, 'No Ossie, not there. Don't go there, it's a bit of a dodgy area! Our stadium is a bit further on.'

"When we got them into the team situation, we found we had a bit of a problem. They were both ball-playing midfielders but neither of them was very good when we didn't have the ball. I said to Keith, 'We're gonna get murdered: teams are going to come straight through us.' The first home game against Aston Villa, we got thrashed 4-1, despite all the fanfare and ticker tape, and we knew it was going to be a long haul. What did we need to do, could we cope with what we had or did we need to bring in a ball winner?

"It took a while for them to accommodate themselves into our system. But they also passed on quite a lot to us, and me as a coach. Ricky, for instance, would get out wide. We knew he wasn't just going to cross the ball to the back post, let the keeper come and say, 'Thanks very much'; he would dribble back in and lay off a pass. 'That's good,' we thought; if we can get someone on the edge of the box as he drills it across we could be in. It was case of learning from each other.

"Ossie was the best player I ever coached or managed. People think it would have been Glenn, but Ossie could do everything. He could run with the ball on his feet, make runs, get the ball back. If he was to be analysed by ProZone, it would be phenomenal to see the ground he covered. He was outstanding. Never went out on the pitch to do a warm-up – he used to sit inside the dressing room doing the crossword. Me and him at a quarter to three. He'd say, 'Pete, what's this clue, nine across?' And then go out and be the best player on the field."

Ardiles and Villa fitted into the "silky soccer" philosophy, but it was tested when the newly promoted team suffered that infamous thrashing at the hands of Liverpool. "I was taking the reserve team that day, but when the score came through – 7-0 – it brought into sharp relief that there are only two things that happen in a game: you either have the ball or you don't. When we didn't have it, we were crap. We had to keep the ball or do our utmost to get it back. We started to do more training sessions on closing people down, getting fitter, working harder. It wasn't all about pass, pass, pass."

"By 1980, we had more of a mix with Argentinians and a Scotsman and a couple of northerners, but we still had the same belief about the way we wanted to play football – it had to be about passing and movement. We signed good players that fitted into that system. And meanwhile Keith and I developed into a good partnership. Our contrasting characters complemented each other. Keith was a very good manager, I was a very good coach – we knew that and used each other's strengths.

"If you're the manager, you have to deal with the player knocking on the door – the usual comments of, 'Why aren't I in the team?' from players, or getting offers for players that are accepted by the club but the player doesn't want to go. You have to deal with the media, the board – who, I have to say, were fabulous then, just a group of businessmen who loved the club. But there are all sorts of things that are important but aren't a great deal of pleasure.

"Keith would have to deal with all that when what he really wanted was to be out there with me and the players on the training ground. Instead he got all the phone calls. I would take training more often than not, though it should be noted that Keith was a very good coach – that's what he was brought to the club as. But the other part of his job got in the way.

"Keith would seek advice but make his own decisions, I could never tell him what team to play. He was the boss. He picked the players and then it was my job to make them into the best unit we could possibly have. Keith would listen but you don't become a good manager by listening to other people all the time; you have to be the boss, and he was a good boss. But it was a good part-nership and we're good friends now; we still argue on the phone about various things – strictly football I should point out. We've always bounced off of each other."

The specifics of coaching are something of an unknown quan-tity. Fans know that plenty of work is done behind the scenes away from games, but it is rare to hear from coaches as to what actually happens day to day. Over 25 years on, Shreeve sheds light on the ideas and practical work that he and Burkinshaw did to make Tottenham tick.

"To have a good team you had to make sure your tent pole made your tent secure: in other words, you had to have a very good goalkeeper of real stature; we needed two centre halves – we had that in Roberts and Miller so we had two solid defenders who, when the other team had the ball, we could get it back. We didn't want them coming out from the back anyway, we would say to them, 'Don't think you're Beckenbauer; you're Paul Miller from the East End – just give it to the Hod Carrier and you'll be all right.' That's what we called Glenn – the Hod Carrier.

"Steve Perryman was an excellent, excellent player. Nobody really appreciated how good he actually was. I've taken international sides – I was Welsh coach for a few years and saw some great players – but Steve Perryman would always get in my top ten. His technique was brilliant. He had a great jam tart and loved the club – he would have slept there if he could.

"With those tent poles in place, we went to work. Specific training would vary – at that time we won more often than not so you would work on different things than if you were losing, but normally on a Monday we would get the lads together. The boys would have had a sherbet over the weekend – that wasn't a problem, they were young men and that's how it was – so on the Monday we would get in amongst them a bit and play eight-a-side. As soon as those games started the competitive spirit would come to the fore and they would put the physical effort in. The quality would be top class. And the commitment . . . sometimes I would have to keep it in check saying, 'Steady on, we don't get a win bonus today.'

"We would do a lot of work with the two strikers. Keith would ask me to take a bunch of apprentices with them. I would put the strikers in white shirts and the others in blue, say. I would then ask questions of the strikers. 'How can you help your partner? What do you want from him and what does he want from you?' Then I'd develop little situations and routines. I would tell Archibald, 'When the ball comes to you, you have got to hit it to me first time; you have no other choice.' I'd say to Garth, 'In that situation, what are you going to do to help him'? He would have to provide an outlet, draw away a defender or make a run. This was my natural way of coaching. I talked this way to international players, but I knew that I knew more than them – well, I'm not quite saying that, but I determined what we worked on.

"We'd work on all these little things so that they would become part of what players did. We were hoping that after this training session finished at lunchtime the two front players would have developed more of an understanding, that they would appreciate how to work as a pair rather than two individuals.

"Another day we'd work with Tony Galvin on his crossing because in the previous game he'd been hitting too many crosses into the crowd. We didn't have any players in the crowd so that wasn't what we wanted. We'd be playing balls out to him under pressure and make him clip his cross in – making him repeat the exercise again and again.

"We'd vary it, keep them interested. Once we'd done those little bits with individuals, we'd do something with the midfield players, on their choice of passes. Glenn could hit a ball 50 yards no problem. We used to get him in the right-half position and to hit a ball out to Tony on the back of the full back. In one fell swoop we'd got in behind the opposition – that's silky soccer because we had got a ball at distance where it was effective and hurt the opposition.

"Then we'd say, 'All right Glenn, we're playing so-and-so this week; they are going to mark you man for man. I'm going to put a young kid against you. He can't kick you but he'll have a go at you.' 'Don't worry Pete, that's all right,' he'd say. But every time he got the ball there was someone on him. But our golden rule remained: Glenn must have the ball. Players could not say, 'He's marked, I can't give it to him' – they still had to feed him, as he was our best player and would make the best decisions for the team.

"We didn't bring all these details together until the last 20 minutes. We'd say to the front two, 'Right, put it into practice; Tony, make sure it stays in play; get close on Glenn, don't kick him because we want him fit but let's see how he copes with it.' This would have been the daily routine."

Coupled with the on-pitch training was the off-pitch innovation that Spurs became renowned for. Like Perryman and the players, Shreeve pays generous tribute to John Syer's sports psychologist team. "We all learned. I learned so much from them, as a coach. In the meetings they organised, we would split the players up according to formation – defenders together, strikers in a group, etc – and tell them to talk to each other.' 'What about?' they'd say. 'What do you mean 'what'? Talk. Talk about football. What do you want from each other? What do you want from the midfield and the back four?' They would have their discussion and then we'd bring them together. Then they'd all have to say what they wanted. Voices would get raised, but we worked it out that with all the people and various permutations involved, we could have about 100 conversations and set-ups with everyone's antennae going off – what does the right full back want from the central midfielder, what does he want from the centre half etc.

"It was to make us a better team. We were communicating at the highest level. I have to give John and his colleagues great credit. We were into man management, but they taught us a lot. They would talk about what music to have playing in your car before coming to a game. They'd say to Glenn, 'Who's your favourite artist at the moment?' He'd say, 'Christopher Cross.' When we went up Wembley Way two years running we had him playing on the tape. It started because one day Glenn had a particularly good game and he said he'd been listening to Cross on the way in. He scored two goals. So it was the association of getting in the right frame of mind.

"It was about preparation and thinking positively. I managed to get an edited videotape of some of our best bits of play in the dressing room on a TV before a match. So when Archie was doing his bootlaces up, he'd look up and see himself smashing the ball in the net from 25 yards. We never lost a game in the dressing room. Because they were all thinking good things – positive mental attitude it was called, or PMA."

Shreeve was also forward-thinking with his focus on nutrition. "That was us being a little bit before our time, maybe. We gave them the correct food at the training ground before anyone knew what 'correct food' was. Before we made changes, anyone in the first team used to get steak for their pre-match meal and the youth team got eggs on toast. But the eggs were much better for you. We changed it around and some complained but we were adamant and said, 'No, those days are over.'"

For all the devotion to the ideal of silky soccer, Burkinshaw and Shreeve worked the players hard, with arduous cross-country runs in Cuffley Woods just down the road from Cheshunt. It was there, however, that the real importance of football was brought into sharp relief. "The runs became famous within the club. Everyone was pleased once they'd done them but not while they were doing it. Whenever I think about that place though, there's a very sad memory associated with it concerning when Pete Southey died.

"It chokes me now to think about it. He was a good player. I was the old boy – well, I was around 40, but I was quite fit. Nonetheless Peter, at one of the Cuffley runs, was jogging alongside me. I said, 'What are you doing here? You should be up the front?' He said, 'I don't feel very good, gaffer.' I told him he would have to drive on if he wanted to progress. In the end I said to the doctor that I was a bit worried about Peter. So he gave him a blood test and it came back that he had leukaemia. The doc said, 'There is no nice way of saying this – the boy's days are numbered.' When I recalled that I had had a go at him for not keeping up with the lads, well, it struck home.

"Peter's death showed how the club was really together. When he died everyone who worked at Tottenham got on a coach and we went over to his funeral in Putney. It bonded us, showing this respect for our young colleague. He was an England youth international. It was such a fantastic thing – no one said they couldn't make it; we all wanted to be there. His old man worked at Heathrow. Every time we landed there he knew about it and he would come to the plane as it landed and shake hands with all the lads; he knew the club had done well by his boy."

Southey's tragic death came in 1983, shortly after Garry Brooke's career-ending crash. They were two of the players Shreeve had nursed through to the first team squad, their fates providing a sobering reminder of the vagaries of life and putting football into true perspective. Up until then, however, Shreeve had experienced all the good things the game had to offer. Back in 1980, he saw that the team was coming together and, playing a full part in its success, it would furnish him with his happiest football memories.

"I knew we had a very good team. We had Glenn, Tony Galvin – an unsung hero, whose work rate was phenomenal; Stevie P's record speaks for itself; Maxie and Robbo – when I became manager for the second time a few years later, everyone used to say, 'Why haven't we got two centre halves like Miller and Roberts?' Yet when I was there when Maxie and Robbo were playing people would say, 'They are no good. They can't play.' As soon as they were missing, people realised how good they were and that they *could* play. We had Chris Hughton, an elegant, right-footed and left-footed full back who would pay one-twos with the centre forward. With Ossie and Ricky and the two up front it was coming together.

"But to be frank, going into the 1981 final we had been pretty average. In the build-up to the game I did my homework on Man City. I told the lads, 'They are going to stop us playing, you know that?' I used to compile my own dossiers and did a lot of research on other teams but I didn't pass that on to the players; I just summarised things for them. Footballers have short attention spans and 20 minutes before a game you need to drive the message home quickly and succinctly.

"Man City had a midfield destroyer, Gerry Gow. I was wise enough to suggest that our midfield would not be given any space. Glenn said to me, 'It's at Wembley; they won't be able to get near us on that big pitch.' 'Excuse me? I said. 'That pitch is about the same size as any other.' To be fair, Glenn half said after the first game, 'Pete, I doff my hat to you; you called it right. They stopped us playing.'

"If you look back from a Man City point of view, they were unlucky not to win the first game. Steve Mackenzie who scored that fantastic equaliser for them in the second game – he could have been a Spurs player. I had him as a boy in the youth team, but I couldn't win his old man over, and he signed for Palace. But we were fated to win the replay after all that had happened with Ricky being taken off.

"On the Friday before the first game, unusually, I gave a little talk to the boys. I always had something to say but this was more of a speech on my part. The boys have said years afterwards, 'That was great what you said.' And it went something like this: 'Do you remember when you were ten years old? Playing in the playground, ball on the penalty spot? What did you imagine? I know what you thought – last minute at Wembley. 'Peter Shreeves strides up, yes! Strikes it right in the corner!' I bet you all did that, imagining you were scoring, didn't you?' They all nodded. 'Well,' I said 'you *are* playing at Wembley on Saturday – it's the cup final, you're there! You're not ten any more, you're a man and all the world is going to be looking at you.' I translated that fantasy to reality. Archie always reminds me of that. It was just something I wanted to say because I loved football.

"I used to play in the five-a-sides as I wasn't a bad player and could hold my own. I used to say 'Gimme the ball; leave that mug Hoddle out; don't give it to him, give it to me. I've got a plan.' I always used to say that: 'I've got a plan.' That became a bit of a catchphrase for the lads – 'Give it to Shreevsie; he's got a plan.' It was me having a laugh, encouraging a bit of banter. 'Don't give it to that mug Ardiles; he'll only give it away. Give it to me; I've got a plan.'

"Going into the first game the plan was we were going to win, so we booked the Hilton Hotel in Park Lane for a reception afterwards. We'd only drawn but we still had to go to the Hilton – no one had planned for that. It was such a flat evening, but me and Keith started talking. We thought we were lucky to have gotten away with it, but we'd been given a second chance. He told me then that he had already spoken to Ricky and told him he was going to play in the replay. 'OK,' I thought, but we'll need to do some different work with him and the boys to get them better prepared.

"There were no big speeches before the replay. The preparation was that we said, 'We could have lost that chaps; we could be crying in our milk. But we've got a second chance. All these fans are coming, your families will be here, you have the chance to go down in history here.' We did some light training on the Wednesday. But the real worry was Stevie Perryman. Not many people know it but he very nearly didn't play. On the morning of the match on the Thursday I took him down to Cheshunt to do a fitness test – to be honest, what we thought would be a 'no hope' test. I was experienced in conducting them and as soon as I asked a player how he felt and he said 'Not too bad' I knew he was not going to make it because the 'Not too bad' is a negative thing and an indication there was doubt in his mind. I took Steve through his paces. He side-footed the ball. 'How's that?' I asked. 'Yeah, it's good' he replied. So Steve played, but with a thigh strain that I thought would rule him out. I don't know how he possibly made it because he could hardly run the day before.

"We knew then that we had three or four days to get Steve

physically fitter. The mental thing with Ricky was something different. We had to be positive. For cup finals in those days you could not go out on the pitch and warm up. You could have a walk around in your suits but not a warm-up. The first time players saw the pitch when in their kit was when they walked up the tunnel for the presentations and the kick off. But in the replay – you could have a warm-up.

"So for the replay I went out with Ricky while the band was still marching up and down playing. I said to Ricky, 'Go the other side of the band and chip the ball over them towards me.' He looked a bit dubious and said, 'Ooh no, I might hit someone.' 'No you won't,' I said. 'You're a great player; you'll be fine. Chip the ball over that band and see how you shape up.'

"What I was trying to do was boost his confidence. By the time we got to kick off, Ricky was up for it, raring to go. His mind was right. It was ludicrous that at Wembley for the first game you couldn't warm your team up because the procedure and ceremony was more important than the result: 'We can't disturb the royal box' and all of that. But for the replay we had more of the genuine football fans, not so much the prawn sandwich brigade there for the 'event'.

"I think we got Ricky in the right frame of mind. He knew that he had let the club and the fans down on the Saturday – and Argentina. He was a very, very proud man was Ricky and he was broken-hearted at his performance, thinking he had let the whole world down. We had to take him from that frame of mind to be confident in the space of four or five days. It was good man management."

Bursting with renewed confidence, Villa weaved his way to football immortality. The details of his winning goal and the reaction it caused are well known, but hitherto the thoughts of the Tottenham management team have been something of a secret. Here, Shreeve conveys what it meant to him and the professionalism he and

Burkinshaw displayed in the immediate aftermath of incredible sporting drama.

"It was the greatest moment of my career. Euphoric. It started when Ricky picked the ball up almost on the half-way line, ran on and went past an opponent, and I said to Keith, 'He's gonna have a run here.' Every time he went past a player, I was nudging Keith with my shoulder or arm, mirroring what Ricky was doing each time he dipped his shoulder; I knocked Keith about four times. I said, 'He's effing going to score, I'm telling yer!' Eventually he did score and well, what joy. But my professional instincts immediately kicked in. Keith remained calm, sitting on the bench and allowing himself a brief round of applause. I got up on my feet thinking, 'We haven't won this yet; there's still time to go.'

"An experienced coach is almost programmed to respond that way. For that first minute after scoring, the players were on cloud nine, so we had to apply a golden rule we had developed. Whenever we had scored and the opponents kicked off, if we hadn't regained the ball after two tackles or challenges from us, the third tackle had to be either us winning possession or conceding a free kick. If we gave away a free kick in their half of the field it was to our advantage.

"Picture the scene: the opposition kick off and the pass normally goes back. I used to say to our players, 'Go in and rattle them.' We may concede a free kick, but we will then be automatically focussing on defending. The instruction was always, 'Either win it back or stop them getting it forwards.' It focused people's minds, made them think about getting into position or picking up their player. So the moment when we scored was pure elation but very quickly we had to get back to business.

"Sometimes at Wembley the game can pass you by; you are that hyped up that you don't 'see' the game. The final whistle goes and you think, 'Well, what happened there?' In the first game we were all too busy waving to wives and family up in the stands and all that pomp-and-circumstance nonsense. The first thing I said on the Thursday was 'I don't want to see anyone waving at anybody. We're here to win the game, and you can kiss your wife after we've won.' Even now when players are at Wembley, they still wave to their wives; as soon as I see a team do that I know they're in trouble.

"But winning the cup gave me huge professional satisfaction. There's no denying it, it was the single best day of my life in football. We won the cup the next year – we got lucky again really, beating QPR – and we won the UEFA Cup, but that first victory was the best. We went back to the Chanticleer afterwards and we were there till the morning. For all of us, apart from Stevie, it was our first big trophy. None of us had worked at a club that had won the FA Cup.

"On the coach coming away from Wembley, Ricky went up to Don McAllister and gave him his winners' medal. Ricky said 'You deserve this, you should have been playing.' Don was really upset that he had been left out of the final squad and I think that momentarily Don accepted the medal, it was such a nice thing for Ricky to do. But eventually we said to him that he'd won the FA Cup Final and they'd be talking about his winning goal for years, so he must have the medal to show for it. Don said, 'Of course I'll give it back to him.' But what a fantastic touch."

Shreeve went on to help mastermind further success as assistant to Burkinshaw, but the title eluded them. Given that his players have had their say as to why they missed it out, it seems reasonable to ask Peter for his view. The disciple of silky soccer is typically honest in his appraisal.

"If you ask me now who will win the league next season it will be one of only four teams. Back in the early '80s Spurs got close but from a position when we hadn't even threatened. You don't suddenly win the league from the position of tenth the season before. You have to establish that pedigree and experience of winning things. We said to ourselves, 'We're pretty good at winning these cups, but in the day-to-day grind of churning out wins in the league we aren't. We thought we had a good chance but when it came to the moment, we were found wanting. It was just a long, long course coming out on top after 42 games as it was then, carrying injuries without cover.

"Keith, and I as well, we played very fair on team selections. In those days, when we had an injury to a left midfielder, the reserve team player in that position came in – Ian Crook; when it was the left back, Mark Bowen stepped in. We always replaced like for like, we never put square pegs in round holes. On reflection, maybe we should have done – we should have had more physical power in the team and used a more experienced player out of his natural position rather than putting in a young boy. We said to these lads, 'You've earned the right to play.' Otherwise the youngsters would all think, 'What chance have I got?' But maybe we should have been more ruthless.

"After '81 we knew we had a good team. We made some additional signings, Ray came in as a keeper, other players started to come through. The team was packed with internationals, yet I still used to do half an hour's work on technique with them every day. I would say, 'I'll stop getting on at you to do this when you *can* do it.' I've spoken to them since and they say they couldn't believe it that as internationals I was still trying to drum this stuff into them. We were flying high in the league and cups, but every day I insisted – 'Left foot, right foot, chest, play it this way, play it that way.'"

Such a philosophy was perhaps out of step with the rest of domestic football, but Shreeve is adamant that the team still retained fundamental British attitudes. "When we were in Europe, we had a hell of a good side, but the foreign teams were terrified of us; they expected that when they came to Tottenham the pace would be intense, the tackles would be flying in. So I used to say to the players, 'Don't disappoint them on that; let's display the physical side of things; when they've got the ball, get in amongst them. But when we've got the ball, it's time for silky soccer.' They would not be able to cope with the hustle and bustle of a London or an English side. That more or less brought all our success. Eventually, European teams got fitter and then it was purely a case of technique.

"We had a potent mix. I used to go and watch all the teams we played in Europe; Ajax, Real Madrid. I would come back and tell the boys what they needed to know. I would say to Stevie P, who was a marvellous, marvellous captain, 'Steve, their number 7 is a bit tasty, you're going to have to get close to him'. He understood fully what I meant. The first time their number 7 got the ball, Steve Perryman would rattle his cage and that fella knew he was not going to get much time to show his array of skills.

"When we had the ball, we had a clear-cut plan that what I called the foot soldiers had to give the ball to the connoisseurs – the Paul Millers of this world had to get and give the ball to the ball players. I would say to Maxie, 'I don't want you to be hitting 50 yard passes – give it Glenn Hoddle and he can do that, he can drop it on a sixpence.' I would say to Glenn, 'Don't forget the very fact they are giving you the ball to deliver it; don't look down on him because he's done the hard work to get the ball off the other team.' We had to encourage a set up where the players had respect for their team-mates in what they could do – and at Tottenham we had that.

"But a side like Liverpool were more ruthless. The major turning point in the 1982 League Cup final game was Graeme Souness going over the top and taking Tony Galvin out of the game. That was Liverpool knowing how to win – playing a bit ugly if you like.

"When I left Spurs and went to other clubs, I realised that were ten ways of winning a game. At Spurs we only had two or three and they were all variations on silky soccer. Some games, especially away, we needed to shut up shop a little bit. We thought we would play teams off the park and in most cases we did because we had a good team. But there were times when a different formation or slightly different style of play might have accumulated more points. Keith *was* a purist but I shared his belief in how the game should be played."

The Glenn Hoddle-inspired demolition of Feyenoord early in the victorious '83/'84 UEFA Cup campaign was a case in point. "I'd been out there and seen that they had some good players, but Cruyff made such a pig's ear of the preparation. He wasn't the manager, just a player, but he went to the papers and said, 'I've heard about this young Hoddle; he won't get a kick; I'll mark him out of the game.' If Glenn ever produced 45 minutes' football that was better than that night then I wasn't there to see it, and I saw every game Glenn played including his internationals. He was unplayable. He was hitting balls above his neck 40 yards to someone on the run and getting it perfect. It was like a matador's performance; he had that cape in that hand and he was more or less saying to Cruyff, 'Where are you? Where are you, son. You're nowhere near me.'

"At 4-0 they were dead and buried. But they took Cruyff off and brought on a couple of midfielders; they changed their tactics, kept it tight and got a couple of goals back. I still knew we'd go through, we got a result out there with Chris Hughton scoring one of the goals, a fine goal playing a one-two. But the home leg was the five-star performance. That European run was superb."

The trophy was secured with a well-managed victory in the final since, at the end of a long and punishing season, Burkinshaw and Shreeve had to marshal their injury-hit resources to beat a very good Anderlecht side. Shreeve reveals a story arising from that game, however, which shows how even the best laid plans can be undone by the most unpredictable of circumstances.

"They had a sweeper at the back who I later tried to sign for

Spurs when I became manager, the Danish international Morten Olsen. I thought the system was the way ahead. Anderlecht always played with one marker and one sweeper at the centre of defence and I thought Olsen would be the one for us.

"I went out with Irving Scholar to sign him. We met Olsen at the hotel in Copenhagen, we spoke at length and it was a done deal. He then said to me, 'What about my dogs?' 'Excuse me?' I said. He said, 'I've got these two dogs!' I said to him, 'I know the rule in England and I'm telling you now, they'll have to go into quarantine for six months.' 'You mean I can't have them in the house?' said Olsen. 'No, no. When we find you a place to live, we might be able to arrange it so it's only a hundred yards down from some kennels where the dogs will have to stay.' But he wouldn't have it – the deal broke down because of his dogs. Obviously we couldn't publicly say we couldn't sign this great player because he would miss his pets, so we came out with some other reason for the press. So the truth is finally out. I stayed good friends with him though. We thought he would have been a key player for us. We tried Ian Crook in that sweeper role, and he was very good at it, but he didn't have the expertise that a player like Olsen had.

"It was us wanting to become a modern club, if you like, because all the top clubs on the continent at that time nearly always played with a spare defender and three markers, and the spare defender was always an immaculate footballer and an expert passer."

Shreeve's attempt to introduce the sweeper system came as he took the reins of power after Burkinshaw's departure. It was a proud moment for the former youth team coach to make the step up, and represented some welcome continuity at a time when the club was undergoing a period of uncertainty after the arrival of new owners with significantly different ideas.

"Keith had made it quite clear he didn't like the way a modern club board worked. He thought the time had come to up sticks and he got a fantastic offer to go and be the manager of Bahrain.

Naturally, I knew in advance that he planned to go. I didn't want to be seen to be disloyal to the man I had almost shared a bed with, but I didn't want to go to Bahrain. I had a young family. I'd done well at Tottenham, I didn't know I would be appointed, but I knew I was a strong member of the coaching staff and had a chance.

"The club went on the trip to Swaziland in the close season. There was a lot of speculation as to who the new Spurs manager was going to be. Obviously I was a candidate, but I wasn't an international name. Everyone else's name was being bandied about. We landed at Johannesburg airport and for the first time I got to learn about how the press worked. We were in transit and a reporter came up to me saying, 'There's a news item broken in London that you are going to be the new Spurs manager – what's your reaction?' I should have said, as I learned when I became more experienced in dealing with the media, 'I have no detail of this, I can only deal with facts, until I have those facts I have no comment.' What I did actually say was, 'Well, no disrespect to any other candidates but I know the club better than anyone else; the players all know me; I'd be delighted to get the job.' That comment nearly cost me the job, because the club wanted to control the news and issue a statement. This reporter knew the score better than me, and realising it was a story he could earn money on, he sold it down the line to London. My quotes were in the papers the following morning.

"Thankfully Irving wasn't dissuaded, said to me that I'd done well and that the job was mine. The players were happy because it meant there wouldn't be somebody else coming in with all new ideas and the proof was in the pudding. We finished third in the first season and were at the top for quite a while; we went close to winning the league, so my time as manager was time well spent.

"Everybody who has been in that situation will say that becoming manager after being coach is a difficult step to take. Everyone will also say, 'Be yourself.' I was determined not to change. We all worked hard together when I was coach so why should I do any different as manager? But there's an inevitable difference when you change roles. When I was the youth team coach, for example, I was 'Uncle Peter'; when I became first team coach, I was 'that so-and-so Shreevesie'. The level of demand was that much higher – we needed to produce victories, not defeats. Some people might say I was a better Uncle Peter than I was the other, which might be fair comment. Most of them did well for me and looking back it was a fantastic time."

Burkinshaw was a hard act to follow, but it is easy to forget now that Shreeve's side was one of the best Spurs have produced for many years, and the third place finish in his first season has been equalled only once since. The pivotal game in that 1984/85 season was the 2-1 home defeat by eventual champions Everton.

"We were there or thereabouts. On reflection the defeat at home against Aston Villa when we had senior players missing hurt us. But Everton were a good side. When I was working with the Welsh national side, I spent a lot of time with Neville Southall. He used to talk me through that game every time. 'Do you remember that save I made off Falco?' he would say. Mark had a shot destined for the top corner, yet somehow Neville kept it out. 'How the hell did you keep that out?' I would ask him. He'd say, 'I'm a top goalie Pete, you know that.' We became good friends. And every time I see an Evertonian, they'll say, 'You're that Peter Shreeves. You did all right at Tottenham. You weren't as good as us though, were you?'

"The Talksport presenter, Mike Parry, whenever I see him, he immediately comes up and his recall of anything to do with Everton, and particularly of that season, inspires him and he gives me every detail – the teams, the matches, every incident. 'You was unlucky there, lad, you had a good season.' 67 years old and he calls me 'lad'!

The weight of expectation fell on Shreeve's shoulders, but in his view that came with the territory, rather than it being a specifically

Spurs thing. It wasn't just Peter who had to bear the pressure but his family as well.

"I was outgoing but I didn't look for publicity; I just got on with it. I used to deal with the press no matter what the result was and more often than not it was a pleasure because we won. I would return calls and because of that they gave me a fair ride, they thought I was a straight bloke. But always, always, always there is pressure if you are the manager, whatever the club. There were always phone calls to make, problems to address. I was top of the league in my first season and I was still under pressure. You had to be 100 per cent clean in your private life, you had to be careful who you were spotted smiling with or what you said because they [the media] had people watching you all the time. People were always trying to pull you down. That is the less pleasant side of the game that all managers had to deal with. Touch wood I was clean so nothing ever came out but I was constantly worrying about it.

"The truth of the matter is I've got lovely kids and three lovely grandchildren, but I never saw my daughters and son grow up. I used to go to their school functions and I was this 'famous dad', but I missed out on so much. I never got to take them to the zoo or do things I'm doing with my grandchildren now because I was always at a game or on a plane somewhere.

"I used to go over to Holland every Sunday morning and go and see their best sides. I saw Frank Rijkaard make his debut for Ajax as a 16-year-old centre half. The scouts we had in Holland sent me to watch Frank Arnesen who's at Chelsea now. He was a good midfielder; he played against us for Anderlecht. But I saw this kid playing the same day and thought 'Wow', a superb athlete and a real prospect. I came back and Irving said to me, 'How was Arnesen?' I said, 'Irving, he was OK, but this kid Frankie Rijkaard, he was absolutely magnificent.' When they found out he was only a young kid it didn't go any further.

"But I knew the Dutch set-up very well because I studied it

and devoted time to it. I used to work six days a week as coach but I gave up the seventh day as manager to go and watch Dutch football. It was all-consuming."

Despite the demands made upon him personally and missing out on both Olsen and Rijkaard, albeit for contrasting reasons, Shreeve doesn't harbour any resentment towards the then owners of the club. "My feeling was that as long as they didn't interfere with the football side of things I was OK. Chairmen now ring up and say, 'Are you playing so-and-so at the weekend?' But as manager at Spurs I never experienced anything of that nature. I was totally in charge of the team, training, and the buying and selling of players.

"There were always other people outside of the club telling you who you should have signed. Take the Argentinian centre forward Mario Kempes, the star of the 1978 World Cup. The agent flagged up that he was available. I asked Ossie what he thought of him. He said, 'He's a world class player, Pete, but, I've got to be honest with you, he's just beginning to go a bit.' 'OK', I said, 'we'll see.' He was looking for a club. You know that if someone is looking for a club, as opposed to all the clubs chasing him, you know that they might be struggling. But in the World Cup he had been fantastic.

"He came on pre-season trips with us and we finished against Monaco. We were playing amateur teams and winning 8-0 with Kempes scoring four goals. Everybody was raving about him. But I could see the opposition was so weak I could have scored a goal. When we got to Monaco, he gave me his watch. He couldn't speak English but he indicated for me to look after it. I put it on and I said to Ossie, 'How much is this worth?' He said, 'Oh, about 14 grand.' I made my mind up there and then. How was he going to be Tuesday night at Middlesbrough in the middle of an English winter with a 14 grand watch on? That might seem silly, but I never signed the boy and he struggled to find a club. It was big story at the time that we were going to sign him, but we were right not to.

"We did sign some good ones, though, like Clive Allen, his cousin Paul, John Chiedozie, though he didn't quite work out, lovely lad though he was. Chrissie Waddle came, he became my soulmate and went with me to Sheffield Wednesday. I paid £495,000 for him and he was sold for over £4 million. So I didn't owe them any money when I left," chuckles Shreeve.

The third-place finish in 1985, however, was to be Shreeve's high-water mark as Spurs manager. The club finished tenth the next season and changes were swiftly rung. Like the break-up of the team, the managerial dynasty that could trace a direct line back to Bill Nicholson came to an end abruptly and without sentiment, amid changing football times.

"We struggled a bit the second year, but if you add that to the previous season's third and divide it by two, it meant my record was sixth and a half place in the table. That would be half decent nowadays. But if you're the manager of Tottenham Hotspur, you're under pressure to deliver. This was at a time when they expected to be challenging. Arsenal weren't ten years further ahead of us then. I had a very good record at Highbury actually. We won 2-1 on Boxing Day in 1984 and we went top.

"But fans know how it is. It's especially marked today – everybody's looking for that quick fix, this new wonder coach. Times were changing. My success at Tottenham had been built on knowing the players and being a big part of their development. Their salaries were good but it wasn't beyond the realm; they earned good money but nothing silly. They were working class lads who didn't have over-the-top motors. I didn't need to go into the dressing room to try and impress them. As time went on, managers found that players became richer, less ambitious. They thought just arriving at a club was all that was needed. I saw a change in the lifestyle of professional footballers, their affection for the club and the manager as a person.

"Agents became a necessary evil. Managers would speak to a

player and he would immediately say, 'Talk to my agent.' The large amounts of money they have taken out of the game – some of them have deserved it, some of them, well, it's scandalous. No one ever said to me when I was dealing with players, 'You'll have to speak to my agent.'"

As to how the end came, there is no rancour on Shreeve's part and he recalls it with typical professional fatalism. "The posse catches you up. In a John Wayne film the cowboys get together and go off and hunt the villain as a posse. It doesn't matter who you are, how good you are, the posse catches up with you. It's one of my sayings. Circumstances come together and they get you. That is when they say, 'All the best Pete; fantastic, but see you later.'

"I wasn't going to be manager of Tottenham Hotspur all my life. I was there 13 years – 13 fantastic years. They flew by. The job was made for me and I was made for the job. Dealing with all these youngsters, seeing them develop, and meeting people all over the world – what a life."

Shreeve's life since then has been full of eventful and enjoyable challenges. It included a brief and unsuccessful return as Tottenham manager during the turmoil of the Venables years in 1991/92, but he had more successful spells as either coach or manager at QPR, Sheffield Wednesday, Barnet and Chelsea where he assisted his former charge Glenn Hoddle. "We got to a cup final and got beat by Man U so I had three FA Cup finals. I actually went to Wembley with my teams ten times, when you include Charity Shields and semi-finals when they shifted to Wembley. So while some football people never get to Wembley, I went there loads of times. I don't mean to show off but when you go there for the eighth time, you don't know which suit to wear," he laughs.

Ever the coach, he now combines a variety of training jobs – from work at an Essex-based academy run by former Spur John Moncur to recent coaching of players from the Premier India Football Academy – with his work as referee's delegate for the

Premier League and the Professional Game Match Officials Board, headed by his good friend Keith Hackett, who officiated in the 1981 final. With the PGMOB, he assesses the performance of officials at Premier League games, liaising with managers and addressing their concerns by going into the minute details of how their game was refereed. It suits Shreeve down to a tee, not only exploiting his wide-ranging and respected football expertise, but enabling him to travel the country watching football, and meeting football people.

"The standard of football is not that great," he feels. "I go to Premier League games and I come away shaking my head at the pace and intensity. Down the leagues, there is too much long-ball football – tin hats football, we call it. It's not my style, but I understand the pressure the manager is under to get a result. Survival is the name of the game.

"But I love being part of the football family. I can go to any ground, say somewhere like Rotherham or Brighton and there'll be someone there ready with a smile and a 'Hello Pete, how you doing?' It's a lovely feeling. Football is now a business, but the camaraderie between a group of football people, that sometimes will include reporters who you know won't turn you over, gives you so many good laughs.

"We've had so many reunions with the Spurs players of the 1980s. But as soon as you get there, the piss-taking and the nicknames all start up again, like it's yesterday, not over 25 years ago. Everybody remembers little details and stories, all those laughs. I go to White Hart Lane when players get inducted into the Hall of Fame. It always strikes me at those events that the supporters love all the banter around the club."

It's a happy note on which to end Shreeve's recollections of those golden years. But Peter 'Smooth' Shreeve, the man who enjoyed the best years of his life being a central part of the great Tottenham Hotspur team of the 1980s mentions one last story that seems to encapsulate the bond between the men who made all that success happen. At the end of the 2007/08 season, Exeter City and their director of football Steve Perryman made it to Wembley for the Conference play-off final, beating Cambridge United 1-0 and so regaining their football league status. On a day of triumph for Perryman, it was fitting that his former managers and coaches, Keith Burkinshaw and Peter Shreeve, were among his proud guests.

"Steve apologised because he wanted to give two of the seats in the royal box to Keith and his wife, and he could 'only' give me a seat amongst the fans. It was still a great seat though and a lovely touch. I said to him, 'Don't worry Steve, I'm normal and don't mind being in with the normal people.'"

Shreeve laughs when he tells the story, but the fact is this was anything but normal – it was a reunion of Spurs heroes. Things had come full circle, and 27 years on from that magical evening at the same venue, when the night air rang to the strains of Glory Glory Hallelujah, three of the famous Boys from White Hart Lane were together, unified in victory once more.